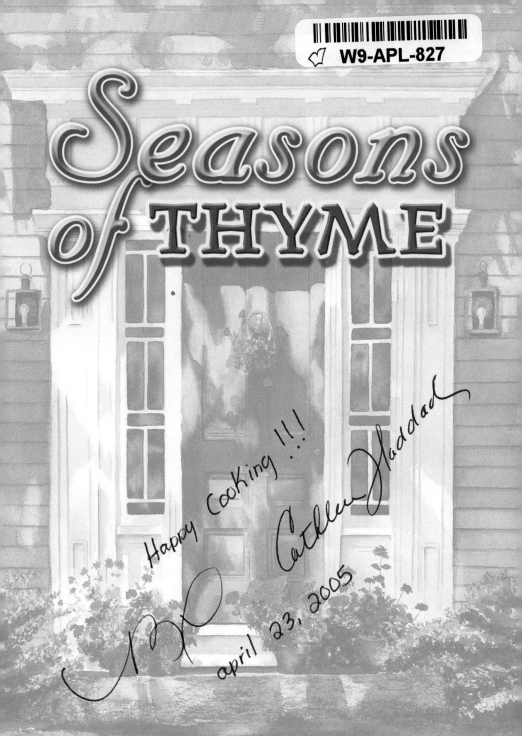

Seasons of THYME

Happy Cooking !!!

Cathleen Haddad

april 23, 2005

Savoring the Traditions of Sutton, Massachusetts

Barbara MH Daigneault and Cathleen Haddad

These recipes are a collection of favorites from our families and friends and reflect upon people who have passed through the doors of many kitchens in Sutton, Massachusetts. We do not claim these recipes are original. Some of the titles have been changed to conform to the overall theme of the book. These recipes have been personally tested, many of them several times. We could not have possibly used all the recipes that were given to us; however, we feel we have selected a wonderful variety to create a cookbook for everyone's enjoyment.

We will donate ten percent (10%) of the proceeds from the sale of this cookbook to a fund for charitable purposes. The fund, administered by the authors, will help meet special needs not covered by existing programs for residents of Sutton, Massachusetts.

Information on obtaining additional copies of *Seasons of Thyme* may be found at the back of the book or by contacting the information listed below. Artwork is available by visiting our website.

Seasons of Thyme
P.O. Box 463
Sutton, Massachusetts 01590
www.seasonsofthyme.net
(508) 865-2438

WIMMER
COOKBOOKS

ConsolidatedGraphics
1-800-548-2537

Table of Contents

You're Invited

The Home of Peter and Kimberly Hunkeler, Boston Road

When Cathleen thought about the cover for *Seasons of Thyme*, this classic Greek revival period entrance was perfect. Cathleen loved how the shadows from the huge old maple tree danced across the front of the home. This home was originally built in 1835 by Colonel Zadok Woodbury and was willed to his niece Frances J. Woodbury Freeland. Frances was a member of the first class to graduate from Sutton High School, she later taught at the Eight Lots School.

A Culinary Journey Through the Seasons of Thyme

You are invited to take a culinary journey with us along the picturesque country roads of Sutton, Massachusetts. As you travel through the *"Seasons of Thyme,"* you will find beautiful artwork and a collection of outstanding recipes which were gathered from those with relationships to this township. As Sutton celebrates its 300th birthday, we have collected these recipes to evoke memories of life in this charming rural community.

Sutton, Massachusetts is a quaint town where people gather to celebrate a heritage. Annual celebrations such as a Chain of Lights event on a snowy day, Waters Farm Days in the autumn air or the Civil War Encampment on a sultry summer weekend marks our history. Our senses come alive as we recall the aromas of freshly mowed hay, the sight of hoof prints from a deer in a freshly fallen snow or the sounds emanating from the Little League parade marching along the flag-adorned historic Boston Road.

As we reflect on our childhood and friendship over 33 years, we treasure our memories of growing up in this close community. In our adulthood, we want to capture the true beauty of our quaint little town through the flavors and aromas of yesterday and today. The warm feelings of our childhood inspired us to remember the people who have walked through the kitchen doors before us. We wish to hold fast to those relationships and embrace our new neighbors as we all share the best of our community through family traditions and memories of our favorite foods.

We savor the fond memories and traditions of yesterday and today as we joyfully anticipate the seasons of tomorrow. We invite you to join us on this journey as we all travel through the *"Seasons of Thyme"*.

Barbara MH Daigneault
and Cathleen Haddad

Acknowledgements

We are grateful to so many individuals who have helped make this cookbook a dream come true. We extend our heartfelt acknowledgement to the following individuals.

To our husbands, Robert A. Daigneault, Sr. and Wayne Haddad, we thank you for your outpouring of love, support, guidance, encouragement, enthusiasm, partnership and patience. Without you none of this would have ever become a reality.

To all the people who graciously gave their favorite recipe(s). Each one of you generously gave your time by writing out recipes, sharing memories and encouraging us along the way. Without you, your time and your effort, we would not have had such a wealth of information to create this beautiful cookbook.

To Cheryl Bedard, Lisa Sarmento and Cheryl Scott, also known as the "Cookbook Queens," these ladies have spent a countless number of hours assisting us with selecting, reviewing, editing, baking, cooking and sampling recipes. You have unselfishly given of your time and talent with dedication, support, enthusiasm and patience. We are so grateful to have you as our friends.

To Jane KH Walsh, for her time, energy and creative writing skills.

To the ladies mentioned in this book that have gone on before us, we thank God for their lives. When you see this symbol ✗, we recognize these ladies with fond and loving memories. These ladies and so many others were pillars in our community and such a great influence as we were children growing up. They unselfishly gave their time and energy to help make Sutton a special place to live. They have warmed our hearts and kitchens in so many ways.

To our families, we never would have completed this book if it weren't for your interest, support, patience and encouragement over the past few years.

To Peter and Kimberly Hunkeler, Robert and Joan Johnson, Patricia M. Morse, Edward J. Mingolla and Linda Sinacola for the opportunity to capture the beauty of the seasons.

To William Griffiths, at the Worcester Art Museum, for his years of encouragement and guidance.

To Ralph "Bud" W. Gurney, Jr., for sharing his wealth of knowledge and love for the Town of Sutton.

To God, for creating the beauty of the earth and place we call home ... "Sutton, Massachusetts".

Barbara MH Daigneault and Cathleen Haddad

About The Authors

Barbara M. (Hebert) Daigneault

A native of Sutton, Massachusetts, Barbara has always enjoyed inviting family and friends into her home for social gatherings. Her passion for the art of casual and fine entertaining has inspired her to create simple yet elegant menus.

Well-organized and eager to give back to a community from which she has gained so much, Barbara created a partnership with her childhood friend and local artist, Cathleen Haddad, to create *Seasons of Thyme*. Barbara is the stepmother of three children and five grandchildren. She and her husband, Robert, reside in Sutton.

Cathleen (Morse) Haddad

Cathleen has learned to express her passion of art through her paintings since she was a young girl - a gift for which she thanks God. Over the years, she has shown her works at many regional and national exhibitions and has won numerous awards. Cathleen studied watercolor to develop her skills at the Worcester Art Museum under the teachings of well-respected artist, William Griffiths.

Her strong desire to capture the beauty of Sutton through her work inspired her to team with Barbara in creating *Seasons of Thyme*. In her spare time, she continues to freelance for local and national businesses and organizations. Moving to Sutton in 1970, Cathleen, one of nine children growing up, developed her culinary skills as a necessity. She and her husband, Wayne, have four children.

Sutton, Massachusetts

Sutton is a lovely, residential community located southeast of Worcester, Massachusetts. The town was located in 1704, and settled in 1716. The origin of the name of the town is unknown, however research has proven that some of our early settlers have roots traced back to Sutton, England.

It is the birthplace of General Rufus Putnam and home of the furniture maker Nathan Lombard. Many prominent figures have passed through the doors of Sutton: John Hancock, Ben Franklin, Daniel Webster, General Lafayette and many more. Many stayed overnight at the proper Lazarus LaBaron Tavern, built in 1796 (the current home of Wallace E. Johnson on Boston Road) as they traveled on their stage routes from Boston to New York. Ben Franklin stayed in a private home, also on Boston Road.

Sutton is well known for many area attractions: Historic Waters Farm (a living history), Pleasant Valley Country Club (home of thirty-three PGA Tour events and fourteen LPGA tournaments), Eaton Farm Confectioners' (one of America's oldest candy makers), Purgatory Chasm State Reservation (a unique natural landmark), Vaillancourt Folk Art (world renown for its Christmas ornaments and collectibles), and Blackstone National Golf Club (championship Rees Jones golf course). Sutton is also naturally beautiful with several active farms, three large lakes, streams, ponds and has lots of open space to farm and grow crops. These are just a few of the many attractions in our town.

Sutton still retains much of the rural beauty. The seasons in Sutton have some of the most beautiful scenes in New England.

In early spring, for a tranquil and peaceful experience, a simply glorious view is to stand at Waters Farm overlooking the stillness of Lake Manchaug as the sun rises. In the summertime, drive along any of the back roads of Sutton, and you are sure to capture spectacular glimpses of the beautiful gardens throughout the town. Enjoy the panorama of Whittier's Farm as you travel along Town Farm Road through the hills and vales into West Sutton. The view is breathtaking during the splendor of fall foliage. On a cold winter's evening in December, gaze across the Town Common and see the warm lights aglow in the windows of Polly's Antiques after a long hard days work for the Chain of Lights.

Now that we've whet your appetite to the beauty of Sutton, turn the pages and enjoy the many creations within them and start making your own memories.

Appetizers

Gathered Together

The Memorial Garden at Waters Farm, Waters Road

In 1974, Dorothea Waters Moran donated her family's summer home, the "Waters Farm", to the Town of Sutton. The home at Waters Farm was built circa 1757. This Memorial Garden was dedicated in the Fall of 2002 in memory of seven ladies who gave their personal time as Hearthkeepers to the support and development of the Farm and in particular, the house, featured in the background of this picture. Ruth Shaw Putnam designed the garden plan, which includes a teakwood arbor and two teakwood benches. She did this with warmth and love.

The ladies are:

Ada Valentine Waters	1874-1953	Barbara Gurney Weaver	1922-2000
Dorothea Waters Moran	1895-1987	Barbara Batcheller Beaton	1914-2001
Belle Putnam Smith	1907-1996	Ruth Cotton Gurney	1919-2001
Shirley Putnam Johnson	1922-1999		

Appetizers

Olive and Jack Dip

Cathleen Haddad

1   medium onion, chopped
2   tablespoons vegetable oil
2   tomatoes, peeled and chopped
½   cup chopped black olives
2   tablespoons chopped hot
    peppers
1   (10-ounce) package frozen
    chopped spinach, drained
2   cups shredded Monterey Jack
    cheese
1   (8-ounce) package cream
    cheese, softened
1   tablespoon red wine vinegar
1   cup half & half
    Salt and pepper to taste

1. Sauté onions in oil until tender. Add the tomatoes and sauté for 2 minutes.

2. In a large bowl, combine remaining ingredients and mix well with a hand mixer. Add the onion and tomato mixture.

3. Pour into an ovenproof serving dish. Bake at 400° for 35 minutes or until bubbly.

4. Serve warm with your favorite crackers.

Italian tomatoes work best.

Baba Ghanouj (Eggplant Dip)

Judy Conley

2   eggplants, average size
4   tablespoons tahini
½   teaspoon salt
3   cloves of garlic, pressed
2-3 lemons

1. Pierce eggplants with a fork and bake at 350° for 35 to 45 minutes, until skin becomes brittle. Remove skins and place eggplant into a food processor.

2. Combine remaining ingredients and blend until you have a whipped mixture. Serve with pita bread cut into triangles.

Hummus

Agnes Garoian Davagian

Hummus is an appetizer brought to the U.S.A. by my family from the "old country", no doubt via Ellis Island. We always serve this at family parties and important occasions.

1 (15-ounce) can chickpeas, drained (reserve liquid)
4 cloves garlic, pressed
3 tablespoons tahini
3 tablespoons lemon juice, freshly squeezed
¼ teaspoon cumin
¼ cup canola oil
 Salt to taste
 Sliced red onion for garnish
 Chopped black olives for garnish

1. Place all ingredients into a food processor or blender. Process until smooth. Add a little reserved liquid, if needed, to desired consistency. (Should be thick.)

2. To serve, pour into bowl and garnish with red onion and black olives.

3. Serve with pita bread cut into triangles.

Mrs. Davagian was the Home Economics teacher at Sutton High School from 1953 to 1979.

Mock Keyma

Nancy Lee Sarkisian

1 cup bulgur wheat
2 (8-ounce) cans tomato sauce
¼ cup lemon juice, freshly squeezed
¼ cup canola oil
½ bunch parsley, finely chopped
1 medium onion, finely chopped
 Pepper to taste

1. Mix all ingredients by hand and refrigerate at least 1 hour before serving.

2. Serve with pita bread cut into triangles.

It's better served the next day. Keeps in refrigerator for two weeks.

Hot Clam Dip

Carmen O'Brien

3 (6.5-ounce) cans chopped clams, drained
3 cloves garlic, minced
4 tablespoons butter, melted
¼ teaspoon oregano
½ cup seasoned bread crumbs
1 cup shredded mozzarella cheese, divided

1. Combine all ingredients, except ¼ cup mozzarella cheese. Mix well and place in a baking dish. Sprinkle with remaining mozzarella cheese.

2. Bake at 350° for 15 minutes.

3. Serve with crackers.

Hot Crabmeat Dip

Trina Chirchigno

1 (8-ounce) package cream cheese
2 tablespoons crab juice
1 (8-ounce) can crabmeat, drained
1½ cups shredded Swiss cheese
¾ cup mayonnaise
2 teaspoons dried onion
½ teaspoon salt
Dash of Worcestershire sauce

1. Combine all ingredients. Mix well.

2. Bake at 375° for 15 to 20 minutes or until bubbly.

3. Serve with crackers.

Guacomole (Avocado Dip)

Cheryl Scott

3-4 ripe avocados, peeled and
    pitted
1   cup sour cream
1   cup hot salsa
    Juice of ½ lemon
    Tabasco Sauce to taste

1. Coarsely mash avocado with a
fork.

2. Mix all ingredients together.
Serve with tortilla chips.

Harvest Pumpkin Dip with Cinnamon Chips

Cheryl Bedard

Surprisingly light. Looks great served in a carved out pumpkin.

1   cup packed canned pumpkin
½   cup sour cream
¼   cup packed brown sugar
½   teaspoon cinnamon
1   cup Cool Whip, thawed
¼   cup pecans for garnish

1. Mix all ingredients together and
sprinkle chopped pecans on top.

2. Serve with Cinnamon Triangle
Chips.

Put dip in dish before placing in pumpkin.

Cinnamon Chips

1   tablespoon ground cinnamon
⅔   cup sugar
1   package flat bread, medium
    size

1. Mix cinnamon and sugar.

2. Lightly mist the flat bread with
water and then sprinkle the
cinnamon/sugar mixture on top.

3. Cut the bread into triangles (a
pizza cutter works great) and place
on a cookie sheet. Crisp the bread
at 400° for 10 minutes.

*This dip is also great served with apple
wedges. To prevent the wedges from
browning, soak them in pineapple juice for
several hours, then drain to serve.*

Blue Cheese Onion Celery Dip

Linda Hendrikse

I found this recipe in an old Bon Appetite *magazine. This makes lots and is a real crowd-pleaser. Serve with veggies or crackers. The longer it sits the better.*

1   (8-ounce) package cream
      cheese
1   cup crumbled blue cheese
1   cup mayonnaise
1   cup sour cream
½   cup finely chopped onion
½   cup finely chopped celery
2   cloves garlic, minced
1   teaspoon celery salt
1   teaspoon ground black pepper

1. In a large bowl, combine all ingredients.

2. Mix with electric mixer until well blended.

3. Cover and chill for 1 hour or up to 3 days.

Taco Dip

Cheryl Scott

12 ounces cream cheese, softened
½   cup sour cream
2   teaspoons chili powder
1½ teaspoons ground cumin
⅛   teaspoon ground red pepper
½   cup salsa
2   cups shredded lettuce
1   cup shredded Cheddar cheese
1   cup shredded Monterey Jack
      cheese
½   cup diced plum tomatoes
⅓   cup sliced green onions
¼   cup sliced black olives
¼   cup sliced pimiento-stuffed
      green olives
      Tortilla chips and blue corn
      chips

1. In a large bowl, combine cream cheese, sour cream, chili powder, cumin and red pepper. Mix until well blended. Stir in salsa.

2. Spread onto 10-inch serving platter lined with lettuce. Top with cheeses, tomatoes, green onions and olives.

3. Serve with chips.

Serves 10.

Margo's Cheese Spread

Anne Sweeney

2 (8-ounce) packages cream cheese
2 tablespoons chopped garlic
3 tablespoons chopped onion
3 tablespoons dried parsley
¾ teaspoon dried basil
1 (4-ounce) jar red pimientos
½ cup olive oil
½ cup white vinegar
Salt and pepper to taste

1. Combine all ingredients and mix well. Refrigerate for 24 hours.

2. Serve with crackers.

Spicy Black Bean and Corn Salsa

Cathleen Haddad

My friend Sue shared this recipe with me and it is my absolute favorite appetizer.

1 (16-ounce) can black beans, drained
1 (16-ounce) package frozen corn kernels
½ cup chopped fresh cilantro
¼ cup chopped green onions
¼ cup chopped red onions
⅓ cup lime juice, freshly squeezed
3 tablespoons vegetable oil
1 tablespoon ground cumin
Salt and pepper to taste
½ cup chopped ripe tomatoes, drained
Red leaf lettuce for garnish
Fresh cilantro sprigs for garnish

1. In a large bowl, combine beans, corn, cilantro, green onions, red onions, lime juice, oil and cumin. Season with salt and pepper.

2. Cover and chill at least 2 hours or up to overnight.

3. Just before serving, stir in tomatoes. Spoon mixture over lettuce. Garnish with cilantro sprigs.

4. Serve with tortilla chips.

Almond Pine Cone

Penny Thompson

A must for holiday entertaining. This recipe originated with my mother, Fran, but each of her five daughters claims it as her own! Guests may help themselves by dipping into the pine cone formation with a toasted almond. Also, fill a colorful serviette lined basket with a mixture of crackers and use this as a spread as well.

1¼ cups whole almonds (skins on)
5 slices bacon, cooked crisp
1 green onion, cut into 2-inch pieces
1 (8-ounce) package cream cheese
½ cup mayonnaise
Salt and pepper to taste

1. Spread almonds on a cookie sheet, bake at 350° for 10 to 15 minutes or until toasted. Turn with spatula and bake another 5 minutes.

2. In a food processor, chop bacon, onion and add cream cheese mayonnaise, salt and pepper. Cream together until smooth.

3. Chill mixture slightly and shape into a pine cone on a serving platter.

4. Starting at stem end of pine cone formation, push toasted almonds into cone in an attractive pattern. Decorate with some pine greenery and whole cranberries.

Best to make the day ahead; arrange almonds just before serving.

Olive and Egg Spread

Evelyn L. Morris

A very close friend, a second mother to me gave me this recipe. It's a tasty hors d'oeuvre.

1 (8-ounce) package cream cheese
1 (8-ounce) jar Spanish olives, finely chopped
2 hard-boiled eggs, finely chopped
½ small onion, chopped
Tabasco Sauce to taste

1. Combine all ingredients and mix well.

2. Serve with crackers.

Best if made the day before.

Cocktail Cheese Wafers

Penny Thompson

I like to serve these with my Deviled Seafood Casserole (page 209).

1 (8-ounce) package Imperial cheese (red container)
2 sticks butter, softened
Dash of salt
Dash of Tabasco Sauce
¼ teaspoon Worcestershire sauce
1½ cups flour
4 cups rice crispies

1. In a food processor, cream cheese and butter.

2. Add salt, Tabasco Sauce and Worcestershire sauce.

3. Blend in flour and rice crispies, mixing well.

4. Shape into balls. Press down with a fork dipped in cold water. Chill.

5. Bake at 350° for 15 to 20 minutes or until lightly browned.

These store well in tins. They also freeze well and are best made ahead of time.

Melted Brie with Winter Fruit

Kathy Dugan

¾ cup chopped pitted dates
1 small apple, peeled, cored and chopped
1 small firm pear, peeled, cored and chopped
½ cup raisins or currants
½ cup chopped pecans
⅓ cup rosé wine or apple juice
1 (16-ounce) wheel of Brie cheese, chilled
Thin baguette slices or crackers

1. In a small bowl, combine dates, apple, pear, raisins, pecans and wine. Mix well and let stand for 2 hours.

2. Slice Brie in half horizontally. Place bottom half cut side up, in a shallow 10-inch round baking dish. Spread with 2½ cups of fruit mixture.

3. Cover with top half of Brie, cut side down. Spoon remaining fruit on top.

4. Bake, uncovered, at 350° for 25 minutes or until cheese melts at edges.

5. Spread on baguette slices or crackers.

I have tried an assortment of other fruit and nut combinations such as chopped apricots, almonds, cranberries and/or walnuts and always receive compliments. Fruit mixture can be made 2 days ahead. Cover and chill.

Serves 16.

Savory Sun-Dried Tomato Cheesecake

Donna LaCava

3 tablespoons seasoned bread crumbs

4 (3-ounce) packages cream cheese, softened

3 eggs

½ cup half & half

2 cups shredded Jarlsberg cheese

3 scallions, chopped

2 tablespoons chopped marinated sun-dried tomatoes

¼ teaspoon Italian seasoning

¼ teaspoon ground pepper

1. Coat a 9-inch springform pan with cooking spray, then dust with bread crumbs.

2. In a large bowl, beat together cream cheese, eggs and half & half until smooth.

3. Stir in remaining ingredients.

4. Pour into prepared pan. Bake at 325° for 45 minutes or until knife is inserted 1-inch from center and comes out clean. Cool on wire rack.

Serves 12.

Asparagus Cheese Roll-Ups

Jayne Swart

1 (16-ounce) loaf thin white bread, crusts removed

1 (8-ounce) package cream cheese, softened

3 ounces blue cheese

1 egg, beaten

1 pound asparagus, steamed but still crunchy

Melted butter

1. Flatten bread slices using a rolling pin.

2. Mix cream cheese, blue cheese and egg together. Spread 1 to 2 tablespoons of cheese mixture on bread.

3. Place 1 asparagus spear diagonally across bread. Roll up corner to corner. Use a dab of the cheese mixture to secure bread.

4. Lightly brush with melted butter and place on a cookie sheet. Bake at 400° for 10 minutes.

Can be made ahead of time and just as good without the melted butter.

Serves 16.

Sun-Dried Tomato and Pesto Torta

Eileen Pastner

*You can make this up to three days
ahead; be sure to start at least one day in advance.*

4   cloves garlic
1½ cups packed fresh basil leaves
¼   cup pine nuts
2   tablespoons extra-virgin olive
      oil
1   teaspoon fresh lemon juice
2⅔ cups cream cheese, softened
      and divided
¼   cup grated Parmesan cheese
1⅓ cups oil-packed sun-dried
      tomatoes, drained
⅓   cup tomato paste
¾   cup butter, room temperature
      Basil sprigs for garnish
      Toasted pine nuts for garnish
      Baguette slices, toasted

1. Finely chop garlic in processor. Add basil, pine nuts, oil and lemon juice. Process until well blended. Add ⅓ cup cream cheese and ¼ cup Parmesan cheese and pulse until blended. Transfer pesto mixture to medium bowl.

2. Coarsely chop tomatoes in processor. Add tomato paste and process until almost smooth. Add ⅓ cup cream cheese and blend well.

3. Using electric mixer beat remaining 2 cups cream cheese and butter in a large bowl until fluffy, season with salt and pepper.

4. Spray a 6-cup soufflé dish with non-stick spray. Line with plastic wrap, extending plastic over sides. Spread ¾ cup cream cheese-butter mixture evenly over bottom of prepared dish. Top with ½ tomato mixture, then ½ cup cream cheese-butter mixture, then ½ pesto mixture.

5. Repeat layering with ½ cup cream cheese-butter mixture, remaining tomato mixture, ½ cup cream-cheese-butter mixture and remaining pesto.

6. Top with remaining cream cheese-butter mixture. Cover and chill overnight. Can be made 3 days ahead. Keep refrigerated.

7. Invert torta onto platter. Peel off plastic. Garnish with basil sprigs and toasted pine nuts. Serve with baguettes.

Serves 20.

Tomato Basil Tart

Sandy Paul

½ (15-ounce) package folded refrigerator pie crust (1 crust)

1½ cups shredded mozzarella cheese, divided

5 Roma tomatoes

1 cup loosely packed fresh basil leaves

4 cloves garlic

½ cup mayonnaise

¼ cup grated Parmesan cheese

⅛ teaspoon ground white pepper

1. Place crust in a 9-inch quiche dish, flute edges, prick with fork and pre-bake according to instructions. Remove from oven, sprinkle with ½ cup mozzarella cheese and cool on wire rack.

2. Cut tomatoes in thick slices; drain on paper towel. Arrange tomatoes on top of melted cheese.

3. In a processor, combine basil and garlic until coarsely chopped. Sprinkle over tomatoes.

4. In a medium bowl, combine remaining 1 cup mozzarella cheese, mayonnaise, Parmesan cheese and pepper. Spoon cheese mixture over top of basil and spread to evenly cover the top.

5. Bake at 375° for 35 to 40 minutes or until top is bubbly.

Serves 4 main dishes or 8 appetizers.

Spanakopita (Spinach Pie)

Paula Carafotes

*This is a traditional Greek recipe. I loved it growing up
and I now frequently make it for my family. Great for the Holiday's!*

1 (10-ounce) bag fresh spinach
1 stick butter, melted
1 cup vegetable oil
5 eggs
1 pound feta cheese, crumbled
2 cups cottage cheese
1 small white onion, finely chopped
1 (16-ounce) box phyllo dough

1. Wash and dry spinach; remove stems.

2. Melt butter and pour into vegetable oil.

3. Beat eggs, add feta cheese, cottage cheese, onion and fold in spinach. Set aside.

4. With a pastry brush, brush oil and butter into bottom and sides of 13 x 11-inch baking dish. Brush 8 to 10 pieces of phyllo dough and layer into bottom of pan. You will have to fold some edges so they fit.

5. After layering bottom, pour spinach mixture into the pan. Butter remaining phyllo dough (another 8 to 10 pieces) and layer the top of the pie. Using a serrated knife, cut into 2 x 3-inch squares before baking.

6. Bake at 375° for 1 hour or until tops are golden brown. Cool 15 minutes before cutting and serving.

Frozen spinach can be used, but you must drain out water and squeeze to dry.

Serves 10 to 15.

Winnipesaukee Crab Cakes

Cheryl Scott

1 (8-ounce) package lump crabmeat, fresh or frozen

1 egg, slightly beaten

6 tablespoons Italian style bread crumbs, divided

1 tablespoon finely chopped green onion

2 tablespoons mayonnaise

¾ teaspoon dry mustard

¼ teaspoon Tabasco Sauce

2 tablespoons cooking oil
  Lemon wedges for garnish

1. Thaw the crabmeat in refrigerator if frozen. Drain.

2. In a medium mixing bowl combine eggs, 4 tablespoons of bread crumbs, onion, mayonnaise, dry mustard and Tabasco Sauce. Gently stir in crabmeat just until combined.

3. With wet hands, gently shape mixture into four, ½-inch thick patties, about 3½-inches in diameter.

4. Place remaining bread crumbs in a shallow dish, coat both sides of patties with crumbs.

5. In a large skillet heat oil over medium heat; add crab cakes. Cook about 3 minutes on each side or until golden brown and heated through.

6. Serve immediately with lemon wedges and tarter sauce, if desired.

Serves 4.

Mouth Watering Stuffed Mushrooms

Cindy King

12 whole fresh mushrooms, medium size
1 tablespoon minced garlic
1 tablespoon vegetable oil
1 (8-ounce) package cream cheese, softened
¼ cup Parmesan cheese
¼ teaspoon freshly ground pepper
¼ teaspoon onion powder
¼ teaspoon cayenne pepper

1. Wash and dry mushrooms with a damp paper towel. Carefully break off stems. Chop stems extremely fine, discarding tough ends.

2. Sauté mushroom stems and garlic in oil over medium heat until moisture has disappeared, taking care not to burn the garlic. Set aside to cool.

3. When mushroom mixture is cool, stir in cream cheese, Parmesan cheese, pepper, onion powder and cayenne pepper. Mixture should be very thick. Using a little spoon, fill each cap with a generous amount of stuffing.

4. Arrange caps on a cookie sheet coated with non-stick spray. Bake at 350° for 20 minutes or until the mushrooms are piping hot and liquid starts to form underneath.

Serves 6 to 8.

Wild Mushroom Timbales

Audrey Mingolla

A rich and elegant appetizer.

1 ounce dried porcini mushrooms
½ cup hot water
5 ounces fresh shiitake mushrooms
4 tablespoons butter, divided
½ cup thinly sliced shallots
12 ounces button mushrooms, chopped
3 tablespoons dry white wine
1 cup chopped fresh parsley
Salt and pepper to taste
1½ cups whipping cream
4 large eggs
2 large egg yolks
¼ teaspoon ground nutmeg

1. Soak porcini mushrooms in ½ cup hot water for 20 minutes. Strain porcini mushrooms and chop. Set aside. Chop half of shiitake mushrooms and slice remaining shiitake mushrooms.

2. In a large skillet, melt 2 tablespoons of butter. Sauté shallots and button mushrooms until mushrooms are brown and dry, stirring occasionally, about 15 minutes.

3. Add wine and boil 1 minute. Transfer mushrooms to a medium bowl.

4. Melt 1 tablespoon of butter in same skillet over medium-low heat. Add porcini mushrooms and chopped shiitake mushrooms. Cover and cook until tender, stirring occasionally, about 10 minutes. Add porcini mixture to button mixture. Stir in parsley and season with salt and pepper.

5. In the same skillet, melt remaining 1 tablespoon of butter and sauté sliced shiitake mushrooms. Set aside for garnish. (Can be prepared 1 day ahead. Cover mushrooms separately and refrigerate.)

6. In a large bowl combine cream, eggs, egg yolks and nutmeg. Season with salt and pepper.

7. Butter eight ¾-cup ramekins. Place ⅓ cup mushroom mixture in each ramekin. Pour ⅓ cup custard mixture into each. Arrange ramekins in a large roasting pan, spacing evenly. Pour enough hot water into pan to come halfway up sides of ramekins.

8. Bake at 350° for about 40 minutes or until custard is set.

Sauce

1	cup low-salt chicken broth
¼	cup whipping cream
6	tablespoons butter
1	tablespoon minced fresh parsley
	Pernod, a few drops
	Tarragon and shallots to taste

1. Boil broth and cream until reduced to ⅓ cup, about 15 minutes. Gradually whisk in butter, stir in parsley and add seasonings.

2. Reheat sliced shiitake mushrooms.

3. Run small sharp knife around sides of ramekins and invert timbales onto plates. Spoon sauce over and garnish with sliced shiitake mushrooms.

Serves 8.

Tex Mex Dip

Brenda Morse

*This recipe was first served at the Morse family's
4th of July party in 1991. It was such a hit that it has been a tradition ever since.*

1 pound hamburger
1 pound hot Italian sausage, casing removed
Garlic to taste
1 (32-ounce) block Velveeta cheese, cubed
1 (16-ounce) jar hot salsa
1 can cream of chicken soup
Tortilla chips

1. In a large frying pan, brown hamburger and sausage. Add garlic while browning. Drain excess fat.

2. Add cheese, salsa, soup and meat to crockpot on high heat. Cook until cheese is melted.

3. Serve in crockpot on low heat. Stir occasionally. Serve with tortilla chips or corn chips.

Can be made with cream of mushroom soup as well.

Serves 10 to 15.

Artichoke Stuffed Mushrooms

Lisa Sarmento

1½ pounds fresh stuffing mushrooms, washed, dried and stems removed
¼ cup chopped onion
2 cloves garlic, chopped
1 tablespoon olive oil
¼ cup dry white wine
¼ cup soft bread crumbs
1 (14-ounce) can artichoke hearts, drained and chopped
3 green onions, chopped
¼ cup grated Parmesan cheese
½ cup mayonnaise
¼ teaspoon salt
¼ teaspoon pepper

1. Finely chop mushroom stems.

2. In a large pan, over medium heat, heat olive oil and sauté mushroom stems, onion and garlic until onion is tender.

3. Add wine and cook until liquid evaporates. Stir in bread crumbs, remove from heat and cool. Combine onion mixture, artichokes and remaining 5 ingredients. Spoon 1 heaping teaspoon into each cap.

4. Place on a lightly greased rack in a roasting pan. Bake at 350° for 12 to 15 minutes or until golden brown.

Yields 25 to 30 appetizers.

Mini Cherry Pepper Quiches

Cheryl Scott

24 fresh red mild cherry peppers
1 egg, slightly beaten
½ cup whipping cream
¼ cup finely chopped fresh
   mushrooms
2 tablespoons finely chopped
   green onion
½ teaspoon Dijon-style mustard
¼ teaspoon salt
⅛ teaspoon pepper
⅓ cup shredded Swiss cheese

1. Cut off tops of peppers and use a small spoon to remove seeds. Place each pepper in a 1¾-inch muffin cup. Use a small crumpled piece of foil to keep peppers upright.

2. In a small bowl, combine egg, cream, mushrooms, onion, mustard, salt and pepper. Mix well. Spoon about 1½ teaspoons of the mixture into each pepper. Sprinkle tops with cheese.

3. Bake at 375° for 15 minutes and until filling is puffed and golden brown. Cool 5 minutes. Remove from pans and serve warm.

Yields 24.

Spinach Balls with Spicy Mustard Sauce

Audrey Mingolla

Spinach Balls

2 (10-ounce) packages chopped frozen spinach, thawed and drained
2 cups herb stuffing mix
1 cup grated Cheddar cheese
1 stick butter
1 small onion, finely chopped
3 eggs
   Dash of nutmeg

1. Mix all ingredients together. Form into small balls.

2. Place on a greased cookie sheet. Bake at 350° for 10 to 12 minutes.

Spicy Mustard Sauce

½ cup dry mustard
½ cup white vinegar
¼ cup sugar
1 egg yolk

1. Combine mustard and vinegar. Let stand at room temperature for 4 hours.

2. Add sugar and egg yolk. Cook in saucepan until thick. Cool.

3. Refrigerate until ready to serve with spinach balls.

Makes about 70.

Pepperoni Pinwheels

Alexandra V. Smith

*I came across this recipe when I was a newlywed.
I made it for a family gathering and everybody loved it. Now it is a family
tradition at my children's birthday parties or any gathering.*

1 cup finely chopped pepperoni
1 cup shredded mozzarella or
    Cheddar cheese
½ teaspoon dried oregano
1 egg, slightly beaten
2 (8-ounce) cans refrigerator
    quick crescent rolls

1. Combine first 4 ingredients and mix well.

2. Separate crescent dough into 16 triangles. Firmly press perforation to seal.

3. Spread ¼ cup of pepperoni mixture on each rectangle. Starting at shorter side, roll up and seal. Cut each roll into 6 to 8 pieces.

4. Place cut side down on ungreased cookie sheet. Bake at 375° for 12 to 15 minutes or until golden brown.

Serves 10 to 12.

Marinated Shrimp Skewers

Linda Erickson

1-2 pounds large shrimp, peeled
    and deveined
¼ cup olive oil
    Juice of 1 lime
1 tablespoon garlic salt
3 cloves elephant garlic, chopped
2 tablespoons chopped fresh
    parsley
1 pound maple or hickory
    smoked bacon

1. Peel the shrimp and put into a bowl. Add the olive oil, lime juice, garlic salt, garlic and parsley. Mix well. Marinate for several hours.

2. Cut bacon strips in half. Wrap each shrimp in a strip of bacon and put on skewer.

3. Grill over medium heat for about 10 minutes on each side. Make sure the bacon is cooked and shrimp is a light pink.

Works well as a main course too.

Cataumet Shrimp for Two

John L. Greene

*Fond memories of a lovely evening in Boston's North End dining
with a poised and charming Suttonian inspired me to attempt this recipe at home.
My home is in Cataumet, Massachusetts by the sea. A little taste of Grand Marnier
for the cook to start and voila, Cataumet Shrimp for Two sets the
mood for a romantic dinner for two.*

1   egg
3   ounces Grand Marnier, divided
2   tablespoons flour
    Salt and pepper to taste
1   dozen large shrimp, peeled and
    deveined
2   tablespoons olive oil
    Parsley sprigs for garnish
    Lemon wedges for garnish

1. In a small bowl, beat egg with 1-ounce of Grand Marnier.

2. Place flour in a shallow bowl and season with salt and pepper. Dip the shrimp in egg mixture, then coat with flour mixture.

3. In a small skillet, heat oil over medium-high heat. Sauté shrimp for 3 - 5 minutes, turning once. Add remaining Grand Marnier to pan just before finishing the cooking process.

4. Serve on individual plates and garnish with parsley and lemon wedges.

Serves 2.

Sautéed Shrimp over Spinach Greens

Linda Davidson

1   pound fresh large shrimp,
    peeled and deveined
½   teaspoon dried thyme
½   teaspoon dried oregano
1   teaspoon dried tarragon
¼   teaspoon dried ground
    coriander
¼   teaspoon freshly ground
    pepper
⅛   teaspoon cayenne pepper
2   tablespoons virgin olive oil

Spinach Greens
2   tablespoons virgin olive oil
10 ounces trimmed spinach,
    washed and drained
¼   teaspoon salt
¼   teaspoon freshly ground
    pepper

1. Sprinkle shrimp with dried ingredients. Place in a single layer in a dish and sprinkle with olive oil.

2. Heat an aluminum or black iron skillet until very, very hot. Place the oiled shrimp in one layer in the skillet and cook over high heat for 1 minute, turn and cook for 1½ minutes on the other side.

1. In a saucepan, heat olive oil and sauté spinach for 2 minutes or until wilted. Add the salt and pepper. Divide among 4 plates.

2. Place 4 shrimp on top of the greens.

3. Deglaze saucepan with 2 tablespoons of water and pour juices over the shrimp and serve.

Serves 4.

Grilled Pizza with Wild Mushrooms and Asiago Cheese

Ron Kolodziej

Pizza on a gas grill? You won't believe how easy and delicious. A favorite for kids!

1 pound assorted fresh mushrooms, oyster, shiitake and chanterelle
¼ cup virgin olive oil
6 ounces pizza dough
½ teaspoon minced garlic
½ cup shaved Asiago cheese

1. Slice cleaned mushrooms and sauté over medium-high heat in olive oil for 3 to 5 minutes. Set aside.

2. On a large, oiled, inverted baking sheet, spread and flatten pizza dough with your hands into a 10 to 12-inch free form circle ⅛-inch thick. Lift and drape dough on a pre-lit gas grill.

3. Within several minutes the dough will bubble, the underside will stiffen and grill marks will appear. Using tongs, flip crust over onto oiled baking sheet. Brush grill surface with olive oil. Scatter garlic, Asiago cheese and mushrooms onto pizza.

4. Slide pizza back onto grill. The pizza is done when cheese is bubbly and melted.

Yields 1 pizza.

Oven-Fried California Quesadillas

Cheryl Scott

2½ cups shredded Monterey Jack cheese

1 (6-ounce) jar marinated artichoke hearts, drained and chopped

1 (2¼-ounce) can sliced ripe olives, drained

⅔ cup picante sauce

¼ cup loosely packed, chopped cilantro

8 (8-inch) flour tortillas

3 tablespoons melted butter

Additional picante sauce for serving

Lime wedges for garnish

1. Combine first 5 ingredients in a bowl. Mix well.

2. Brush one side of 4 tortillas with butter and place buttered side down on baking sheet. Place 1 cup cheese mixture on each tortilla and spread to within ¾ inch of edge.

3. Top each with remaining tortillas, pressing firmly. Brush tops of tortillas with butter.

4. Bake at 450° for 10 minutes or until tops are lightly browned. Remove from oven and let stand 3 to 5 minutes. Cut each into 8 wedges.

5. Serve with additional picante sauce and lime wedges.

Refried beans can be substituted for artichokes.

Yields 32 appetizers.

Citrus Marinated Scallops Wrapped in Bacon

Evelyn L. Morris

Super hors d'oeuvres. I've had many compliments on this one.

1	pint small bay scallops
3	ounces lemon juice
½	pound bacon
½	cup brown sugar

1. Marinate scallops in lemon juice for 4 hours.

2. Cut bacon strips in thirds. Wrap each scallop with bacon and secure with toothpick. Place on rack in a shallow pan. Sprinkle with brown sugar.

3. Bake at 425° for 30 minutes or until bacon is browned.

Garlic Ginger Chicken Strips

Sandi Roy

¼	cup sherry or chicken broth
¼	cup reduced-sodium soy sauce
3	cloves garlic, minced
1	tablespoon honey
1	tablespoon minced fresh basil
½	teaspoon ground ginger
½	teaspoon Chinese five-spice powder
¼	teaspoon crushed red pepper flakes (optional)
¼	teaspoon pepper
1	pound boneless, skinless chicken breasts, cut into 1-inch strips

1. Combine first 9 ingredients. Remove 3 tablespoons for basting and cover and refrigerate.

2. Place chicken in a large resealable plastic bag; add the remaining marinade. Seal bag and turn to coat. Refrigerate for at least 4 hours.

3. Drain and discard marinade.

4. Broil chicken 3 to 4-inches from the heat for 3 minutes; turn strips over. Baste with reserved marinade. Broil 4 to 5 minutes longer or until chicken juices run clear, turn occasionally.

Serves 4.

Chinese Chicken Wings

Pam Jernberg

*This recipe was created by an American Airlines pilot and his wife -
Ed and Beth Beck. They loved wings and enjoyed experimenting with flavors.*

3-4 packages chicken wings or wingettes
2 cups soy sauce, divided
Garlic salt to taste
1 clove garlic, minced
¼ teaspoon dry mustard
¼ teaspoon ground ginger
1 tablespoon butter

1. Place wings in large baking pan and sprinkle generously with 1 cup soy sauce, then garlic salt. Cover tightly with aluminum foil.

2. Bake at 500° for 10 minutes. Reduce heat to 250° and bake 1½ hours or until very tender.

3. Drain juices and place wings on a cookie sheet. Heat remaining 1 cup of soy sauce, garlic, mustard, ginger and butter. Brush mixture generously over wings, broil until skins brown and crisp.

Chicken Nuggets

Jean Nilsson

A delicious appetizer!

3 boneless, skinless chicken breasts
½ cup unseasoned bread crumbs
¼ cup grated Parmesan cheese
2 teaspoons seasoned salt
2 teaspoons salt
1 teaspoon dried thyme
1 teaspoon dried basil
½ cup melted butter

1. Cut each chicken breast into 6 to 8 pieces to form a nugget.

2. Combine bread crumbs, cheese, seasoned salt, salt and herbs. Dip chicken in melted butter then roll in crumb mixture.

3. Place on foil lined cookie sheet in single layer. Bake at 400° for 20 minutes.

Bruchetta

J. Cichy-Natoli

1 pint grape tomatoes, cut in
half
2 celery ribs, diced
¼ cup sliced black olives
⅓ cup sliced green olives
¼ cup minced fresh parsley
1 clove garlic, minced
1 large carrot, julienne sliced
⅓ cup finely minced sweet onion
½ cup cubed mozzarella cheese
1 tablespoon virgin olive oil
½ tablespoon balsamic vinegar
Salt and pepper to taste
Italian or French bread

1. Combine all ingredients. Adjust
seasonings to taste if needed. Let
stand at room temperature for
30 minutes.

2. Serve over grilled sliced Italian or
French bread.

Shrimp and Artichoke Marinade

Pam Adams

2 pounds medium shrimp,
cooked, peeled and
deveined
2 (14-ounce) cans artichoke
hearts
15-20 small mushrooms
¾ cup olive oil
¼ cup tarragon vinegar
2 tablespoons water
2 cloves garlic, crushed
1 teaspoon sugar
½ teaspoon freshly ground pepper
1½ teaspoons salt
1½ teaspoons dry mustard

1. Combine shrimp, artichokes and
mushrooms in a container with a
seal.

2. Combine the remaining
ingredients in a screw top jar,
shake well and pour over the
shrimp mixture. Cover tightly and
refrigerate overnight.

3. Stir 2 or 3 times during the
marinating process. Drain off the
marinade and serve.

*You can substitute white wine vinegar for
tarragon vinegar.*

Serves 12 to 15.

Madison Marinated Shrimp

Barbara MH Daigneault

Shrimp and champagne. Yummy and what a great combination. This was served at a Rehearsal Dinner at a friend's parent's home in Madison, Connecticut. The medley of shrimp and artichokes is so pleasing to the palate. Everyone wants this recipe. I have only shared it with a few very close friends over the years, it's one of those "best kept secret" recipes you'll just want to keep to yourself.

1   pound (31-40 count) shrimp, peeled and deveined

1   (14-ounce) can artichoke hearts, drained and halved

½   small red onion, peeled and sliced thinly into rings

1   (8-ounce) can sliced water chestnuts, drained

Marinade

½   cup canola oil

¼   cup white wine vinegar

3   tablespoons dry white wine

2   tablespoons snipped parsley

½   teaspoon sugar

¼   teaspoon salt

¼   teaspoon paprika

⅛   teaspoon whole black peppercorns

½   clove garlic, minced

1. Bring a medium pan of water to a boil. When the water boils, add the cleaned shrimp and bring the water back to a boil for 1 minute. Remove from heat, drain and rinse under cold water.

2. After the shrimp cool, put into a large food storage bag along with the artichoke hearts, onion and water chestnuts.

1. Place all ingredients in a screw top jar. Cover and shake well. Pour over shrimp mixture. Marinate for 24 hours turning several times.

You must use fresh shrimp and cook them yourself. A little more work, but worth the extra flavor.

Serves 6.

Mousse of Sole with Sauce Salpicon de Joinville

Audrey Mingolla

2 pounds filet of sole
7 egg whites
1½ cups heavy cream
½ teaspoon salt
3 drops Tabasco Sauce

1. Puree all ingredients in food processor.

2. Grease 8 individual molds and fill with mixture.

3. Bake at 350° in water bath about 40 minutes or until done.

Sauce Salpicon de Joinville
½ cup shrimp, diced
½ cup scallops, diced
1 cup lobster meat, diced
1 stick plus 1 tablespoon butter, divided
1 cup brandy
2 cups heavy cream

1. Sauté seafood in 1 tablespoon of butter. Flame seafood in brandy until flame burns out.

2. Add cream and remaining butter and cook until slightly thickened.

3. Invert mousse from molds onto individual plates and top with sauce.

Caryl Masiello's Pecans

Audrey Mingolla

1 egg white
1 tablespoon cold water
1 pound pecans
1 cup sugar
1 teaspoon cinnamon
1 teaspoon coriander
  Dash of salt

1. Beat together egg white and water until frothy. Add pecans and coat evenly.

2. Mix together dry ingredients and coat pecan mixture.

3. Spread of a greased cookie sheet. Bake at 300° for 30 minutes. Stir frequently while baking.

Tortilla Tucks

Ann Bouvier Achorn

*I first tasted this recipe at a friend's cocktail party a number of years ago.
There was quite a gathering around one particular area and people couldn't seem
to get there fast enough. This hors d'oeuvres was the magnet. This is always a hit
and people always request the recipe. Because this must be made ahead,
it is served directly from the refrigerator and is easily portable.
It is an easy selection for the cook as well.*

10 (6-inch) flour tortillas
2   (8-ounce) packages cream
     cheese, softened
9   ounces Cheddar cheese,
     shredded
2   cups thick salsa
5-6 green onions, chopped
1   (16-ounce) can black olives,
     drained and chopped

1. Spread each tortilla with a layer of cream cheese. Sprinkle with Cheddar cheese, salsa, green onion and olives.

2. Roll up as tightly as possible and place seam side down on flat dish. Cover with plastic wrap and refrigerate 8 to 48 hours.

3. To serve, slice into 1-inch pieces.

Black beans can be substituted for olives.

Harvest Spiced Nuts

J. Cichy-Natoli

1   egg white, slightly beaten
1   teaspoon cold water
4   cups mixed nuts, salted
     (no peanuts)
1   cup sugar
2   tablespoons pumpkin pie spice

1. Combine egg white and water. Add nuts and toss to coat.

2. Combine sugar and pumpkin pie spice. Toss into mixture.

2. Spread on a lightly greased cookie sheet. Bake 300° for 20-25 minutes. When cooled, break apart.

Sesame-Crusted Shrimp
with Tahini-Ginger Dipping Sauce

Cheryl Bedard

*A very unique Asian appetizer and simple to make. This recipe was
an immediate hit with family and friends. It has become one of my favorites.*

24 medium shrimp, peeled and
    deveined, tails intact
2 teaspoons vegetable oil
¼ teaspoon kosher salt
⅛ teaspoon freshly ground
    pepper
1 tablespoon black sesame seeds
    or 2 tablespoons white
    sesame seeds

1. Toss the shrimp in a bowl with
the oil, kosher salt and pepper. Dip
one side of each shrimp in the
sesame seeds. Place on a foil-lined
baking sheet, sesame seed side up.

2. Bake at 450° for 5 to 7 minutes
or until shrimp are opaque. Finish
under broiler to toast sesame
seeds.

3. Serve warm with dipping sauce.

Dipping Sauce
½ cup mayonnaise
⅓ cup tahini
2 tablespoons mirin
    (sweet rice wine)
2 tablespoons soy sauce
2 tablespoons seasoned rice
    vinegar
2 tablespoons lime juice
2 tablespoons grated peeled
    fresh gingerroot
1 tablespoon sesame oil

1. Combine all ingredients in a
food processor and process until
smooth. Refrigerate until chilled,
about 2 hours.

*The dipping sauce can be prepared 3 days
in advance. The shrimp can be prepared
up to 8 hours in advance and refrigerated.*

Makes 24 shrimp.

Beverages, Accompaniments & Condiments

Welcome Additions

The Garden at Robert and Joan Johnson, Westview Drive

This garden was featured at the 2002 Sutton Garden Club's "Inspirational Gardens" tour. This statue welcomes you into a lovely rose garden where one can reflect upon the beauty of the season. Hidden behind the rose garden are impressive water gardens and koi ponds. In 1956, Mr. and Mrs. Johnson purchased a house lot for $1,100.00 from Ernest MacDonald. This land was part of a dairy farm where cows were led to pastures to graze. Being the first home on the street, the Johnson's had the privilege of naming it "Westview Drive".

Beverages, Accompaniments and Condiments

Apricot Slush

Patricia M. Morse

This can be made up ahead and stored in the freezer. Great for drop by guests in the summer. We keep it on hand at the camp all summer long.

2	tablespoons instant ice tea mix
8	cups hot water
1	(12-ounce) can frozen orange juice concentrate
1	(12-ounce) can frozen lemonade concentrate
1½	cups sugar
2	cups apricot brandy
	Ginger ale
	Mint leaves for garnish

1. Mix all ingredients mixing brandy in last.

2. Pour into plastic containers. Cover. Freeze.

3. Put a few scoops in glass, add ginger ale and garnish with a mint leaf.

Eggnog "Quinn Nog"

Jennifer Quinn

My husband's aunt gave this recipe to me. It has been in his family for many years. This eggnog is usually served around Thanksgiving and Christmas. Everyone loves it, but it's deadly! Beware!

12	eggs, separated, reserve whites
1½	cups super fine sugar
1	quart whole milk
1½	quarts heavy cream, divided
1	quart bourbon
½	cup dark rum
2	cups cognac
	Grated nutmeg

1. Beat egg yolks for approximately 10 minutes, until thick and yellow.

2. Gradually add sugar then beat in milk and 1 quart cream. Add liquor. (This portion can keep in refrigerator until ready to serve.)

3. Just before serving, allow egg whites to come to room temperature and then beat until stiff. Fold into other mixture. Whip remaining ½ quart cream and fold in.

4. Serve topped with grated nutmeg.

This can also be made without the liquor.

Banana Brunch Punch

Patricia M. Morse

I make this over the holidays and everyone (all ages) loved it! Fabulous!

6 medium, ripe bananas
1 (12-ounce) can frozen orange juice concentrate
1 (12-ounce) can frozen lemonade concentrate
3 cups warm water, divided
1 cup sugar, divided
1 (46-ounce) can pineapple juice
3 (2-liter) bottles lemon-lime soda
Orange slices for garnish

1. In a blender add bananas, orange juice and lemonade, blend until smooth. Remove ½ of mixture and set aside.

2. Add 1½ cups water and ½ cup sugar to mixture in blender. Blend until smooth.

3. Repeat with remaining banana mixture. Pour into containers, cover and freeze until solid.

4. One hour before serving, take punch base out of freezer.

5. Just before serving, place in large punch bowl. Add pineapple juice and soda. Garnish with orange slices.

Add a little rum for a great summer drink!

Serves 20.

Glugg

Cheryl Bedard

*I received this recipe from my first roommate when I was
19 years old (when the drinking age was 18). I make a batch every winter just to fill
the house with the wonderful aroma! It tastes great on a cold winter evening.*

12 ounces Burgundy wine	1. Mix all ingredients and simmer
4 ounces apricot brandy	15 to 20 minutes. Do not boil.
1 orange, quartered (do not peel)	2. Serve warm.
9 cloves	
3 cinnamon sticks	
4 ounces honey	

Slushy Piña Coladas

Patricia M. Morse

*These are a big hit at our annual 4th of July party.
Keeps in freezer for weeks. Enjoy lakeside or wherever!*

1 (48-ounce) can pineapple juice
3½ cups light rum
1 (8-ounce) can coconut milk
    Ginger ale or lemon-lime soda

1. Combine first 3 ingredients. Pour into a 13 x 9-inch plastic pan with cover so mixture is no more than 1½-inch thick. Freeze.

2. When ready to serve, scoop out 2 to 3 tablespoons of the frozen mixture into a glass of your choice.

3. Top with ginger ale or lemon-lime soda to taste.

Summertime Punch

Janet O'Neill

I have been asked to make this punch for many special occasions, baby or bridal shower, holiday brunch or teachers' luncheons. It looks as good as it tastes and is very easy to make. My cousin sends me lemon leaves from his backyard tree in Cotati, CA and I store them year round in my freezer.

1 (64-ounce) bottle raspberry-cranberry drink, chilled
3½ cups water, divided
2 large lemons
2 large limes
1 medium nectarine
½ pound seedless green grapes
½ cup raspberries
  Lemon leaves
5 tea bags
¼ cup sugar
1 (1-liter) bottle lemon-lime soft drink, chilled
1 (6-ounce) can frozen lemonade concentrate

Early in the day or day ahead

1. Mix together 3 cups raspberry-cranberry drink and 2 cups water. Pour 3½ cups of this drink mixture into 6-cup ring mold and freeze. Refrigerate remainder.

2. Cut a continuous 1-inch wide strip of peel from each lemon and lime; reserve peels.

3. Squeeze juice from lemons and limes to equal ¼ cup each and refrigerate to use in punch later. Trim white membrane from lemon- and lime-peel strips. Form each strip into a rose by rolling it tightly, skin-side out, around finger and secure with a toothpick. Cover and refrigerate.

4. When juice ring is frozen, cut nectarine into wedges and separate grapes into small clusters. Discard toothpicks from citrus peel roses and arrange them with nectarine wedges, grape clusters, raspberries and lemon leaves on frozen ring for garnish. Pour in half of remaining drink mixture and freeze about 1 hour to set garnishes. Add remaining drink mixture and freeze.

5. In 4-cup glass measuring cup, pour boiling water over tea bags to equal 4 cups. Let steep 10 minutes. Discard tea bags. Cover and refrigerate until ready to complete punch.

Just Before Serving

1. In 6-quart punch bowl, mix sugar, lemon-lime drink, undiluted lemonade, tea, remaining cranberry drink, lemon and lime juices and remaining 1½ cups cold water.

2. Place punch bowl on tray. Add mold to punch.

The mold can also be made without the leaves.

Serves 16.

Irish Whiskey Cream

Mark Campbell

Excellent for mornings and evenings during the holidays!

3 eggs	1. Put all ingredients in blender for 2 minutes. Serve.
2 tablespoons chocolate syrup	
1 (12-ounce) can sweetened condensed milk	*Keeps in refrigerator for 4 to 6 weeks.*
¼ teaspoon coconut extract	
1 quart frozen non-dairy coffee creamer, thawed	
1 cup whiskey	

Margaritas by the Pitcher

Cindy Wolodkin

1 cup gold tequila
½ cup lemon juice, freshly squeezed
¼ cup lime juice, freshly squeezed
2 tablespoons sugar
½ cup triple sec
¾ cup Grand Marnier

1. All the ingredients can be blended with ice or simply served on the rocks.

You also have the option of blending in the Grand Marnier or floating it on top of the finished drink.

Whispering Smiths

Patricia M. Morse

1 (12-ounce) can frozen pink lemonade, thawed
12 ounces vodka
18 ounces ginger ale or Sprite
   Additional ginger ale or Sprite for serving

1. Mix all ingredients and pour into a plastic shallow pan. Cover and freeze.

2. When ready to serve, add 2 scoops of frozen mixture to glass and add ginger ale to taste.

This can be made ahead of time and stored in the freezer until needed. I use the lemonade can to do the measurements.

Apple Ginger Chutney

Rita Dignan

2 Granny Smith apples, peeled, cored and chopped
1 cup minced onion
¾ cup apple cider vinegar
¾ cup firmly packed brown sugar
½ cup golden seedless raisins
2 tablespoons peeled and minced gingerroot
1 red bell pepper, minced
½ teaspoon dry mustard
½ teaspoon salt
½ teaspoon dried red pepper flakes

1. In a saucepan combine all ingredients. Bring the mixture to a boil stirring constantly.

2. Cook over moderate heat, stirring occasionally for 40 minutes or until it thickens.

3. Spoon chutney into glass jars with tight-fitting lids.

The chutney keeps covered and chilled for two weeks.

Makes 3 cups.

Flank Steak Marinade

Lisa Sarmento

For an outstanding piece of grilled flank steak, pour this marinade over the top and marinate overnight. Delicious!

⅔ cup ketchup
½ cup water
⅓ cup lemon juice
1 teaspoon celery seeds
2 teaspoons Worcestershire sauce
1 bay leaf
½ teaspoon dried basil
¼ teaspoon pepper
Dash of Tabasco Sauce

1. In a small saucepan, combine all ingredients. Simmer for 10 minutes.

2. Cool and pour over flank steak.

Jalapeño Pepper Jelly

Beatrice Sobaleski

This jelly is great spread over cream cheese and served with crackers.

5   medium whole jalapeño chili peppers
2   medium green bell peppers
1½ cups white vinegar
1   package powdered pectin plus 2 well rounded teaspoons
6   cups sugar
10 drops green food coloring

1. Rinse and chop all peppers. Retain half of jalapeño pepper seeds.

2. Place peppers and vinegar in blender and puree. (May have to do in a couple of batches.)

3. Put pureed ingredients in a 5-quart saucepan. Add pectin and bring to a rolling boil over high heat, stirring constantly.

4. Add sugar and food coloring and bring to a rolling boil once again. Boil exactly 1 minute.

5. Pour into jelly jars and seal.

Red peppers and red food coloring can be substituted for red jelly.

Makes 5 half-pint jars.

Ponzu

Jack Strouse

A Japanese sauce made with citrus juices that is great for basting chicken or fish.

1   cup orange juice
½   cup sake
¼   cup sugar
¼   cup soy sauce
2   tablespoons lime juice, to taste
¼   teaspoon red pepper flakes
1   tablespoon cornstarch

1. In a saucepan, mix all ingredients, except cornstarch. Bring to a boil and lower heat.

2. Mix cornstarch with ¼ cup cold water to create slurry. Add to orange juice mixture and simmer until slightly thickened.

3. Pour over chicken or fish before cooking.

Oaky Smokey Barbecue Sauce

Gary Edwin Mosher

This recipe is from my mother-in-laws first cousin, Betty Lu Schwarz. Betty put together a cookbook and gave it to all her children. We love this recipe for its simplicity when we are grilling and need a quick sauce. Great with spareribs, chicken and lamb.

¼ cup vinegar
½ cup water
2 tablespoons sugar
1 tablespoon mustard
½ teaspoon pepper
1½ teaspoons salt
½ teaspoon cayenne pepper
1 thick slice of lemon
1 onion, sliced
4 tablespoons butter
½ cup catsup
2 tablespoons Worcestershire sauce
1½ teaspoons liquid smoke

1. Mix first 10 ingredients in a saucepan and simmer 20 minutes uncovered.

2. Add catsup, Worcestershire sauce and liquid smoke and bring to a boil.

You may substitute Tabasco Sauce for cayenne pepper and a lime for a lemon. This recipe can be doubled.

Yields 1¾ cups.

Steak Baste

Debbi Abbott Holmgren

Everyone, who has had this, loves it! I recommend using this for gas grill or charcoal cooking.

1 cup soy sauce
¼ cup Gravy Master
2 large onions, coarsely chopped
2 tablespoons chopped garlic
2 teaspoons Italian herb seasoning mix

1. Combine all ingredients in a blender and blend until pureed.

2. Marinate steak for 1 to 2 hours at room temperature, being sure to coat both sides. Baste while cooking.

This recipe can be halved. Any leftover steak baste can be refrigerated in a glass jar. This could also be used to marinate pork as well.

Yields 2½ cups.

Singletary Farm Raisin Sauce

From The Kitchen of Mary Stevenson Benjamin
submitted by her daughter Betty Benjamin LeClaire

This recipe was used in 1940 in the "Singletary Supper" of baked ham. The supper included fresh fruit with sherbet, mashed potatoes, raisin sauce, fresh vegetables, salad, relishes, assorted rolls, ice cream with sauces or sherbet and cakes. The cost was $1.00. Barbara Beaton, Marthena King and Ruth Putnam were among the waitresses who served it. They made $1.00 a night plus shared tips. In addition to serving, they also did the dishes.

1   cup light brown sugar
3   tablespoons flour
½   teaspoon pepper
    Pinch of cloves
    Pinch of salt
3   tablespoons cider vinegar
½   cup water
2   tablespoons butter

1. Combine the dry ingredients and add liquids.

2. Add butter and cook over medium heat, stirring as needed until mixture comes to low boil and thickens.

You may add raisins to suit your taste or make a "raisinless" sauce. Can be made ahead of time and kept in the refrigerator. A little water may have to be added to reheat.

Fresh Tomato Salsa

Linda Erickson

3 large vine ripe tomatoes, chopped
1 medium red onion, chopped
1 small green bell pepper, chopped
2 cloves elephant garlic, diced
2 teaspoons minced fresh
   jalapeño peppers, to taste
1 tablespoon olive oil
   Garlic salt, to taste
   Fresh chopped cilantro, to taste
   Fresh chopped parsley, to taste

1. Mix all ingredients and refrigerate for at least 1 hour before serving.

2. Serve with tortilla chips.

Cindy's Sweet and Spicy Mustard

Cindy King

This recipe is the "best kept secret" you will ever want to pass on! This has a real bite to it!

½ cup white vinegar
½ cup Colman's English dry
   mustard
1 cup sugar
2 eggs, slightly beaten

1. Mix together vinegar and mustard and let sit overnight in a covered saucepan.

2. The next day, add the sugar and eggs. Cook over medium heat with wooden spoon. Stir constantly until the mustard starts to bubble and thicken, about 20 to 30 minutes.

3. Pour into ½-pint canning jars and seal.

4. Serve with round buttery crackers and extra sharp cheddar cheese.

Overcooking will make the mustard hard.

Makes 3 half-pints.

Mom's Raw Cranberry Relish

Beverly B. Anderson

As long as I can remember, my mother would serve this dish with all the fixins' for Thanksgiving dinner. I have made this a traditional dish every year of our 36-year marriage. It brings back happy memories to take out the old family grinder and enjoy the taste and compliments of this "made from scratch" cranberry dish.

2	large oranges
4	cups fresh cranberries
2	red apples, cored (do not peel)
2	cups sugar
½	cup chopped walnuts

1. Peel oranges and reserve half of one peel.

2. Coarsely chop all fruit, including peel, in a food processor. Transfer fruit to bowl, add sugar and mix well.

3. Refrigerate several hours or overnight.

4. Add nuts just before serving.

I use an old-fashioned food chopper and attach it to a butcher-block table.

Serves 10 to 12.

Gingered Cranberry Relish

Kathy Dugan

One of my sisters shared this recipe years ago at Thanksgiving - it has become a family "favorite".

1½	cups dried cherries
1	cup fresh cranberries
1	cup sugar
¼	cup coarsely chopped crystallized ginger
½	cup plus 2 tablespoons orange juice
1	tablespoon finely grated lemon zest
6	tablespoons water

1. Combine all ingredients in a saucepan and bring to a boil over moderately high heat. Reduce heat slightly and cook until cranberries pop open (about 8 minutes), stirring frequently.

2. Transfer to a bowl and let cool.

3. Serve at room temperature.

Hot Dog Relish

Anah E. Perry

*Tracy Horne's mother from Manchaug, Massachusetts gave
this recipe to Alden Perry when he delivered milk. We have made it ever since.
50+ years! It is so good! Everyone loves it!*

5 cups seeded, finely chopped
   cucumbers (do not peel)
3 cups all purpose onions, finely
   chopped
2 red or green jalapeño peppers,
   finely chopped
¾ cup salt
1½ quarts of water
1 quart white vinegar
3 cups sugar
2 teaspoons mustard seed
2 tablespoons celery seed

1. Put cucumbers, onions, jalapeño peppers, salt and water in an aluminum kettle and soak overnight.

2. Drain the next day and rinse with water.

3. Place back in kettle and add vinegar, sugar, mustard seed and celery seed. Bring to a boil for 10 to 15 minutes.

4. Seal in jars.

*No yellow cucumbers. Red jalapeños give
a little color.*

Makes 7 pints.

Sweet Refrigerator Pickles

Nancy Perry

This is a good way to use all the cucumbers from your garden. I received this recipe from Elizabeth Froh when we lived on Hough Road. Betty received The Boston Post cane when she was 98 for being the oldest Sutton resident. At 103 years old, she still maintains her own home.

2 quarts (about 6 medium) thinly sliced cucumbers (do not peel)
2 onions, sliced
2 tablespoons salt
1 cup white vinegar
1½ cups sugar
1 teaspoon dill seed

1. Mix cucumbers, onions and salt. Let stand 2 to 3 hours. Drain and rinse well.

2. Mix vinegar, sugar and dill seed; pour over cucumbers and onions. Stir until sugar dissolves and the syrup is thin.

3. Pour into containers. Refrigerate or freeze.

Ripe Cucumber Pickles

From the Kitchen of Mildred A. Hutchinson
submitted by her daughter Norma Baker

4 quarts cucumbers, peeled, seeded and sliced
4 medium onions, sliced
2 red or green bell peppers, sliced
4 teaspoons salt
4 teaspoons white mustard seed
3 cups white vinegar
3 cups sugar
1 teaspoon dry mustard
1 teaspoon turmeric

1. Bring all ingredients to boil in a large pot. Cook between 5 and 10 minutes.

2. Pour into canning jars and seal.

Breads & Breakfast

Morning Greetings

The Barn at the Home of Patricia M. Morse, Wheelock Road

The sun rises over the hills of Sutton Center and what better way to greet each morning than with the call of a rooster. This barn was built in 1784. It is a very large and spacious barn built from native Sutton chestnut trees, a wood that was in abundance and very resistant to decay. Chestnut wood is known for its longevity and durability.

Breads and Breakfast

Daisy Putnam's Brown Bread

Gretel Smith

This recipe originated with my grandmother, Daisy Putnam. My mother, Albertine Putnam, made this recipe frequently to have with baked beans on Saturday night. She always had a supply for the hunters to take to Maine every fall.

1   cup all bran
1   cup sour milk
½   cup raisins
1   tablespoon molasses
½   cup sugar
1   cup flour
1   teaspoon baking soda
¼   teaspoon salt

1. Grease and flour the inside of a 1 pound coffee can. Use a kettle with cover and rack, deep enough to hold the coffee can. Pour in water to come half way up the can.

2. In a bowl, combine all bran and sour milk. Let stand 3 to 5 minutes or until cereal softens.

3. Stir in raisins and molasses. Add dry ingredients, mixing well.

4. Pour into prepared can. Cover can with aluminum foil. Place kettle on stove and boil gently for 3 hours. Add water to kettle as needed.

5. Remove can to a rack, place upside down and allow to cool for 20 minutes. Loosen sides with a long knife and let the bread slide out.

To sour milk, add 5 teaspoons of vinegar to 1 cup of milk.

Yields 1 loaf.

Steamed Brown Bread

Deb Hebert

This recipe is a favorite addition to a ham and baked beans dinner. The recipe comes from The New American Cookbook published in 1941. We found this book in a summer camp on Lake Singletary. It is fascinating to reflect on history through a cookbook. For example, this book offers menu planning for a liberal diet ($3,000 or over annual income), a moderate-cost adequate diet ($2,000 to $3,000 annual income) and a minimum-cost adequate diet ($1,000 to $2,000 annual income).

1 cup white flour
1 cup whole wheat flour
1 cup cornmeal
1½ teaspoons salt
½ cup sugar
1 teaspoon baking soda
½ cup molasses
1½ cups buttermilk
2 tablespoons oil
½ cup raisins (optional)

1. In a large bowl, blend white flour, whole-wheat flour, cornmeal, salt and sugar together.

2. In a small bowl, mix soda and molasses together. Add molasses mixture and buttermilk to the dry ingredients. Add oil. Mix well.

3. Fill a greased pudding mold ¾ full and steam on top of the stove in a water bath for 3 hours.

For raisin brown bread, add ½ cup of flour dredged raisins and reduce the sugar to ¼ cup.

Yields 1 loaf.

Finnish Coffee Bread

Nancy Rice

1 cup scalded milk

½ cup plus 2 tablespoons butter, divided

½ cup sugar

1 teaspoon salt

2 eggs, beaten and divided

1 package dry yeast

½ cup lukewarm water

10 cardamom seeds, crushed

5 cups flour

1 tablespoon confectioners' sugar

1 tablespoon almond extract

1. Pour scalded milk over ½ cup butter, sugar and salt. Cool until lukewarm.

2. Add eggs, reserving 1 tablespoon of beaten egg.

3. Dissolve yeast in ½ cup lukewarm water and add to milk and egg mixture along with cardamom seeds.

4. Add 5 cups flour and knead. Cover and let rise until double.

5. Divide dough in half. To shape the bread, roll each piece into rectangular shapes.

6. Mix together 2 tablespoons melted butter, confectioners' sugar and almond extract. Spread filling onto surface. Roll up bread and place in a 13 x 9-inch pan.

7. Snip top with scissors and fake braid by pressing to left and to right to look like a braid. Cover and let rise again.

8. Bake at 350° for 1 hour.

9. Brush each piece of bread with reserved egg and sprinkle with sugar. Bake until cake tester inserted in center comes out clean.

Yields 1 loaf.

Mother's Homemade Bread

Diane Lavoie

*For those of you who frequented "Henry's Lunch" on Route 146
(the site of the Econo Lodge) back in the 50's and 60's and loved the bread,
here is the recipe. My mother-in-law, Gabrielle Lavoie, couldn't make enough of it
for her customers. She would always run out of bread before the end of the day.
This is one of those recipes that was handed down to her by her mother and never
measured. One day I watched her as she was about to place each ingredient into a
bowl. I would measure it and write it down so the rest of our family could have it.
This bread makes a fantastic toast! Her children (Paul, Marcel, Normand, Andrew,
Maryjean, Madeleine and Raymond) call it "Mother's Bread". To this day
they will tell you no one could make bread like Mother. I think she
added an extra ingredient called "Mother's Love".*

2 packages dry yeast
5½ cups lukewarm water
2 tablespoons salt
2 tablespoons sugar
½ cup milk, scalded
¼ cup shortening
1 (5-pound) bag, plus 1 cup
   flour

1. In a large bowl, soak yeast for approximately 15 minutes in lukewarm water and salt.

2. Add sugar, milk and shortening. Sift the flour into the water mixture, kneading as you go along.

3. Knead together approximately 20 to 25 minutes on a floured surface. Place in a greased bowl and cover. Let rise until doubled.

6. Knead and let rise again. Cut into 5 loaves and place into greased pans.

7. Bake at 375° for 1 hour (when you tap, loaves will sound hollow). Take out of pans and cool on racks. Bottoms should be light brown.

Add 5½ cups of water first and add another ½ cup if it is too dry. I usually find I need to add the rest of it. When it feels nice and elasticity, then it is just right.

Yields 5 loaves.

Oatmeal Molasses Bread

Beatrice Sobaleski

This is my favorite bread!

1 cup quick oats
½ cup whole wheat flour
½ cup brown sugar
2 tablespoons molasses
1 tablespoon salt
2 tablespoons margarine
2 cups boiling water
1 package dry yeast
½ cup warm water
5-6 cups flour

1. In a large bowl, combine oats, whole-wheat flour, sugar, molasses, salt and margarine. Pour the boiling water over all and mix well.

2. When mixture is cooled to lukewarm, dissolve yeast in lukewarm water and add to cooled mixture.

3. When mixture is cool, stir in approximately half of the flour then turn onto a floured surface and knead in remaining flour. Place in greased bowl. Cover and let rise until double.

4. Punch down and shape into two loaves. Place in greased bread pans and let rise again.

5. Bake at 350° for 30 to 40 minutes.

Yields 2 loaves.

Grandma's Farm Cornbread

LaDona Coll

This is my favorite recipe from my grandmother who lived in Ohio. Her cornbread always tasted the best, perhaps it was the iron skillet she used to bake with.

1	cup flour
1	cup cornmeal
1¼	cups sugar
4	teaspoons baking powder
½	teaspoon salt
1	egg
1	cup milk
¼	cup shortening, melted

1. In a large bowl, combine dry ingredients and mix well.

2. In a smaller bowl, mix together egg, milk and shortening. Combine moist mixture to dry ingredients and mix until blended. Be careful not to over mix.

3. Pour into a greased 8 x 8-inch pan. Bake at 400° for 25 to 30 minutes.

French Breakfast Puffs

Nancy Perry

This isn't a fancy recipe, however it's my children's favorite for Christmas morning.

⅓	cup shortening
1	cup sugar, divided
1	egg
1½	cups flour
1½	teaspoons baking powder
¼	teaspoon nutmeg
½	cup milk
⅓	cup butter, melted
1	teaspoon cinnamon

1. In a large bowl, mix shortening, ½ cup sugar and egg.

2. In a separate bowl, combine flour, baking powder and nutmeg, mix alternately with milk and add to shortening mixture.

3. Fill greased muffin pans ⅔ full. Bake at 350° for 20 minutes.

4. Roll each muffin top in melted butter, then in remaining ½ cup sugar mixed with cinnamon.

Yields 12 muffins.

Frigidaire Dinner Rolls

From the Kitchen of Faith Smith
submitted by her daughter Hope Stockhaus

My mom made these rolls for many special meals.
The kids would fight over who was going to punch the dough.

1	yeast cake
½	cup sugar
1	teaspoon salt
2	cups lukewarm water
1	egg
7	cups sifted flour, divided
5	tablespoons shortening, melted

1. In a large bowl, crumble yeast. Add sugar, salt and water to dissolve.

2. Add egg.

3. Sift flour before measuring. Add half the flour and beat well.

4. Add melted shortening and mix in remaining flour. Let rise to double its size. Punch down.

5. Shape into rolls and place on greased pan. Let rise slowly once again to double.

6. Bake at 425° for 20 to 25 minutes.

Cranberry Walnut Bread

Linda Bjorn

2	cups flour
1	teaspoon baking soda
1	teaspoon salt
¾	cup sugar
1	egg
⅓	cup orange juice
3	tablespoons white vinegar plus water to make ⅔ cup
¼	cup vegetable oil
1	cup raw cranberries, halved
1	cup chopped walnuts

1. In a large bowl, sift together dry ingredients.

2. In a medium bowl, beat egg with a fork. Stir in orange juice, vinegar with water and oil. Add all at once to dry ingredients. Stir until flour is moistened. Add cranberries and nuts.

3. Pour mixture into a greased loaf pan. Bake at 350° for 60 to 70 minutes.

Yields 1 loaf.

Gooey Pecan Rolls

From the Kitchen of Ethel Hutchinson
submitted by her niece Norma Baker

These rolls evoke fond memories of Thanksgiving at my aunt's house. She had the perfect Thanksgiving house. Her old walnut table sat all 17 of us comfortably in her colonial dining room. Her rolls were always prepared to perfection. I only make them for special holidays and they always remain a treat.

½ cup milk

1 teaspoon salt

1 tablespoon plus ¼ cup sugar, divided

1 yeast cake

1 egg

2 tablespoons shortening, softened

2-2¼ cups sifted flour

1 tablespoon soft butter

1 teaspoon cinnamon

¼ cup melted butter

¼ cup brown sugar

1. In a large pan, heat milk. Remove from heat and add salt and 1 tablespoon sugar. Crumble yeast cake into mixture and stir until dissolved. Stir in egg and shortening.

2. Mix in enough flour to handle easily. Mix dough with hands until moderately stiff. Roll out dough into 12 x 7-inch oblong.

3. Spread surface with butter then sprinkle with remaining ¼ cup sugar and cinnamon. Roll up and cut into 12 slices.

4. Place in a 9-inch round pan coated with melted butter and brown sugar. Cover and let rise about 30 minutes.

5. Bake at 400° for 20 to 25 minutes or until golden brown. When done, turn pan upside down onto serving plate.

Yields 12 rolls.

Wake Up and Smell the Rolls

Cheryl Bedard

Make these the night before and pop them into the oven in the morning. They are so delicious and easy!

1 cup coarsely chopped walnuts or pecans
1 cup raisins (optional)
1 (24-count) package frozen dinner rolls (do not thaw)
Ground cinnamon
1 (6-ounce) package vanilla pudding (not instant)
½ cup packed brown sugar
1 stick butter

1. Layer nuts and raisins on the bottom of a greased 13 x 9-inch pan.

2. Roll frozen dough balls in cinnamon and place in the pan, spacing evenly. Sprinkle dry pudding and brown sugar evenly over the top.

3. Melt the butter and pour over the rolls. Cover and place in a cold oven overnight to rise.

4. In the morning, uncover the pan and place it back into the cold oven and start the oven, cooking at 350° for 30 minutes.

5. Once done, loosen rolls from the sides of the pan with a knife. Place a large platter on top of the pan and flip the rolls upside down onto the platter. Serve warm.

You can also put these in the oven overnight, not covered with plastic wrap and set the oven to auto start.

Yields 24 rolls.

Lemon Poppy Seed Pound Cake

Audrey Mingolla

3 cups flour
¼ teaspoon baking soda
¼ teaspoon salt
1½ cups unsalted butter, room temperature
3 cups sugar
6 eggs
Grated rind of 2 lemons
2 teaspoons pure lemon extract
¼ cup poppy seeds
1 cup sour cream
Confectioners' sugar for dusting

1. Sift together flour, baking soda and salt. Set aside.

2. In a large bowl, cream butter until light and fluffy. Add sugar and beat until well blended. Add eggs, one at a time, beating well after each. Add lemon rind, lemon extract and poppy seeds. Beat for 2 minutes.

3. Add the flour mixture into the batter alternating with sour cream, beginning and ending with the flour mixture.

4. Spoon the batter into a greased 10-inch tube pan. Tap the pan once on the counter to settle any air pockets. Bake at 300° in center of oven for 1½ hours or until the cake pulls away from the edge of the pan or until a toothpick inserted in the middle comes out clean.

5. Cool on a wire rack for 30 minutes. Remove from pan and cool completely before dusting with confectioners' sugar.

Perfect Pumpkin Bread

Albertine M. Putnam

This bread is especially tasty when spices are fresh!

⅔ cup shortening
2½ cups sugar
4 eggs, beaten
2 cups pumpkin
⅔ cup water
1 teaspoon baking soda
3½ cups flour
3 teaspoons baking powder
1 teaspoon cloves
1 teaspoon cinnamon
⅔ cup dates or raisins
⅔ cup chopped walnuts or pecans

1. Cream shortening and sugar. Add eggs and mix well. Add pumpkin, water and baking soda.

2. Sift remaining dry ingredients and add to creamed mixture. Stir in dates and nuts.

3. Pour mixture into 2 greased and floured loaf pans. Bake at 350° for 1 hour or until a toothpick inserted in the center comes out clean.

Yields 2 loaves.

Rhubarb Bread

Karen Matson

A great bread to make when visiting family or friends. This recipe makes 2 loaves and my three sons are always happy when I leave one behind.

1 cup brown sugar
½ cup plus 2 tablespoons sugar
⅔ cup vegetable oil
2 eggs
1 cup milk
1 teaspoon vanilla
1 teaspoon salt
2½ cups flour
1½ teaspoons baking powder
½ teaspoon baking soda
1½ cups diced rhubarb
½ cup chopped nuts (optional)

1. Mix together sugars and oil. Add eggs and milk. Blend well.

2. Stir in remaining ingredients. Fold in rhubarb and nuts.

3. Pour batter into 2 greased loaf pans. Bake at 350° for 1 hour.

Yields 2 loaves.

Strawberry Bread

Jennifer Quinn

Great snack for any time of the day!

3 cups sliced strawberries
4 eggs
1¼ cups vegetable oil
3 cups flour
2 cups sugar
3 teaspoons cinnamon
1 teaspoon baking soda
1 teaspoon salt
1 cup chopped walnuts
   (optional)

1. In a medium bowl, combine strawberries, eggs and oil. Mix well.

2. In a large bowl, combine all dry ingredients, including nuts. Add strawberry mixture to dry mixture and stir until just blended.

3. Pour into 2 greased loaf pans. Bake at 350° for 1 hour.

Yields 2 loaves.

Zucchini Bread

Patricia M. Morse

3 eggs
1 cup brown sugar
1 cup sugar
1 cup vegetable oil
2 cups finely grated zucchini
1 teaspoon vanilla
2½ cups flour
½ cup wheat germ
3 teaspoons cinnamon
1 teaspoon salt
1 teaspoon baking soda
1 teaspoon baking powder
   Whole walnut halves

1. Beat eggs until light and fluffy. Add sugars, oil, zucchini and vanilla. Mix well.

2. Add dry ingredients, except the walnuts. Mix well again.

3. Pour into greased and floured loaf pan. Lay a row of nuts down center of the bread. Bake at 325° for 1 hour.

Yields 1 loaf.

Sour Cream Coffee Cake

From the Kitchen of Betty B. Windle
submitted by her daughter-in-law Cynthia C. Windle

My mother-in-law wrote to her daughter, "Dear Connie, here is my favorite recipe. It is quick and easy, needs no frosting and it can be eaten warm or cool."

½ cup packed light brown sugar
1 teaspoon cinnamon
½ cup chopped walnuts
1 stick margarine
1 cup sugar
2 large eggs
1 cup sour cream
2 cups flour
1 teaspoon baking powder
1 teaspoon baking soda
½ teaspoon salt
1 teaspoon vanilla

1. In a small bowl, mix brown sugar, cinnamon and walnuts and set aside.

2. In a mixer, cream margarine, sugar, eggs and sour cream.

3. In a medium bowl, sift together flour, baking powder, baking soda and salt. Add sifted ingredients to cream mixture and beat at medium speed until smooth. Add vanilla and blend.

4. Pour half the batter into a greased tube pan. Top with ½ the nut mixture, followed by remaining batter and top with remaining nut mixture. Bake at 350° for 40 minutes.

This cake freezes well.

Serves 10 to 12.

Cranberry Yogurt Coffee Cake

Darylene Perry

*This is one of the many recipes I received when I visited the
Ocean Spray kitchen. I love cranberries and this recipe is delicious.*

1 (18½-ounce) box yellow cake mix
1 (3½-ounce) package vanilla instant pudding
4 eggs
¾ cup plain yogurt
1 cup vegetable oil
1 (16-ounce) can Ocean Spray whole berry cranberry sauce
½ cup chopped walnuts

1. In a large bowl, blend cake mix, pudding mix, eggs, yogurt and oil. Beat with electric mixer on high for 3 minutes.

2. Grease and flour a 13 x 9 x 2-inch pan. Pour ⅔ of batter in pan. Spoon cranberry sauce evenly over it. Spoon remaining batter evenly over cranberry sauce. Sprinkle with nuts.

3. Bake at 350° for 55 to 60 minutes. Cool on rack 35 minutes before serving.

Serves 20.

Harvest Loaf

Lee Wenc

3½ cups flour
1 teaspoon salt
½ teaspoon cloves
2 teaspoons baking soda
1 teaspoon nutmeg
2 teaspoons cinnamon
½ teaspoon ginger
2 sticks butter
2 cups sugar
4 eggs
1 (15-ounce) can pumpkin
1½ cups chocolate chips
1½ cups chopped walnuts

1. In a medium bowl, mix first 7 ingredients.

2. In a large bowl, cream butter and sugar. Beat at high speed until light and fluffy. Add eggs, dry ingredients and pumpkin. Beat together.

3. Stir in chocolate chips and walnuts.

4. Pour into 2 greased loaf pans. Bake at 350° for 60 minutes.

Yields 2 loaves.

Sunrise Apricot Orange Muffins

Gladys L. Stewart

1 cup chopped dried apricots
1 cup boiling water
1 stick butter or margarine, softened
1¼ cups sugar, divided
¾ cup sour cream
2 cups all-purpose flour
1 teaspoon baking soda
½ teaspoon salt
1 tablespoon freshly grated orange peel
½ cup chopped walnuts or pecans
¼ cup orange juice

1. Combine apricots and water. Let stand for 5 minutes. Drain and discard liquid, set apricots aside.

2. In a large bowl, cream butter and 1 cup sugar until fluffy. Add sour cream and mix well.

3. In a separate bowl, combine dry ingredients and add to the creamed mixture until just moistened. Fold in orange peel, nuts and apricots. The batter will be very stiff.

4. Fill greased muffins pans ¾ full. Bake at 400° for 18 to 20 minutes or until muffins test done.

5. Combine remaining ½ cup sugar and orange juice. Dip tops of warm muffins in this mixture.

Yields 1 dozen.

Simple and Delicious Banana Muffins

Karen Arakelian Weldon

This also makes great banana bread!

1 stick butter
2 cups sugar
3 eggs
3-4 bananas, mashed
3 cups flour
2 teaspoons baking powder
   Pinch of salt
1 teaspoon baking soda
1 cup milk
½ cup chopped nuts (optional)

1. In a large bowl, cream butter and add sugar. Mix well. Add eggs and bananas.

2. Sift together flour, baking powder and salt.

3. Dissolve baking soda in milk. Add flour and milk alternately to the banana mixture. Beat well. Add nuts if desired.

4. Spoon into greased muffin tins. Bake at 375° for 20 to 25 minutes.

For banana bread, pour into a greased loaf pan and bake at 350° for 45 minutes to 1 hour.

Yields 2½ dozen.

Blueberry Muffins with Streusel or Glaze

Rebecca Smith

Two different muffins combined into one!

1 cup sugar
1 stick margarine
2 eggs, slightly beaten
1 cup sour cream
1 teaspoon vanilla or almond extract
2 cups flour
1 teaspoon baking powder
½ teaspoon baking soda
¼ teaspoon salt
2 cups fresh blueberries

1. In a large bowl, cream together sugar and margarine. Mix in eggs, sour cream and extract.

2. In another bowl, combine flour, baking powder, baking soda and salt.

3. Mix blueberries into flour mixture. Combine dry and liquid ingredients.

4. Spoon into greased muffin tins. If you wish to use the streusel topping, it must go on before baking. Bake at 375° for 20 to 25 minutes.

Streusel Topping

¼ cup sugar
3 tablespoons flour
½ teaspoon cinnamon
1 tablespoon butter, melted

1. Combine all topping ingredients until mixture is crumbly. Sprinkle on top of muffins and bake.

Glaze

¾ cup confectioners' sugar
½ teaspoon vanilla or almond extract
3 teaspoons hot water

1. Mix all glaze ingredients until smooth and drizzle over baked muffins.

Yields 12 muffins.

B & B Bran Muffins

Chris Rice

Many years ago, I had these muffins at a Bed and Breakfast in Maine and added this recipe to my collection. Our family loves them and I love having the batter in the refrigerator to be able to serve warm muffins every morning.

2 cups boiling water
6 cups all bran, divided
2 sticks butter or margarine
2½ cups sugar
4 eggs
5 cups flour
2 teaspoons salt
5 teaspoons baking soda
1 quart buttermilk

1. Pour boiling water over 4 cups of cereal. Set aside to cool.

2. In a large bowl, cream together butter and sugar. Add eggs and beat well.

3. Add dry ingredients alternating with buttermilk. Stir in remaining dry cereal and cooled cereal into batter. Blend thoroughly.

4. Bake at 400°, in greased muffin tins, for 25 to 30 minutes.

Batter keeps in refrigerator up to 2 weeks.

Yields 48 muffins.

Morning Glory Muffins

Lynn Murphy O'Neal

An all time favorite that originated in Nantucket some 20 years ago.

1 ¼ cups sugar
2 ¼ cups flour
1   tablespoon cinnamon
2   teaspoons baking soda
½   teaspoon salt
½   cup shredded coconut
½   cup raisins
2   cups grated carrots
1   apple, peeled and shredded
1   (8-ounce) can crushed
      pineapple, drained
½   cup chopped walnuts or
      pecans
3   eggs
1   cup vegetable oil
1   teaspoon vanilla

1. In a large bowl, sift together sugar, flour, cinnamon, baking soda and salt. Add coconut, raisins, carrots, apple, pineapple and nuts. Stir to combine.

2. In a separate bowl, whisk eggs, oil and vanilla. Pour into the dry mixture and blend well.

3. Spoon batter into muffin tins lined with papers, filling to the brim. Bake at 350° for 35 minutes. Cool muffins in the pan for 10 minutes then turn out and finish cooling on wire rack.

These muffins freeze well.

Yields 16 muffins.

Light Scones

Pam Adams

2 cups flour
2 tablespoons sugar
3 teaspoons baking powder
1 teaspoon salt
¼ teaspoon baking soda
½ cup raisins
½ cup yogurt
¼ cup oil
3 tablespoons plus ¼ cup milk, divided
1 egg, beaten
Brown sugar for sprinkling

1. In a large bowl, combine first 7 ingredients and mix well.

2. Add oil, 3 tablespoons milk and egg and stir well until dough clings together.

3. On a well-floured surface, toss dough and knead 10 to 15 times. Divide dough in half. Put each ball into a 6-inch circle with a slightly rounded middle.

4. Brush with remaining ¼ cup milk and sprinkle with brown sugar. Cut each circle into wedges.

5. Place on a greased baking sheet. Bake at 425° for 12 to 14 minutes.

This recipe can be made with sour cream instead of yogurt.

Serves 4.

Asparagus and Yellow Pepper Frittata

Cheryl Scott

An awesome Sunday morning treat! Try different combinations. Ham and Vidalia onion are excellent too!

2 pounds thin asparagus
2 large yellow bell peppers
1 medium zucchini
3 scallions
3 shallots, minced
1 tablespoon unsalted butter
10 large eggs
½ cup heavy cream
3 tablespoons chopped fresh Italian parsley
1½ teaspoons salt
¼ teaspoon freshly ground pepper

1. Trim asparagus and diagonally cut into ¼-inch wide slices. Cut peppers into ¼-inch wide strips. Halve zucchini lengthwise and diagonally cut both zucchini and scallions into thin slices. Have ready a bowl of ice and cold water.

2. In a large saucepan of boiling salted water, blanch asparagus 1 minute and drain in colander. Immediately transfer asparagus to ice water to stop cooking. Drain asparagus well in colander and pat dry.

3. In a large skillet, cook peppers and shallots in butter over moderately low heat, stirring occasionally until peppers are softened, about 10 minutes.

4. In a large bowl, whisk together eggs, cream, parsley, salt and pepper. Stir in asparagus, pepper mixture, zucchini and scallions.

5. Pour custard into a greased 13 x 9 x 2-inch glass baking dish. Bake at 350°, in middle of oven until golden and set, about 35 minutes. Cool frittata on a rack.

Frittata may be made 1 day ahead and chilled, covered. Bring frittata to room temperature before serving.

Serves 12.

Basil Breakfast Strata

Susan Koopman

I first had this at a baby shower. It is a jazzed up version of the classic egg and cheese strata. This is delicious, especially in the summer with fresh tomatoes.

1	cup milk
½	cup dry white wine
1	loaf day old bread, cut into ½-inch slices
8	ounces prosciutto, thinly sliced
2	cups arugula leaves
3	tablespoons olive oil
16	ounces goat cheese, crumbled
3	ripe tomatoes, sliced
½	cup pesto
4	eggs, beaten
	Salt to taste
	Freshly ground pepper to taste
½	cup heavy cream

1. On the day before serving, mix the milk and wine in a shallow bowl. Dip 1 or 2 slices of bread in the milk mixture. Squeeze as much liquid out of bread without tearing.

2. Place the bread in a 12-inch round or oval au gratin dish and cover with a slice of prosciutto, several arugula leaves dipped in olive oil, some crumbled goat cheese and a few tomato slices. Drizzle sparingly with pesto.

3. Repeat the layering process again, overlapping the bread slices slightly, until the dish is filled.

4. Beat the eggs with salt and pepper and pour evenly over the layered bread. Cover with plastic wrap and refrigerate overnight.

5. The next morning remove the dish from the refrigerator and let warm to room temperature. Drizzle top with cream.

6. Bake at 350° for 45 minutes to 1 hour or until puffy and browned. Serve immediately.

Swiss peasant bread or French bread is recommended.

Serves 6 to 8.

Canadian Bacon Brunch Eggs

Debbi Abbott Holmgren

12 slices Canadian bacon
12 slices Swiss cheese
12 eggs
1 cup whipping cream
⅓ cup Parmesan cheese
   Pepper to taste
   Paprika to taste
   Chopped fresh parsley to taste

1. Place Canadian bacon in a single layer in a greased 13 x 9 x 2-inch baking dish and top with Swiss cheese.

2. Gently break the eggs into the dish, spacing evenly, then pour whipping cream over everything.

3. Bake at 450° for 10 minutes.

4. Remove from oven and sprinkle with Parmesan cheese, pepper, paprika and parsley. Bake an additional 8 to 10 minutes until set. Let stand for 5 to 10 minutes before serving.

Serves 6 to 8.

Eggs Rebel

Helen L. Crewe

This casserole can be made the night before. It also doubles easily.

6 slices bread, cubed
1 pound smoked sausage, cut-up or diced ham
6 eggs, slightly beaten
2 cups milk
1 cup shredded Cheddar cheese
1 teaspoon salt
1 teaspoon dry mustard

1. Place the bread in the bottom of a greased casserole dish and top with the meat. Pour eggs over meat.

2. Mix remaining ingredients with a mixer and pour over the bread and eggs. Cover and refrigerate overnight.

3. Bake, uncovered, at 350° for 40 to 45 minutes.

Serves 6.

Broccoli-Salmon Quiche

Diane Lavoie

Great for brunches.

1 (9-inch) pastry shell
1 tablespoon vegetable oil
1½ cups chopped broccoli
⅓ cup chopped onion
⅓ cup chopped red bell pepper
½ cup shredded Swiss cheese
1 cup flaked canned or cooked
  salmon
3 eggs, beaten
1¼ cups milk
1 teaspoon dried tarragon
¼ teaspoon salt
⅛ teaspoon freshly ground
  pepper

1. Place a piece of foil inside pastry shell and partially fill with uncooked beans or rice, to keep shell from rising. Bake at 425° for 10 minutes. Remove foil and beans. Continue baking 5 minutes or until lightly browned. Remove from oven and let cool. Reduce oven temperature to 375°.

2. Heat oil in a medium skillet over medium heat. Add broccoli, onion and bell pepper. Cook and stir 3 to 4 minutes or until crisp-tender. Set aside to cool.

3. Sprinkle cheese over bottom of pastry shell. Arrange salmon and vegetables over cheese.

4. In a medium bowl, combine eggs, milk, tarragon, salt and pepper. Pour over salmon and vegetables.

5. Bake 35 to 40 minutes or until filling is puffed and knife inserted in center comes out clean. Let stand 10 minutes before cutting.

Serves 6.

Light Broccoli-Chicken Quiche

Diane Elizabeth Burke

Quick and easy, this takes less than 5 minutes to prepare. The crust is self-made.

1½ cups diced, cooked chicken
1 (10-ounce) package frozen chopped broccoli, thawed and well-drained
1 cup light ricotta cheese
½ cup low-fat plain yogurt
1 egg
1 egg white
¼ cup all-purpose flour
½ teaspoon baking powder
½ teaspoon salt
¼ cup grated Parmesan cheese
2 tablespoons margarine, melted

1. Lightly spray a 9-inch pie plate with nonstick cooking spray. Combine half of chicken and half of broccoli in pie plate.

2. Puree remaining ingredients in a blender. Pour over chicken in pie plate. Scatter remaining chicken and broccoli on top.

3. Bake at 350° for 30 to 45 minutes or until wooden toothpick tests clean. Let stand 10 minutes before slicing.

Serves 6.

Faux Quiche

Eric C. Biemiller

*A friend, Candence (Candy) Rennell, gave this recipe to me.
This beauty makes its own crust.*

3 eggs
1 cup milk
½ cup Bisquick
3 tablespoons butter, melted
Dash of pepper
Dash of nutmeg
3 ounces ham, shrimp or crab
1 cup grated Swiss or Cheddar cheese
⅓ cup grated Parmesan cheese
1 small green bell pepper, chopped
1 small onion, chopped

1. In a blender, combine eggs, milk, Bisquick, butter, pepper and nutmeg and blend for about 1 minute. Fold in remaining ingredients.

2. Pour into a 9-inch greased pie plate. Bake at 350° for 35 to 40 minutes.

If you use a 10-inch pie plate, bake for 30 to 35 minutes.

Blueberry Stuffed French Toast

Karen Arakelian Weldon

This is a make-the-night-ahead recipe.

1 loaf English style toasting bread, crust discarded, cut in 1-inch cubes
2 (4-ounce) containers Mascarpone cheese, softened
1 cup fresh blueberries
12 eggs
2 cups milk
⅓ cup maple syrup

1. Arrange half the bread cubes in a greased 13 x 9 x 2-inch baking dish. Spoon Mascarpone cheese over bread. Sprinkle blueberries over cheese.

2. Arrange remaining bread cubes over blueberries.

3. In a large bowl, whisk together eggs, milk and syrup. Pour egg mixture evenly over bread mixture and chill overnight.

4. In the morning, bake French toast covered with foil at 350° for 30 minutes. Remove foil and bake an additional 30 minutes until puffed and golden.

Blueberry Sauce

1 cup sugar
2 teaspoons cornstarch
1 cup water
1 cup fresh blueberries
1 teaspoon butter

1. In a small saucepan, stir together sugar, cornstarch and water. Cook over moderate heat, stirring occasionally, for 5 minutes or until thickened.

2. Stir in blueberries. Simmer mixture until blueberries burst. Add butter. Stir sauce until butter is melted.

3. Pour over French toast.

If using frozen blueberries, make sure to rinse and drain well.

Serves 8.

Cinnamon Apple Baked French Toast (Casserole)

Barbara MH Daigneault

While visiting my nephew, Alex Hebert, at the University of Vermont, I found this recipe. It is so easy to prepare and must be made a day ahead of time. This casserole is perfect for a crisp fall morning and served with warmed Vermont maple syrup.

1 loaf French or Italian bread
8 large eggs
½ cup sugar, divided
3½ cups milk
1 tablespoon vanilla
6-8 McIntosh or Cortland apples, peeled, cored and sliced
3 teaspoons cinnamon
1 teaspoon nutmeg
2 tablespoons butter
   Warmed maple syrup for serving

1. Slice bread into 1½-inch slices. Place the bread tightly together into a greased 13 x 9 x 2-inch glass baking dish.

2. In a separate bowl, beat together eggs, ¼ cup sugar, milk and vanilla. Pour ½ of egg mixture over bread. Place sliced apples on top of bread to cover. Pour remaining mixture evenly over apples.

3. Mix remaining ¼ cup sugar with cinnamon and nutmeg and sprinkle evenly over top of apples. Dot casserole with butter. Cover and refrigerate overnight.

4. In the morning, remove foil from casserole. Bake at 350° for 1 hour. The casserole will rise high and brown nicely. Remove from oven and allow to stand for 10 minutes before serving. Cut into squares and serve with warmed maple syrup.

Serves 8 to 10.

Pecan and Honey Stuffed French Toast

Barbara MH Daigneault

This is a delicious French toast. I always make it for overnight guests. Easy and elegant.

1   cup coarsely chopped pecans, toasted
¾   teaspoon ground cinnamon, divided
2   tablespoons honey
8   slices country-style bread, 1-inch thick
6   eggs
1   cup milk
1   cup half & half
1½ tablespoons light brown sugar
¼   teaspoon ground nutmeg
    Warmed maple syrup for serving

1. In a small bowl, stir together pecans, ½ teaspoon cinnamon and honey to make a soft paste.

2. Lay bread slices flat. Using a serrated knife, slice bread horizontally through the middle, leaving bread connected at one end to form a pocket.

3. Evenly spread 1 tablespoon pecan mixture inside the opening of each slice.

4. In a large bowl, whisk together eggs, milk, half & half, sugar, remaining ¼ teaspoon cinnamon and nutmeg.

5. Dip the stuffed bread into the egg mixture and evenly coat both sides. Remove promptly and cook on a preheated greased electric griddle until heated through and golden on both sides. Serve with warmed maple syrup.

To toast pecans, place on a piece of foil and bake at 350° about 5 minutes or until slightly browned, being careful not to burn. Stir occasionally.

Serves 4.

Papa's Pancakes

Deb Hebert

*My husband David's family vacationed on Cape Cod at
"Papa's Cape House" every 4th of July. There were always different
combinations of family members on different years. We always cooked at home
rather than going out to restaurants because of the large number of people and the
fun and informality of dining at home. Some of the best memories include the large
family meals. I always brought this pancake recipe. I would combine the dry
ingredients in a food storage bag, adding a small note with a reminder of the
amount of eggs and milk to add and breakfast preparation was easy. Maine
blueberries or apples were a favorite addition to the basic recipe.*

1¼ cups flour
3 teaspoons baking powder
1 tablespoon sugar
½ teaspoon salt
1 egg, beaten
1 cup milk
2 tablespoons canola oil

1. In a large bowl, combine dry ingredients.

2. In a small bowl, combine remaining ingredients and add to dry mixture. Whisk until well blended.

3. Cook pancakes on a non-stick griddle until golden brown.

Serves 4.

Homemade Muesli

Barbara MH Daigneault

*This homemade cereal has become a breakfast staple in our home.
It is so healthy and tastes great. It's even better if you add the milk and
let it stand for 15 minutes before eating.*

4 cups rolled oats
2 cups wheat flakes
½ cup soy protein powder
½ cup oat bran
½ cup slivered almonds, toasted
32 (halves) dried apricots, chopped

1. Combine all ingredients and serve with milk.

*To toast almonds, place on a piece of foil.
Bake at 350° for 5 minutes or until golden
brown. Stir occasionally.*

Yields 16 servings.

Ambrosia

Susan B. Ekstrom

This is a great snack anytime during the day.
It's a wonderful compliment served with brunch.

1 cup sour cream
1 cup pineapple chunks, drained
1 cup Mandarin oranges, drained
1 cup mini marshmallows
1 cup shredded coconut

1. Combine all ingredients. Chill for 4 to 6 hours before serving.

Can be made the day before.

~~~

Mom's Holiday Fruit Cup

Deborah Putnam Reynolds

My mom, Christine Hunt Putnam, was the greatest cook with all kinds
of wonderful dishes. Her holiday fruit cup has graced my holiday table every year
of my life! It is simply tradition. No matter where our family gathers during the
holiday, this fruit cup is always served! Even though my mom is no longer
with us, we always think of her at our holiday table.

2 white grapefruit
2 ruby red grapefruit
4 large juicy oranges
2 large apples, your favorite
1 bunch purple or green seedless grapes
1 jar maraschino cherries, reserve liquid
2 large bananas
½ cup chopped nuts (optional)
1 pint strawberry sherbet

1. Cut the grapefruits and oranges in half. Scoop out the seeds and then cut into cubes. Squeeze remaining juice into bowl. Peel and cut the apples into small pieces. Cut the grapes in half. Cut cherries in half. Slice the bananas.

2. In a large bowl, combine all fruits and reserved cherry liquid. Add walnuts, if desired. Mix well.

3. To serve, put in individual compotes and top with sherbet.

This can be prepared the day before serving and keeps in the refrigerator several days.

Serves 20.

Soups

Comforts of Winter

The Farmer's Porch at the Home of Patricia M. Morse, Wheelock Road

On cold crisp winter days, when the snow is piled up high, Cathleen wanted this painting to capture the true essence of a "nor'easter" as it sweeps across the hills of Sutton. The farmer's porch was added onto this 1870's home in 1995 to replicate a traditional old New England farmhouse.

Soups

Fairview Farm Beef Stew

Marlene Largess

2 pounds stew beef
4-5 potatoes, quartered
1 cup sliced celery
2 cups baby carrots
½ large green bell pepper, diced
1 can tomato soup
2 cups water
2-3 tablespoons quick cooking tapioca
½ envelope dry onion soup mix
2 tablespoons Worcestershire sauce
1 tablespoon sugar
Salt and pepper to taste

1. Combine all ingredients in a casserole dish. Cover tightly with glass lid and bake at 250° for 6 hours.

Can also be cooked at 325° for 3½ hours.

Serves 5.

The Twins Wallabe Stew

Beth Hyder

This recipe was named after a very special set of twins in my life, Jonathan and Keith Hebert. It's their favorite stew on a cold winter's day.

1 pound center-cut bacon, cut into 1-inch pieces
2 cups cubed new red potatoes
1 cup chopped onion
1 cup sour cream
1¼ cups whole milk
1 (10¾-ounce) can cream of chicken soup
1 (8-ounce) can whole kernel corn, drained
¼ teaspoon pepper
¼ teaspoon dried thyme

1. In a large saucepan, cook bacon over medium heat for 5 minutes or until cooked through and a little crisp. Drain off excess grease. Add potatoes and onions.

2. Continue to cook, stirring occasionally until potatoes are tender, about 15 to 20 minutes.

3. Add remaining ingredients. Continue cooking, stirring occasionally, until heated through.

Beef Barley Noodle Soup

Doreen Plante Thornburg

This soup was made by my grandmother and passed down to my mother. My twin daughters love it so much we have named it "Grammy's Soup". I started making it 3 years ago and plan to pass it on to my daughters as a fourth generation recipe.

5-6 small beef soup bones
1 pound beef steak, top round
1 medium onion
1 medium tomato
1 bunch of celery hearts, chopped
½ cup barley
4-5 beef bouillon cubes
6 large carrots, peeled and sliced
1 (8-ounce) package farfalle noodles, cooked

1. Place all bones in bottom of stockpot. Add meat, whole onion, whole tomato, celery hearts and barley. Fill stockpot with 3 quarts water. Bring to a boil over high heat. Once boiling, reduce heat to simmer and cover. Let simmer for 3 hours.

2. Add carrots and simmer an additional hour.

3. Remove bones and marrow from pot and discard. Remove meat, cut into tiny bite-size pieces and add back to stock. Put desired amount of noodles in a serving bowl and place soup on top.

Camping Chili

Jerry and Patti Thomas

This is my favorite chili recipe for just plain eating. This chili recipe has won a Massachusetts state champion 3 times, as well as many state and regional championships. My competition recipe is designed to get the judges attention, but it is a little rich for gluttony. Here is my adapted chili recipe. It's not the real thing (the prize-winning recipe), but it's pretty darn good.

2 pounds lean ground beef or beef, cut into ⅜-inch cubes
1 medium onion, diced
1 green bell pepper, diced
1 (15-ounce) can tomato sauce
1 (15-ounce) can diced, peeled tomatoes, drained
1 (15-ounce) can chicken broth
1 (4-ounce) can diced green chiles
2 jalapeños, minced or 1 teaspoon red pepper flakes
2 (15-ounce) cans beans (kidney, pink or shell), rinsed and drained
6 tablespoons chili powder
2 tablespoons ground cumin
½ teaspoon cayenne pepper
1 teaspoon garlic powder
1½ teaspoons pepper
2 teaspoons salt
1 teaspoon sugar
   Grated Cheddar cheese for topping

1. In a skillet, brown meat and drain.

2. Put all ingredients, except beans, in a large pot and cook until vegetables are tender, about an hour at a low simmer. (If using hand-cut sirloin, this process will take about 3 hours.)

3. Add beans and cook another 30 minutes. Serve.

Serve with crackers. Top with grated cheddar cheese. Any leftovers are great on top of pasta, baked potatoes or hot dogs.

Vegetarian Chili

Barbara MH Daigneault

I have always served this at snowmobile parties. This recipe is quick and easy to put together. As the pot gets low, just keep adding more of the ingredients. Ground turkey or beef can be added for meat lovers.

1 cup chopped onion
1 cup water
½ cup diced green bell pepper
2 tablespoons chili powder
1½ teaspoons ground cumin
2 (14-ounce) cans no-salt stewed tomatoes (do not drain)
1 (15-ounce) can red kidney beans, rinsed and drained
1 (15-ounce) can garbanzo beans, rinsed and drained
¼ cup non-fat sour cream

1. In a large pot coated with cooking spray, cook onion until tender. Add remaining ingredients, except the sour cream.

2. Bring this mixture to a boil. Reduce heat and simmer uncovered for 30 minutes. Top each serving with a dollop of sour cream.

Leek and Mushroom Bisque

Kathy Dugan

1 pound mushrooms, sliced
1 bunch leeks, white part only, sliced
1 stick butter
4 tablespoons flour
1 teaspoon salt
¼ teaspoon pepper
3 (14-ounce) cans chicken broth, divided
1 cup light cream
Parsley for garnish

1. In a large saucepan, sauté mushrooms and leeks in butter until tender, approximately 5 minutes.

2. Stir in flour, salt, pepper and 2 cans broth, stirring constantly until mixture comes to a boil. Lower heat, cover and simmer 20 minutes. Remove from heat and cool slightly.

3. Pour a little at a time into a blender and puree. Return pureed mixture to saucepan. Add remaining can of broth and 1 cup of light cream. Heat until hot. Garnish with parsley.

Serves 4 to 6.

Vegetarian Lentil Stew

Cindy Wolodkin

This is a hearty vegetarian stew. This is great served in the fall and winter months with copious amounts of Grandma's Farm Cornbread (page 60).

5   cups water or vegetable stock
1   cup dry lentils
½   teaspoon thyme
½   teaspoon marjoram
1   bay leaf
3   tablespoons olive oil
2   onions, chopped
4   carrots, peeled and diced
1   (15-ounce) can whole
      tomatoes, cut up
¼   cup dry sherry
      Salt and pepper to taste
¼   cup chopped fresh parsley
      Grated Swiss, Monterey Jack or
      Cheddar cheese

1. In a large pot, bring water, lentils, thyme, marjoram and bay leaf to a boil. Cover and simmer for 20 to 30 minutes or until lentils are tender.

2. Meanwhile, heat the olive oil and sauté the onions and carrots. Cover and simmer until the carrots are crispy-tender. Stir the carrots and onions into the lentil mixture, along with the tomatoes, sherry, salt and pepper. Simmer for 1 hour.

3. Just before serving, stir in parsley. Place the cheese in the bottom of each bowl and fill with stew.

This stew freezes well.

Serves 4 to 6.

Mushroom Artichoke Bisque

Ann Harris

My sister Denise shared this one with me. It's one of my favorites!

2   tablespoons finely chopped onions
1½ cups thinly sliced mushrooms
3   tablespoons butter
2   tablespoons flour
1½ cups chicken broth
2   cups half & half
1   (16-ounce) can artichoke hearts, drained and diced
    Salt and pepper to taste
    Beau Monde seasoning to taste

1. In a large pot, sauté onion and mushrooms in butter for 5 minutes. Stir in flour and cook slowly for 2 minutes.

2. Slowly add broth and half & half. Stir with whisk over low heat to thicken. Stir in artichokes and seasonings. Serve when heated through.

Occasionally, I put some of the mushrooms in a food processor for more texture in the soup. To make a thicker soup, omit some of the half & half.

Serves 4 to 6.

Rich and Creamy Mushroom Soup

Tim Morse

1   stick butter
1   pound mushrooms, sliced
1   cup flour
12 cups chicken broth
1   quart heavy cream
4   slices American cheese
    Salt and pepper to taste
    Onion powder to taste

1. In a large stockpot, melt butter. Add mushrooms and sauté until soft. Add flour and cook 3 to 5 minutes. Add chicken broth and bring to a boil, whisk to remove any lumps.

2. Remove from heat for 10 minutes and stir occasionally. Slowly whisk in cream. Put back on heat and bring liquid to just under a boil.

3. Drop American cheese on top. Once cheese melts, whisk in seasonings to taste.

Serves 6.

Leek and Potato Soup

Pat Nedoroscik

This rich, creamy soup has only 196 calories per serving with 2.9 grams of fat.

2-3 medium leeks, white part only (4 cups)
1 tablespoon olive oil
2 pounds yellow boiling potatoes, peeled
4 cups chicken broth, fat removed
Salt and pepper to taste

1. Rinse leeks, cut in half and thinly slice to make 4 cups. Cut potatoes in half and thinly slice to yield 4 cups.

2. In heavy 4-quart saucepan, heat oil over medium high heat. Add leeks and cook stirring for 3 to 4 minutes until softened. Add potatoes and broth and bring to a boil.

3. Cover the pan and simmer on medium low heat for 25 to 30 minutes or until the vegetables are tender. Add salt and pepper to taste.

I mash this mixture after the cooking time with a hand potato masher, just because I like the texture better. This soup tastes better reheated on low. May substitute vegetable broth for chicken broth.

Cream of Parsley and Almond Soup

Ann Bouvier Achorn

8 bunches Italian parsley
16 cups (4-quarts) chicken stock, preferably homemade
1 cup chopped shallots
4 cups chopped celery
2 bay leaves
4 (4-inch) sprigs thyme
2 cups ground almonds
3-4 cups heavy cream
Salt to taste
Tabasco Sauce to taste
Freshly grated nutmeg

1. Wash the parsley and separate the stems from the leaves. Reserve a handful of the stems.

2. In a large pot, place the chicken stock, shallots and celery. Place the parsley stems, bay leaves and thyme sprigs in a little "purse" fashioned from cheesecloth. Tie with string and add to the pot. Cover and simmer soup for 30 minutes.

3. Remove cheesecloth purse and discard. Add parsley leaves and almonds to the pot. Continue simmering for 20 minutes.

4. In a food processor or blender, puree soup. (This may be completed in advance to this point and refrigerated or frozen.)

5. To finish, return soup to pot and add cream. Slowly reheat to simmer. Do not boil. Season to taste with salt and Tabasco Sauce. Dust with freshly grated nutmeg. Serve immediately.

Yields 12 (1-cup) servings.

Autumn Curried Carrot Soup

Cheryl Bedard

This recipe brought back New England fall memories when I lived in California.

4 cloves garlic, roasted
4 tablespoons butter
2½ cups chopped carrots
2 cups chopped celery
1 cup chopped onion
1 cup diced potato
3 tablespoons flour
2 tablespoons brown sugar
1 cup milk
1 teaspoon dried rosemary
½ teaspoon curry powder
Salt and pepper to taste
2 cups chicken broth
2 cups half & half
Dash of turmeric
2 tablespoons dry white wine

1. Roast whole garlic cloves at 325° for 30 minutes. Peel garlic by squeezing out bulb.

2. In a large pot, melt butter and sauté garlic, carrots, celery, onion and potato. Sprinkle flour and brown sugar over the vegetables and toss to coat. Add milk and stir until blended. Add rosemary, curry powder, salt, and pepper and cook 15 minutes over low heat.

3. Add vegetable mixture, in small amounts to blender and puree with chicken broth.

4. Return to pot and add cream and turmeric and cook for 15 minutes. Add white wine and serve.

Baked Winter Squash Soup

Diane Elizabeth Burke

This soup is so creamy and doesn't have any cream. It is a must to serve at fall dinner parties. Guests will always want more. For a nice touch, serve in a hollowed-out sugar pumpkin.

Squash Soup

2   acorn squash
1   large butternut squash
6   tablespoons unsalted butter
6   teaspoons dark brown sugar
3   carrots, peeled and halved
1   large onion, thinly sliced
48   ounces chicken broth, divided
¾   teaspoon ground mace
¾   teaspoon ground ginger
     Pinch of cayenne pepper
     Salt to taste
     Fresh chopped chives for garnish
     Crème fraîche for garnish

1. Cut squash in half lengthwise. Scoop out and discard seeds. Place squash halves, skin side down, in a shallow roasting pan. Place 1 tablespoon of butter and 1 teaspoon brown sugar in each cavity of squash.

2. Arrange carrots and onions around squash. Pour 2 cups of broth in pan, cover tightly with aluminum foil and bake at 350° for 2 hours.

3. Remove pan from oven and allow vegetables to cool slightly. Scoop out squash pulp and place in stockpot.

4. Add to stockpot the remaining broth, mace, ginger, cayenne pepper and salt. Mix well and bring to a boil. Reduce heat and simmer, uncovered, for 10 minutes.

5. Puree the soup, in batches, in a blender until smooth.

6. Return to stockpot, adjust seasonings and heat thoroughly. Serve each portion garnished with chives and a dollop of crème fraîche.

Crème Fraîche

1 cup fresh cream
2 tablespoons buttermilk

1. Heat cream to 95 degrees and stir in the buttermilk. Pour mixture into a clean glass container. Cover and let sit in a warm place (70 to 80 degrees) for 24 hours. Refrigerate the crème fraîche to allow it to thicken further. It should be ready in 4 hours.

Crème fraîche is a tangy cultured cream similar to sour cream with a lighter texture. It will keep in the refrigerator up to a week and a half.

Serves 12.

Tortellini Escarole Soup

Barbara Morris

A former work associate, Deb B., who was of Italian decent, shared this recipe with me. She grew up in a largely Italian populated section of Bellingham, Massachusetts.

1 onion, chopped
2 (1-inch) cubes salt pork
1 clove garlic, minced
1 (49-ounce) can chicken broth
1 (28-ounce) can crushed tomatoes
  Dried basil, oregano and parsley to taste
1 head escarole, washed and shredded
1 pound tortellini, cooked and cooled
  Freshly grated Parmesan cheese

1. In a large stockpot, sauté onion in salt pork until tender. Add garlic and cook until tender. Add chicken broth, tomatoes and seasonings. Cook for 1 hour.

2. Add escarole and cooked tortellini just prior to serving.

3. Once served, top with Parmesan cheese.

Serve with Italian bread.

Very Veggie Garden Soup

Cheryl Scott

My grandmother used to make this soup with vegetables grown from my grandfather's garden. She would freeze the soup in quart containers. Relatives would raid her freezer all winter long.

3   tablespoons olive oil
1   clove garlic, minced
1   small onion, chopped
2   cups sherry
1   (48-ounce) can chicken broth
1   (14-ounce) can beef broth
1   head broccoli, cut into small pieces, discard stems
1   head cauliflower, cut into small pieces, discard stems
5   carrots, peeled and diced into ¼-inch pieces
5   celery stalks, diced into ¼-inch pieces
1   (28-ounce) can chopped tomatoes with garlic and basil
1   small zucchini, diced
1   small summer squash, diced
1   (8-ounce) package frozen green beans
1   (8-ounce) package frozen corn
1   (15½-ounce) can kidney beans, drained and rinsed
1   (15-ounce) can garbanzo beans, drained and rinsed
3   chicken bouillon cubes
3   beef bouillon cubes
4   servings quick cooking rice, cooked

1. In a large stockpot, heat olive oil and sauté garlic and onion. Add sherry, chicken broth and beef broth. Add all vegetables and simmer until carrots are tender.

2. Add bouillon and enough water to bring soup level back up. Add rice just before serving.

You may substitute any veggies and try barley instead of rice for a change.

Summertime Gazpacho

Patricia M. Morse

*This is an old Spanish dish with hundreds of variations and
after trying several recipes this one turned out to be everyone's favorite.
Gazpacho is a cold refreshing summertime soup with plenty of flavor.*

1 (15-ounce) can garbanzo beans, rinsed and drained
1 (14½-ounce) Italian diced tomatoes (do not drain)
1¼ cups V-8 juice
1 cup beef broth
1 cup quartered cherry tomatoes
½ cup seeded and chopped cucumbers
¼ cup chopped red onion
¼ cup minced fresh cilantro or parsley
3 tablespoons lime juice, freshly squeezed
1 clove garlic, minced
½ teaspoon salt
¼ teaspoon Tabasco Sauce
   Splash of Worcestershire sauce

1. In a large glass bowl, combine all ingredients. Cover and refrigerate until serving time.

Serves 6.

Cold Beet Soup

Barbara Bessette

This was one of my Polish grandmother's favorite recipes.

1 bunch beets, washed and peeled
1 quart water
   Juice of 1 lemon
   Salt to taste
   Sugar to taste
1 cup sour cream

1. Coarsely grate beets.

2. In a large saucepan, boil beets in 1 quart of water until softened. Add lemon juice, salt and sugar. Boil an additional 5 minutes. Stir in sour cream. Mix well. Serve.

This recipe can be served either hot or cold.

Spring Green Soup

Cheryl Bedard

*This soup can either be served directly from
the blender or chilled on a hot summer's afternoon.*

1 cucumber, peeled and halved
  lengthwise
½ pound pencil-thin asparagus,
  trimmed
2 cups cold water, divided
¼ pound spinach, stems removed
  and rinsed well
4 scallions, cut into 2-inch
  lengths
1 ripe avocado, pitted and
  peeled
¼ cup fresh mint leaves, plus
  more for garnish
4-6 fresh sorrel leaves for garnish
  (optional)

1. Cut ½ of cucumber into eighths
and the other into diced ¼-inch
pieces. Set aside. Cut asparagus
spears into 2-inch lengths.

2. Puree in a blender with ½ cup
cold water until smooth. Add
spinach, scallions, cucumber
eighths and another ½ cup water.
Blend until thoroughly pureed.

3. Add avocado, mint leaves and
lemon juice and puree until
smooth, adding remaining water a
little at a time until soup is desired
consistency. Add salt and season
with pepper.

4. Scrape down sides of blender
with a rubber spatula and puree
5 seconds more.

5. Cut sorrel into fine strips, if
using. Divide soup among four
bowls. Garnish each with diced
cucumber, sorrel and a fresh mint
sprig. Serve immediately.

*Add a hint of fresh chopped cilantro for a
different twist.*

Serves 4.

Hearty Cabbage Soup

Diane Lavoie

This is my mother's soup. It always tastes best the next day.
Fresh pumpernickel or rye bread compliment this soup.

5-6 country-style pork spareribs, trimmed

1 (32-ounce) jar sauerkraut, without sugar added

1 small to medium head cabbage, shredded

1 bay leaf

½ teaspoon whole black peppercorns

1 onion

1-2 celery stalks, sliced

2 carrots, sliced

3 cloves garlic

Salt to taste

Sliced kielbasa (optional)

Scant red pepper flakes (optional)

1. Boil spareribs for ½ hour. Add sauerkraut and cook for an additional ½ hour.

2. Add cabbage, bay leaf, peppercorns, onion, celery, carrots and garlic. Season with salt and simmer until vegetables are done, approximately another ½ hour.

3. During the last 10 minutes of cooking, add kielbasa slices and red pepper flakes if desired. Skim off any foam on top and sides. Discard bones and serve.

You might want to rinse the sauerkraut before using. Pork chops can be used in place of spareribs and if soup appears to be too sour, you may add a few pinches of sugar.

Minestrone

Linda Carr

1 tablespoon vegetable oil
½ pound sweet Italian sausage links, sliced
3 cloves garlic, sliced
1 pound carrots, peeled and sliced into ¼-inch pieces
1 pound green beans, sliced into 1-inch pieces
2 pounds zucchini, sliced into 1-inch rounds
1 quart V-8 juice or tomato juice
1-2 quarts water (approximately)
¼ cup chopped fresh parsley
2 tablespoons chopped fresh basil
Pinch thyme
Salt and pepper to taste
1 (15½-ounce) can kidney, white or black beans
½ pound elbow macaroni, cooked

1. In a large stockpot, heat oil over medium heat and sauté sausage and garlic until browned.

2. Add carrots and green beans. Stir every few minutes for 10 minutes. Add zucchini. Stir occasionally for 10 minutes. Add V-8 juice and 1 quart of water. Adjust water to desired consistency. Cook until vegetables are almost tender, about 5 minutes.

3. Add seasonings during last 15 minutes. Add macaroni and beans and heat thoroughly.

If you are not going to serve this right away, leave out macaroni until ready to serve. You may substitute hamburger for the sausage.

Winter Sausage Soup

Rebecca O. Goodwin-Augustus

1½ pounds Italian sausage (sweet or hot)
1 onion, diced
3½ quarts reduced fat, low sodium chicken broth
2 cups chunky Italian plum tomatoes or diced tomatoes
1 cup white rice, cooked
1 cup spinach, fresh or frozen, well-drained
Shredded mozzarella, extra fine

1. Boil sausage and cook well. Remove casings and cut into small pieces.

2. Sauté sausage and add onion. Cook until tender.

3. Add chicken broth and bring to a simmer. Add rice, tomatoes and spinach. Simmer just a few more minutes. Top with shredded cheese and serve.

You may add 1 cup of lentils for a hearty soup.

Spicy Mulligatawny

Heather Daigneault

3 teaspoons olive oil, divided
2 cups cooked, chopped skinless chicken breast
1 cup peeled and chopped apple
¾ cup chopped onion
½ cup chopped carrot
½ cup chopped celery
½ cup chopped green bell pepper
2 tablespoons flour
1 tablespoon curry powder
1 teaspoon ground ginger
½ teaspoon crushed red pepper flakes
¼ teaspoon salt (optional)
2 (15-ounce) cans fat free, low sodium chicken broth
¼ cup tomato paste

1. In a large stockpot, heat 1 teaspoon of oil over medium heat. Add chicken and cook for 3 minutes. Add remaining oil, apple, onion, carrots, celery and green pepper. Cook for 5 minutes.

2. Stir in flour, curry, ginger, pepper flakes and salt. Cook for 1 minute. Stir in broth and tomato paste.

3. Bring to a boil. Reduce heat and simmer for 8 minutes or until thoroughly heated through.

Serves 4.

Healthy Vegetable Soup
with Chicken and Wild Rice

Lisa Sarmento

This recipe is best made the day before serving to allow flavors to mellow.
Serve with Italian or French bread and grated Parmesan cheese. It's a meal in itself.

1	tablespoon olive oil
1	onion, chopped
3	quarts low sodium chicken broth
1	(28-ounce) can diced tomatoes
2	cups fresh corn kernels
2	cups fresh baby spinach, rinsed
6	carrots, peeled and sliced
4	celery stalks, chopped
3-4	cups shredded skinless roasted chicken breast
1	cup wild brown rice, uncooked
	Splash of white vinegar
	Freshly ground pepper to taste

1. In an 8-quart stockpot, heat oil over medium-high heat. Sauté onion until tender.

2. Add remaining ingredients and bring to a boil.

3. Cover and simmer for 2 hours. Add water as needed.

Roasted Chicken and Wild Rice Stew

Carrie Daigneault

*Wild rice, a native American delicacy, is not rice at all
but the seed of a tall aquatic grass. This stew is absolutely delicious,
without all the fat and calories. You will love it!*

1 (6-ounce) box long-grain wild rice
1 tablespoon olive oil
1½ cups chopped red onion
1 cup chopped celery
1 cup chopped carrot
1 (8-ounce) package mushrooms, sliced
¼ cup all-purpose flour
½ teaspoon dried tarragon
¼ teaspoon dried thyme
2 cups water
2 tablespoons dry sherry
2 (14-ounce) cans fat-free, low sodium chicken broth
1 (12-ounce) can fat-free evaporated milk
3 cups skinless roasted chicken breast, shredded

1. Prepare rice according to package directions.

2. Heat oil in a large stockpot. Add onion, celery, carrots and mushrooms, sauté until tender. Stir the flour, tarragon and thyme into the vegetable mixture and cook for 1 minute, stirring frequently. Add water, sherry, chicken broth and evaporated milk.

3. Bring mixture to a boil. Reduce heat and simmer for 20 minutes or until slightly thickened. Stir in cooked rice and chicken. Cook for 10 minutes or until thoroughly heated through.

This soup tastes better the next day.

Serves 8.

Clam Chowder in a Pastry Dome

Cheryl Bedard

Clam Chowder

24 large fresh clams, scrubbed and rinsed well
2 cup dry white wine
2 tablespoons vegetable oil
1 large white onion, diced
1 leek, white and pale green part, diced
2 celery stalks, diced
2 slices smoked bacon, diced
2 Idaho potatoes, diced
1 quart heavy cream
2 tablespoons minced fresh thyme
Salt and freshly ground pepper to taste

1. In a large pot, combine the clams and wine. Bring the liquid to a boil, covered, and steam the clams for about 8 to 10 minutes or until they have opened. Shuck the clams, reserving the juice, and strain the juice through a fine sieve into a bowl. Quarter each clam and transfer to a bowl.

2. In a large stockpot, heat oil over moderate heat. Add the onion, leek, celery and bacon and cook the mixture covered, stirring occasionally, for 5 minutes.

3. Add the reserved liquid and simmer 10 minutes.

4. Add the potatoes, cream, thyme, salt and pepper. Bring to a boil and simmer, stirring occasionally, for 25 to 30 minutes or until potatoes are tender.

5. Stir in the clams and adjust seasoning. Divide the warmed soup among 6 ovenproof bowls.

Pastry Dome

1   (1-pound) package puff-pastry
    dough
1   large egg
1   egg yolk
    Pinch of salt

1. Create an egg wash by beating egg and egg yolk with 1 teaspoon of water and a pinch of salt. Set aside.

2. Cut the puff pastry into circles large enough to cover each bowl. Brush the edge of each circle with egg wash and invert the circles onto the bowls. Pressing the edges of the dough onto the bowl to seal. Brush the tops of the pastry with egg wash, lightly score in a crosshatch design and arrange bowls on a baking sheet.

3. Bake at 400° for 10 to 12 minutes or until dough is puffed and golden.

Serves 6.

P-Town's Lobster Bisque à la Mitch

Diane Lavoie

This comes from the Provincetown Seafood Cookbook by Howard Mitcham.
Mr. Mitcham is Cape Cod's best-known and most admired chef.

3	quarts fish stock or bouillon
2	(1½-pound) live lobsters
1	stick butter
2	onions, chopped
3	scallions with half their green leaves, chopped
1	celery heart, chopped
2	tablespoons flour
1	(8-ounce) can tomato sauce
¼	teaspoon nutmeg
	Salt and freshly ground pepper to taste
1	cup cream
1	cup evaporated milk
¼	cup sherry

1. Place the fish stock or bouillon in the bottom of a pot and bring it to a boil. Plunge the lobsters in, cover and steam for 20 minutes. Remove the lobsters, reserving liquid, and pick out all the meat, fat, tomalley and coral. Dice the meats and set all this aside.

2. Place the lobster shells in a pan and bake at 450° for 20 minutes or until they are well browned but not burned. Remove the shells and pound into small pieces in a mortar, moistening with a little of the stock from the pot.

3. Place the pounded shells and the juice back into the stock in which the lobsters were cooked. Boil it rapidly for about 15 minutes or until approximately 1 quart of the liquid has evaporated. Strain off the liquid through a double cheesecloth and set aside.

4. Melt butter in a skillet and sauté the onions, scallions and celery until soft and golden. Add the flour and stir until it browns lightly. Add the tomato sauce and stir. Add the strained stock and ½ the diced lobster meat, all of the fat, tomalley and coral. Add the nutmeg and adjust salt and pepper. Cook the mixture slowly, stirring constantly until it thickens a little.

5. Put it in a blender and cream it. Fold into this mixture the cream and evaporated milk. Add the remaining diced lobster meat and the sherry.

6. Put it all in a saucepan and heat to the boiling point. Serve in preheated bowls with slices of French or Italian bread.

Evaporated milk will prevent curdling and you won't have to use a double boiler. It also gives backbone and body to either bisques or chowders.

Creamy Chicken and Corn Chowder

Barbara MH Daigneault

I am always looking for a delicious low fat soup that doesn't take a long time to prepare. This chowder is the cream of the crop.

2	tablespoons butter
¼	cup chopped onion
¼	cup chopped celery
1	jalapeño pepper, seeded and minced
2	tablespoons all-purpose flour
3	cups 2% reduced-fat milk
2	cups roasted, chopped skinless chicken breast
1½	cups fresh or frozen corn kernels (about 3 ears)
1	(14¾-ounce) can cream-styled corn
1	teaspoon chopped fresh thyme or ¼ teaspoon dried thyme
¼	teaspoon cayenne pepper
⅛	teaspoon salt

1. In a large pot, melt the butter over medium heat. Add onion, celery and jalapeño. Cook for 3 minutes or until tender, stirring frequently.

2. Add flour and cook 1 minute, stirring constantly. Stir in milk and remaining ingredients.

3. Bring to a boil. Reduce heat, cover and cook until thickened (about 5 minutes).

I like to keep freshly frozen corn on hand. I usually buy a dozen ears of corn at Foppema's Farm. After cooking, what we don't eat I cut off the cob and freeze in food storage bags and enjoy the fresh taste of corn all winter long.

Serves 6.

Sherry Seafood Bisque

Butch Myers

This dish has turned into a favorite at my Wild Game dinners.
I should call it "Lawyer's Bisque", as it is my lawyer's favorite.

1   tablespoon butter
¼   small onion, grated
½   teaspoon salt
½   teaspoon pepper
¼   teaspoon celery salt
¼   teaspoon dried parsley
1   teaspoon flour
2   (32-ounce) cartons chicken or beef broth
3   (8-ounce) cans baby clams, chopped (do not drain)
1   (8-ounce) package fresh mushrooms, sliced
6   cups whole milk
½   pound bay scallops
½   pound shrimp, 31-40 count, peeled and deveined, cut in ¼-inch pieces
4   squares white American cheese
1   cup sherry
    Fresh parsley for garnish

1. In an 8-quart pan, melt butter over medium heat. Add grated onion and cook until tender. Add salt, pepper, celery salt and parsley. Mix well.

2. Add flour and stir to form a paste. Gradually add broth and cook for 7 minutes over medium heat.

3. Add clams, with juice, and mushrooms and cook for 5 minutes. Gradually stir in milk. Add scallops and shrimp.

4. Cut the cheese into ¼-inch strips and add stirring constantly. Do not let boil. Add sherry. Cook a little longer to allow flavors to blend.

You may want to adjust the sherry to your liking. Some people might prefer a stronger taste. This bisque cannot be frozen and reheats nicely.

Serves 12.

Salads

Spring Greens

The 17th Hole at Pleasant Valley Country Club, Armsby Road

Pleasant Valley County Club, an expansive old apple orchard carved into a championship caliber golf course in 1961, is quietly nestled into the rolling hills of Sutton. A nationally recognized establishment, Pleasant Valley has been New England's Home of Professional Golf since 1962. Today, Pleasant Valley a private, 18-hole world-class golf course, bringing to life a tradition ensured by the pride of over 40 years of the Mingolla family ownership.

Salads

Asian Vinaigrette

Cindy King

⅓ cup soy sauce
⅔ cup canola oil
¼ cup rice wine vinegar
3 tablespoons Asian sesame oil
1 tablespoon honey

1. Combine all ingredients and mix for 30 seconds.

Use this dressing with combinations such as bean sprouts, shredded Chinese cabbage, thinly sliced onion and matchstick-cut cucumbers, carrots and red bell peppers.

Yields 1½ cups.

Creamy Blue Cheese Dressing

Ann Bouvier Achorn

¼ sweet onion, such as Vidalia
1 clove garlic, peeled
½ cup mayonnaise
½ cup sour cream
¼ pound blue cheese, coarsely crumbled
1 tablespoon white wine vinegar
1 teaspoon Worcestershire sauce
Dash of Tabasco Sauce
Salt and pepper to taste
1-3 teaspoons water (if necessary)

1. In a food processor, coarsely chop the onion. With the machine running, drop the garlic into the feed tube and process for a few seconds until it is chopped. Add remainder of ingredients, except the water.

2. Pulse gently just until the cheese forms small, irregular chunks. Taste for seasoning. Add more Worcestershire sauce or Tabasco Sauce if you desire.

3. Transfer dressing to a covered container and refrigerate at least 1 hour or up to 5 days. Just before serving, stir mixture and add water if needed to reach desired consistency.

This makes a great dip for crudités also.

Creamy French Dressing

Barbara Bordeaux-Woods

1 can tomato soup
¾ cup canola oil
¾ cup apple cider vinegar
¼ cup water
1 cup sugar
1 tablespoon salt
1 teaspoon black pepper
1 tablespoon Worcestershire sauce
1 tablespoon dry mustard
2 tablespoons onion
1 teaspoon paprika

1. Combine all ingredients in a blender and blend for 10 minutes until creamy. Refrigerate.

Chill at least 8 hours before serving. Keeps in refrigerator at least 1 month.

Yields 1 quart.

Herbed Raspberry Vinaigrette

Ann Bouvier Achorn

⅓ cup raspberry preserves
¼ cup vegetable oil
4 teaspoons rice vinegar
4 teaspoons cider vinegar
1 tablespoon dry white wine
1 teaspoon coarse-grained mustard
2 tablespoons finely chopped fresh parsley, chives, tarragon or chervil
Salt and pepper to taste

1. Combine all ingredients in a bowl, whisking until well blended. Add salt and pepper to taste.

Using a combination of the herbs enhances the flavor. This recipe multiplies well.

Yields ¾ cup.

Poppy Seed Vinaigrette

Cheryl Bedard

Fabulous served over spinach salad.

½ cup sugar
1 teaspoon paprika
½ teaspoon dry mustard
1 teaspoon Worcestershire sauce
1 cup olive oil
1 teaspoon minced onion
½ cup white vinegar
⅛ cup poppy seeds

1. Combine all ingredients in a blender and mix until well blended.

Yields 1½ cups.

Christmas Cranberry Apple Salad

Barbara MH Daigneault

This is a favorite served with our Christmas dinner. The blend of sweet and tart flavors and the crunchy and soft textures are so pleasing to the palate. This recipe compliments roasted turkey or baked ham especially well.

1 tablespoon lemon juice
2 large apples, cut into bite-size pieces (do not peel)
1 large carrot, grated
½ cup currants or raisins
½ cup chopped walnuts
½ cup whole berry cranberry sauce
1 teaspoon freshly grated orange peel

1. Sprinkle lemon juice over apples. Toss lightly. Add carrot, currants and walnuts. Stir in cranberry sauce and orange peel.

2. Chill at least 1 hour before serving.

This recipe doubles well. You can also use cranberry-raspberry sauce in place of cranberry sauce. You may serve as an individual serving in a lettuce cup or in a large bowl for buffet style serving.

Serves 4 to 6.

Classic Caesar Salad

Diane Lavoie

Croutons

2   tablespoons unsalted butter, melted
2   tablespoons extra-virgin olive oil
1   (8-ounce) loaf Italian bread, crust removed, cut into ¾-inch cubes
2   teaspoons coarse salt
¾   teaspoon cayenne pepper
½   teaspoon freshly ground pepper

1. In a large bowl, combine the butter and olive oil. Add the bread cubes and toss until coated. Sprinkle with salt, cayenne pepper and pepper. Toss until evenly coated.

2. Spread the bread in a single layer in a cookie sheet. Bake at 450° for approximately 10 minutes or until the croutons are golden. Set aside.

The croutons are best made no more than ½ hour before assembling the salad.

Salad

2   cloves garlic
4   anchovy fillets
1   teaspoon coarse salt
1   teaspoon freshly ground pepper
1   tablespoon lemon juice, freshly squeezed
1   teaspoon Worcestershire sauce
½   teaspoon Dijon mustard
1   large egg yolk
⅓   cup extra virgin olive oil
2   (10-ounce) heads romaine lettuce, washed and dried
1   cup freshly grated Parmesan or Romano cheese

1. Place the garlic, anchovy fillets and salt in a wooden salad bowl. Using 2 dinner forks, mash into a paste.

2. Using a fork, whisk in the pepper, lemon juice, Worcestershire sauce, mustard and egg yolk. Whisk in the olive oil.

3. Chop the romaine lettuce leaves into 1-inch pieces. Add the croutons, romaine and cheese to the bowl and toss well. Serve immediately.

You may substitute 1 tablespoon of mayonnaise in place of raw yolk.

Serves 4 to 6.

Mandarin Salad

Kathleen M. Handfield

This salad is light and refreshing. It's a perfect compliment to any beef or pork dinner.

Sweet and Sour Dressing

¼ cup vegetable oil
2 tablespoons sugar
2 tablespoons vinegar
1 tablespoon fresh snipped parsley
½ teaspoon salt
Dash of pepper
Dash of Tabasco Sauce

1. In a medium bowl, combine all ingredients and whisk until well blended. Set aside until ready to serve salad.

Salad

½ head romaine lettuce, torn into bite-size pieces
2 medium stalks celery, chopped
2 green onions, thinly sliced
1 (8-ounce) can Mandarin oranges
¼ cup chopped walnuts

1. In a large bowl, combine above ingredients and toss with dressing.

Substitute green onion with red onion. I usually double everything, including the dressing for a larger salad.

Serves 4 to 6.

Cloissoné Salad

Claudine Destino

Taken from my cookbook titled "Confessions of a Kitchen Diva".

A salad as delicious for the eyes as the palate: a beautiful arrangement of colors and flavors. This salad is slightly fussy because of the oranges and almonds. If you must, substitute canned, drained Mandarin oranges and omit the sugar to caramelize the almonds.

Salad Dressing

¼ cup white wine vinegar (preferably Champagne vinegar)

¼ cup sugar

1 teaspoon dried parsley flakes

½ teaspoon salt

¼ teaspoon pepper

1 dash Tabasco Sauce

½ cup vegetable oil

Reserved orange juice (from oranges below)

Salad

1 (10-ounce) bag fresh spinach (about 6 cups)

1 small head Romaine lettuce, thoroughly washed and torn into pieces

2 oranges, sectioned (reserve juice)

1 pint strawberries, sliced

1 apple (Gala or Cortland), julienned

3 tablespoons sugar

½ cup slivered almonds, toasted

1 small red onion, thinly sliced

4 ounces chèvre cheese (mild goat cheese), crumbled (optional)

1. Stir first 6 ingredients of salad dressing together in a small bowl (or mix in a blender). Add oil in a fine stream, stirring briskly until incorporated. Add reserved orange juice. Refrigerate dressing until serving time.

2. Mix greens together; top with orange sections and sliced strawberries. Toss apples with a little dressing to prevent browning; set aside.

3. Place sugar in the bottom of a small, heavy skillet and heat over medium-high until sugar completely melts. As soon as sugar melts, remove from heat (caution: sugar burns easily) and stir almonds in to coat. Remove from the pan and pour on a lightly buttered piece of aluminum foil to cool. When cool, break into small pieces.

4. Toss salad with onions, apples and enough dressing to coat. Divide among individual serving plates. Top with cheese and almonds and serve immediately.

To section an orange, slice off the top and bottom. Stand the fruit on one of the cut ends. Following the contour of the fruit, slice off all the peel and white pith in thick strips. After all peel has been removed, cut along each side of the membrane and orange section while holding the orange over a bowl to catch the sections and any juice. When all sections have been removed, squeeze all the remaining juice from the membranes into the bowl. Discard membranes.

Serves 8.

Seven Layer Salad

Mary B. King

This can be made the day before and refrigerated until ready to serve.

1 head iceberg lettuce, torn into bite-size pieces	1. In a glass container, layer ingredients listed above from lettuce to mushrooms.
½ cup chopped celery	
½ cup chopped red bell pepper	2. Top with mayonnaise and sugar. Then sprinkle with bacon and Cheddar cheese.
½ cup chopped onion	
5 hard-boiled eggs	
1 (10-ounce) package frozen tiny peas, uncooked	*Serves 8.*
1 (8-ounce) package sliced mushrooms	
1 pint mayonnaise	
1 teaspoon sugar	
½ cup bacon, cooked crisp and crumbled	
1 (8-ounce) package Cheddar cheese	

24-Hour Untossed Salad

Lynn Murphy O'Neal

1 pound fresh spinach, washed and dried
Salt and pepper to taste
1 teaspoon sugar
½ pound bacon, cooked crisp and crumbled
6 hard-boiled eggs, chopped
1 head iceberg lettuce, torn into serving pieces
Salt and pepper to taste
1 teaspoon sugar
1 (10-ounce) package frozen tiny baby peas, uncooked
1 medium sweet or red onion, thinly sliced
Julienne strips of Swiss cheese
2 cups mayonnaise mixed with 1 cup sour cream

1. Remove stems from spinach and tear leaves into pieces. Place in a clear salad bowl and sprinkle with salt, pepper and sugar.

2. Starting with the bacon, add a layer of the remaining ingredients in the exact order listed.

3. Cover and refrigerate overnight.

4. Do no toss at any time.

Salt and pepper are used at 2 different times in this recipe. It is not in error that they are listed twice. You may improvise and vary layers with julienne strips of ham.

Serves 8 to 10.

Cranberry-Pear Tossed Salad

Eileen Pastner

⅓ cup apricot nectar
⅓ cup red wine vinegar
⅓ cup canola oil
2 teaspoons Dijon mustard
¼ teaspoon salt
⅛ teaspoon pepper
2 tablespoons sugar
½ cup chopped walnuts
12 cups mixed salad greens
3 medium ripe pears
½ cup dried cranberries
¾ cup crumbled blue cheese

1. In a medium bowl, whisk together first 6 ingredients.

2. In a heavy skillet, melt sugar over medium heat, stir constantly. When sugar is melted, add walnuts and stir to coat. Remove from heat.

3. In a large salad bowl, combine greens, pears and cranberries. Drizzle with dressing. Add nuts and blue cheese.

Serves 12.

Classic Spinach Salad

Liz Donahue Mosher

This salad is a family favorite at gatherings. The dressing is out of this world.

Dressing

½ cup red wine vinegar
¾ cup sugar
⅓ cup ketchup
1 tablespoon salt (optional)
1 cup vegetable oil

1. In a small bowl, combine vinegar, sugar, ketchup and salt. Mix well.

2. Whisking constantly, add oil in a fine stream and whisk until well blended.

Salad

2 (10-ounce) bags fresh spinach, washed, stems removed and torn into bite-size pieces
4 hard-boiled eggs, sliced
½ pound bacon, cooked and crumbled
1 (8-ounce) can sliced water chestnuts
1 Bermuda onion, finely chopped

1. Toss all ingredients and drizzle with dressing just prior to serving.

This salad tastes best if served at room temperature.

Serves 8 to 12.

Spinach Strawberry Salad with Creamy Cashew Dressing

Cindy Wolodkin

This recipe is best with fresh, in-season berries.

½ cup oil
⅓ cup cashews
¼ cup warm water
3 tablespoons honey
1 tablespoon lemon juice, freshly
    squeezed
2 teaspoons white vinegar
1½ teaspoons dried dill
¾ teaspoon soy sauce
2 cloves garlic, minced
   Torn spinach leaves, stems
    removed and washed
   Sliced strawberries
   Sliced mushrooms
   Alfalfa sprouts

1. In a blender, combine first 9 ingredients and blend until smooth and creamy. Chill.

2. On six salad plates, arrange the spinach leaves, strawberries, mushrooms and alfalfa sprouts. Spoon the chilled dressing over the salads.

The leftover dressing will keep in refrigerator for up to two weeks.

Serves 6.

Autumn Avocado and Pomegranate Salad

Diane Elizabeth Burke

This salad is perfect to start a dinner on a cool crisp autumn evening.

Warm Champagne Vinegar Dressing

1 cup Champagne vinegar
2 tablespoons sugar
1½ tablespoons unbleached
    all-purpose flour
2 teaspoons dry vermouth
1 teaspoon Dijon-style mustard
1 egg, beaten
3 tablespoons heavy or whipping
    cream
2 cups olive oil
    Salt and freshly ground
    pepper, to taste

1. In a small saucepan, combine the vinegar, sugar, flour, vermouth and mustard. Heat to simmering over medium heat.

2. Gradually whisk in the egg and cream over low heat. Whisk in the oil in a thin steady stream. Season with salt and pepper. Remove from heat.

Yields 3 cups.

Salad

10 cups torn spinach leaves
1 medium avocado, pitted,
    peeled and thinly sliced
    Seeds of 1 pomegranate
1 cup Warm Champagne Vinegar
    Dressing

1. In a large salad bowl, place the spinach leaves and arrange the avocado slices in a circle around the edge of the salad. Place the pomegranate seeds in the center of the salad.

2. Pour 1 cup of the dressing over the salad at the table, toss and divide between salad plates.

Serves 8.

Tart Greens with Apples, Pecans and Buttermilk Honey Dressing

Leigh Hebert

My fiancé is not a big salad eater but, between the apples and pecans, he hardly recognizes the salad underneath. This salad is his favorite.

Buttermilk Honey Dressing

¼ cup cider vinegar
¼ cup sour cream
¼ cup buttermilk
3 tablespoons honey
1 teaspoon minced garlic
1 scallion, minced
Pinch of ground red pepper
Salt and pepper to taste
½ cup olive oil

1. In a small bowl, whisk together first 8 ingredients. Add olive oil in a slow steady stream, whisking constantly. Set aside.

Tart Greens

4 cups arugula, washed, dried and torn into bite-size pieces
1 small head radicchio, washed, dried and torn into bite-size pieces
2 Belgian endives, sliced lengthwise into long strips
2 Granny Smith apples, cored and thinly sliced
½ cup pecan halves, toasted

1. In a large bowl, combine all the lettuce. Add enough dressing to coat the salad.

2. Divide the greens among salad plates and top with apples and pecans. Serve immediately.

To toast pecans, place on a sheet of foil and bake at 350° for 5 minutes, toss occasionally or until toasted to your liking.

Serves 4 to 6.

A Healthy Waldorf Salad

Barbara MH Daigneault

This is one of those healthy recipes I found in a fitness magazine years ago. A little different twist than your standard Waldorf Salad but the flavors are superb and you needn't feel guilty about eating it.

Yogurt Dressing

⅓ cup nonfat vanilla yogurt
¼ cup reduced-calorie whipped topping
½ teaspoon freshly grated lemon peel
⅛ teaspoon ground nutmeg

1. Place yogurt in a small bowl. Gently fold in whipped topping, lemon peel and nutmeg. Set aside.

Salad

2 cups apples, chopped (do not peel)
1½ teaspoons lemon juice, freshly squeezed
⅓ cup chopped celery
¼ cup raisins
3 tablespoons chopped walnuts

1. Toss apples with lemon juice. Add celery, raisins and nuts.

2. Toss salad with dressing to coat.

Serves 6.

Winter Salad with Gorgonzola and Walnuts

Audrey Mingolla

Dressing

1   tablespoon Dijon mustard
3   tablespoons white wine vinegar
1   tablespoon lemon juice, freshly
      squeezed
½   cup walnut or sesame oil
¼   teaspoon salt
¼   teaspoon freshly ground pepper

1. In a jar with a tight lid, combine all ingredients. Shake well until thick.

Salad

1   head romaine lettuce, washed,
      dried and torn into bite-size
      pieces
½   pound Gorgonzola cheese,
      crumbled
1   cup coarsely chopped walnuts
1   Red Delicious apple, sliced
    Sliced red onion (optional)
    Grated red cabbage (optional)

1. In a large salad bowl, mix all ingredients and toss with dressing.

Serves 6 to 8.

Madhatter Salad

Cathleen Haddad

My friend, Karen Thibodeau, gave this recipe to me.
For years, I had to promise never to share it with anyone, until now.
Everyone will want this recipe. It's perfect for any party.

1   (16-ounce) bag shredded
    cabbage
1   bunch broccoli, finely chopped
8   scallions, finely chopped
1   stick butter
2   (3-ounce) packages ramen
    noodles, plus spice packet
1   cup sunflower seeds
½   cup sugar
2   teaspoons soy sauce
¼   cup apple cider vinegar
½   cup olive oil

1. In a large bowl, combine cabbage, broccoli and scallions. Set aside.

2. In a large skillet, melt the butter and add the noodles, spice packet and sunflower seeds. Cook until golden, being careful not to burn. Set aside to cool.

3. In a small bowl, combine remaining ingredients.

4. Keep all ingredients separate until ready to serve. Just before serving, make sure the dressing is mixed really well. Toss all ingredients together until well blended. Serve immediately.

This salad must be dressed at the last minute.

Crab Louis

Cathleen Haddad

I love to serve this for a luncheon and make your guests feel extra special. This is so easy to prepare, but looks and tastes like you were in the kitchen for hours. Try to use fresh Maine crabmeat, otherwise use frozen Alaska king crabmeat.

Sauce Louis

1	cup mayonnaise
⅓	cup chili sauce
1	tablespoon grated onion
1	tablespoon chopped fresh parsley
½	teaspoon Worcestershire sauce
2	tablespoons lemon juice, freshly squeezed

1. In a small bowl, combine all ingredients. Chill.

Crab Salad

1½	pounds lump crab
1	cup chopped celery
½	cup mayonnaise
	Juice of 1 lemon
	Pepper to taste
4	medium tomatoes
4	hard-boiled eggs
	Lemon wedges for garnish
1	avocado sliced
¼	cup sliced green olives for garnish

1. Remove cartilage from crabmeat. Mix with celery and mayonnaise. Season with lemon juice and a little pepper.

2. Arrange seafood on four plates. Surround with tomatoes and eggs. Cover. Refrigerate approximately 30 minutes.

3. Top each salad with a dollop of Sauce Louis. Garnish with lemon wedges, avocado slices and olives.

Lobster may be substituted for crab.

Curried Chicken Salad

Barbara MH Daigneault

I received this recipe from LaDona Coll. LaDona and I served this along with fresh fruit at a Women's Fellowship Luncheon at the First Congregational Church in Sutton, Massachusetts in the early 1990's. Everyone loved the flavor and it was a huge hit. The flavors and textures all blend together for a most delectable delight. This same recipe was served at the Sutton Garden Clubs year-end party in July of 2003 at my home.

Curry Dressing

- ¾ cup mayonnaise
- 1 teaspoon curry powder
- 2 teaspoons soy sauce
- 2 teaspoons lemon juice, freshly squeezed

1. In a small bowl, combine all ingredients and whisk together well. Set aside.

For those who don't like curry, simply omit it and the taste is still delicious.

Chicken Salad

- 2 cups cooked chicken breast, cut into bite-size pieces
- ¼ cup sliced water chestnuts
- ½ pound green grapes, cut into halves
- ½ cup chopped celery
- ½ cup slivered almonds, toasted
- 1 (8-ounce) can pineapple chunks, well drained

1. In a large bowl, combine all ingredients.

2. Toss with dressing and chill for several hours before serving to allow flavors to blend.

Serve this in a pineapple boat and your guests will really think you outdid yourself. If using the pineapple boat, use the fruit from the pineapple in place of canned pineapple.

Serves 4.

Gingered Pork Tenderloin Salad

Diane Elizabeth Burke

½ cup ginger preserves
⅓ cup rice vinegar
⅓ cup low-sodium soy sauce
1½ tablespoons dark sesame oil
1 pound pork tenderloin
6 cups shredded Napa cabbage
(or other Chinese cabbage)
1 cup thinly sliced sweet red
pepper

1. In a small saucepan, combine first 4 ingredients and bring to a boil over medium heat, stirring constantly. Remove from heat and cool completely.

2. Trim fat from tenderloin and place in a food storage bag. Pour half of soy sauce mixture over tenderloin and reserve remaining mixture. Seal bag and shake until tenderloin is coated. Marinate in refrigerator at least 2 hours, turning occasionally.

3. Remove tenderloin from marinade, reserving marinade. Insert meat thermometer into thickest part of tenderloin, if desired.

4. Place marinade in a small saucepan. Bring to a boil. Remove from heat and set aside.

5. Place tenderloin on grill, coated with cooking spray, over medium heat. Grill, covered, 20 minutes or until meat thermometer registers 160 degrees, turning and basting occasionally with reserved marinade. Let tenderloin stand 10 minutes. Slice diagonally across grain into thin slices.

6. Combine cabbage and red peppers. Pour remaining half of soy sauce mixture over cabbage mixture and toss lightly. Spoon cabbage mixture evenly onto individual salad plates. Arrange tenderloin slices over cabbage.

Serves 4.

Saratoga Broccoli Salad

Barbara MH Daigneault

While living in Saratoga, California in 1994, I received this recipe. Bob and I invited a friend, Doug Keener, for dinner one evening and he wanted to bring along a salad. This is by far the best broccoli salad we have ever tasted and to think Doug made it was even more special. The flavors all blend together and will be a sure hit at any summertime party.

1	head broccoli, finely chopped
4	stalks celery, finely chopped
1	bunch scallions, thinly sliced
1	cup raisins
1	cup chopped walnuts
1	cup mayonnaise
½	cup sugar
3	tablespoons apple cider vinegar
10	slices bacon, cooked crisp and crumbled

1. In a large bowl, combine first 5 ingredients.

2. In a small bowl, combine mayonnaise, sugar and vinegar, whisking until well blended. Pour over broccoli mixture and mix well. Refrigerate at least 4 hours before serving.

3. Just before serving add crumbled bacon and toss.

Marinated Carrot Salad

From the Kitchen of Barbara B. Beaton
submitted by Patricia M. Morse

This is a great addition at a cookout on a hot summer's day. It's a vegetable and salad in one.

2	pounds carrots, cooked and thinly sliced
1	onion, thinly sliced
1	green bell pepper, cut into thin strips
1	can tomato soup
1	cup sugar
¾	cup cider vinegar
½	cup salad oil
1	teaspoon dry mustard
1	teaspoon Worcestershire sauce

1. In a medium bowl, combine carrots, onion and green pepper.

2. In a small saucepan, combine remaining ingredients and cook until the sugar is dissolved.

3. Pour over carrot mixture and marinate at least 24 hours. Drain off sauce, leaving a little behind in serving bowl.

German Potato Salad

Valerie Ciavarra

*My grandmother used to make this potato salad whenever
I would go to upstate New York to visit her. It's my favorite potato salad.*

5 potatoes, peeled
¼ pound bacon
1 onion, finely chopped
1 cup vinegar
3 tablespoons sugar
1 tablespoon cornstarch

1. Boil potatoes about 20 minutes or until tender. Let cool, then dice and set aside.

2. In a skillet, fry bacon until crisp. Set on a paper towel to remove excess grease. Reserve drippings.

3. Add onion to remaining drippings in pan and cook until transparent. Add approximately 1 cup vinegar and sugar to onion mixture and bring to a slow boil.

4. Mix cornstarch to ¼ cup cold water. Add cornstarch mixture to onion mixture to thicken.

5. Pour over potatoes. Crumble bacon and sprinkle over potatoes. Gently stir to mix. Serve warm.

May be refrigerated, reheat to serve.

Serves 8.

Classic Potato Salad

Karen Thibodeau

5 pounds Idaho potatoes
1 cup mayonnaise
2 tablespoons hot horseradish mustard
1 teaspoon garlic powder
½ teaspoon onion salt
½ teaspoon celery salt
½ teaspoon black pepper
½ teaspoon salt
1 dozen hard-boiled eggs, chopped small
Paprika (optional)

1. Peel potatoes and cut into pieces bigger than bite-size. Boil potatoes until firm yet slightly tender, roughly 20 minutes once water returns to boil. Drain and run under cold water to stop further cooking. Drain well.

2. In a small bowl, combine mayonnaise, mustard, garlic powder, onion salt, celery salt, pepper and salt. Mix well.

3. In a large bowl, combine eggs and potatoes. Add mayonnaise mixture and fold in trying not to mush potatoes too much. Add more mayonnaise until you have the consistency you like.

4. Chill if desired. Sprinkle with paprika.

Easy Summer Pasta Salad

Dedee Fisher

Perfect for a hot summer's night barbecue.

1 (8-ounce) box shell or farfalle pasta
1 (16-ounce) container of fresh salsa
1 (4-ounce) package goat cheese
Mustard, amount and type your preference

1. Cook pasta according to package directions. Cool slightly.

2. While still warm, add salsa, cheese and mustard. Serve at room temperature.

Greek Orzo Salad with Shrimp

Beth Willoughby

This recipe is so simple to prepare and is very impressive looking. Shrimp and orzo, rice-shaped pasta, combined with traditional Mediterranean ingredients make for a delicious summer dish. I serve Hummus (page 10) with pita bread as an accompaniment. Remember to chill the white wine.

Dressing

¼ cup plus 2 tablespoons packed fresh dill
1½ cloves garlic
3   tablespoons olive oil
3   tablespoons lemon juice, freshly squeezed
1½ tablespoons red wine vinegar
½   teaspoon salt
    Freshly ground pepper

1. In a food processor, finely chop dill. With machine running, drop garlic through feed tube and process until minced. Scrape down sides of bowl.

2. Add oil, lemon juice, vinegar and salt. Season with pepper. Process until blended, about 5 seconds. Transfer dressing to large bowl.

Salad

¾ cup orzo
1   teaspoon vegetable oil
1   pound large shrimp, peeled, deveined and cooked
3½ ounces feta cheese, crumbled
1   large ripe tomato, seeded and diced
12 kalamata olives, pitted and chopped
2   green onions, sliced
    Red leaf lettuce
    Fresh dill sprigs for garnish
    Kalamata olives for garnish

1. Cook orzo according to package directions. When cooked, rinse and drain well. Toss with 1 teaspoon of vegetable oil and chill.

2. Add shrimp, chilled orzo, feta, tomato, chopped olives and onions to dressing. Toss gently to combine. Adjust seasonings.

3. Line four serving plates with lettuce. Mound salad decoratively atop lettuce. Garnish with dill sprigs and olives.

Salad can be prepared 3 hours ahead. Cover and refrigerate.

Serves 4.

Pasta Salad with Artichokes and Sun-Dried Tomatoes

Eileen Pastner

This salad can be completely prepared the night before.

1 (20-ounce) package fresh three-cheese tortellini
½ cup mayonnaise
½ cup olive oil
¼ cup red wine vinegar
1½ teaspoons Dijon mustard
1 teaspoon sugar
½ teaspoon salt
½ teaspoon ground pepper
¼ teaspoon dried oregano
¼ teaspoon dried thyme
¼ teaspoon dried basil
1 clove garlic, pressed
2 cups chopped celery
1 (13¼-ounce) can artichoke hearts, drained and chopped
¾ cup chopped green onions
½ cup drained, oil-packed, sun-dried tomatoes, coarsely chopped
½ cup kalamata olives, pitted and coarsely chopped
½ cup freshly grated Parmesan cheese

1. Cook pasta in a large pot of boiling salted water until just tender but still firm to bite. Drain. Rinse with cold water to cool quickly. Drain again.

2. Whisk mayonnaise and next 10 ingredients in small bowl until well blended. Season with salt and pepper.

3. Transfer ¾ cup dressing to a large bowl. Mix in celery, artichokes, green onions, sun-dried tomatoes and olives. Add pasta to vegetable mixture, then Parmesan cheese. Toss to blend.

4. Mix in more dressing by ¼ cupfuls, if desired. Season salad with salt and pepper. Serve cold or at room temperature.

Serves 6 to 8.

Pasta Salad with Chicken and Beets

Cathleen Haddad

This is a great summer pasta salad, it's really good! Not only does it taste good but the color from the beets, make it look good too. It can be made without the chicken.

Dressing
1   cup mayonnaise
6   tablespoons sugar
1   teaspoon salt
¼   teaspoon pepper

1. In a small bowl, whisk all ingredients.

Pasta Salad
2   cups diced cooked chicken
1   pound cooked elbow macaroni
1   (10-ounce) bag frozen petite peas (do not thaw)
1   (16-ounce) can pineapple chunks, drained
1   (16-ounce) can beets, rinsed and cubed

1. In a large bowl, combine all ingredients. Toss with dressing. Chill until ready to serve.

Adjust amount of peas added to salad to your liking.

Sunshine Salad (Orange)

Cathy Eaton

⅔   cup sugar
2   (3-ounce) packages orange jello
2   cups boiling water
1   (8-ounce) can Mandarin oranges, drained
1   (20-ounce) can pineapple chunks, not drained in heavy syrup
1   pint sour cream

1. Dissolve sugar and jello in hot water. Add oranges and pineapple chunks and refrigerate for ½ hour.

2. When slightly jelled, mix in sour cream. Pour into a mold and refrigerate overnight.

When you add sour cream, it will appear curdled. Mix slowly with wire whisk until smooth.

Sunshine Salad (Lemon)

Diane Lavoie

This is a perfect summer salad.

1 (3-ounce) package lemon jello
1 cup boiling water
1 (8½-ounce) can crushed pineapple, drained (reserve liquid)
1 tablespoon vinegar
¼ teaspoon salt
1 cup shredded carrot
¼ cup chopped pecans (optional)

1. Dissolve jello in water. Add water to reserved pineapple juice to make 1 cup. Add to jello along with vinegar and salt. Chill until partially set.

2. Fold in pineapple, carrot and pecans. Pour into a mold. Chill until firm.

You can use any type of nut.

Serves 6.

Cranberry-Cherry Salad Mold

Barbara Bordeaux-Woods

1 (6-ounce) package cherry jello
1 cup boiling water
1 cup cold water
1 cup sour cream
1 (16-ounce) can whole berry cranberry sauce
1 (8½-ounce) can crushed pineapple, drained
½ cup chopped nuts
½ cup chopped celery

1. Dissolve jello in 1 cup boiling water. After dissolved, add 1 cup of cold water.

2. Combine remaining ingredients and pour into a mold. Serve when chilled.

Cranberry-Apple Salad Mold

From the Kitchen of Olive Perry
submitted by Nancy Perry

This recipe is from Jeff's grandma, Olive Perry. She was a terrific everyday and special occasion cook! She always doubled the recipe as she had a crowd to feed, whether it was hungry dairymen for lunch or company for supper. Olive and her husband, Norman, owned and operated The Maples on Singletary Avenue in Sutton, Massachusetts.

2 cups cranberries, washed	1. Cook the cranberries with water until skins are broken. Put through a Foley food mill (food processor).
1 cup water	
1 cup sugar	
2 tablespoons gelatin, soaked in ½ cup cold water for 5 minutes	2. Add sugar and bring to a boil. Pour over hydrated gelatin. Stir constantly.
1 cup chopped celery	3. When almost cooled, add celery, apple and nuts. Pour into a mold and refrigerate until ready to serve.
1 cup chopped apple	
½ cup chopped walnuts	

Confetti Cole Slaw Parfait

From the Kitchen of Eunice P. King
Taken from Recipes – Sutton Grange Cookbook, 1978

1 (3-ounce) package lime gelatin	1. Dissolve jello in boiling water. Stir in cold water and vinegar. Gradually add this to Miracle Whip, mixing until well blended. Chill until slightly thickened.
1 cup boiling water	
½ cup cold water	
1 tablespoon vinegar	
½ cup Miracle Whip	
1 cup finely chopped cabbage	2. Fold in remaining ingredients and pour into a 1-quart mold. Chill until firm and serve.
½ cup shredded carrot	
½ cup sliced celery	
⅓ cup raisins	

Serves 6.

Entrées

Welcome Home

The Home of Patricia M. Morse, Wheelock Road

Cathleen never tires of drawing her childhood home. This always stirs up comforting memories of the home cooked meals prepared on their self-supporting farm. Each year the entire Morse family returns home for traditional New England holiday gatherings. This home was built around 1873 for Ella Jane Wheelock, niece of Luther and Calvin Wheelock, and great grandmother of Ralph W. (Bud) Gurney Jr. The Morse family purchased the farmhouse in 1970, where they raised their nine children.

Entrées

Entrées

Cranberry Glazed Chicken Breasts

Jane KH Walsh

Easy to prepare and so moist.

4-6 boneless, skinless chicken breast halves
1 (8-ounce) can jellied cranberry sauce
½ cup brown sugar
¼ cup soy sauce
1 teaspoon salt
1 teaspoon dry mustard
1 teaspoon ground ginger
1 clove garlic, crushed
2 tablespoons lemon juice

1. Place chicken in a greased 9 x 9-inch baking dish.

2. In a small saucepan, heat cranberry sauce and add brown sugar to dissolve. Remove from heat and add remaining ingredients and pour over chicken.

3. Bake at 325° for 35 to 45 minutes.

Serves 4 to 6.

Cranberry Orange Baked Chicken

Ann Junnila

This is a favorite dish for birthday celebrations.

4 tablespoons butter
⅓ cup flour
1 teaspoon salt
4-6 boneless, skinless chicken breasts
1½ cups whole cranberries (fresh or frozen)
¾ cup sugar
¼ cup chopped onion
1 teaspoon grated orange peel
¾ cup orange juice
¼ teaspoon cinnamon
¼ teaspoon ground ginger

1. In a large skillet, melt the butter. Combine flour and salt. Lightly coat the chicken with flour mixture and brown, turning once.

2. In a medium saucepan, combine cranberries, sugar, onion, orange peel, orange juice, cinnamon and ginger. Bring to a boil and pour over chicken. Cover skillet and cook slowly for 10 minutes.

You may use whole berry cranberry sauce, just decrease the amount of sugar. This recipe can also be baked, in a covered casserole dish, at 350° for 45 minutes.

Serves 4 to 6.

Chicken Scaloppine in Lemon-Caper Sauce

Audrey Mingolla

2 pounds boneless, skinless chicken breast
2 lemons
Salt and pepper to taste
Flour (for dredging)
6 tablespoons olive oil, divided
6 tablespoons unsalted butter, divided
2 cloves garlic
10 Cerignola or other large green pitted olives, sliced
¼ cup small capers
½ cup dry white wine
1 cup chicken stock
2 tablespoons chopped fresh parsley

1. Place 2 pieces of chicken at a time between plastic wrap and pound to ¼-inch thick.

2. Squeeze juice from 1½ lemons; cut the remaining half lemon into thin slices.

3. Sprinkle the chicken with salt and pepper. Dredge in flour and tap off excess. In a wide, heavy skillet over medium heat, heat 3 tablespoons of the oil and 2 tablespoons of butter. When the butter foams, add as many scaloppine as will fit without touching. Cook until golden brown on both sides, about 5 minutes total.

4. Remove from pan and drain on paper towels. Wipe out the skillet with paper towels after all scaloppine is cooked.

5. Pour in the remaining oil and butter. Add the garlic and lemon slices, cook for 3 minutes, scraping the bottom of the skillet until the garlic is golden. Remove the lemon slices and set aside. Add the olives and capers and cook for 4 minutes.

6. Pour in the wine and bring to a boil, let the wine reduce to half. Pour in the chicken stock, bring to a boil and cook until the sauce is syrupy.

7. Return the scaloppine and lemon slices to the skillet, turning in the sauce to warm. Sprinkle with parsley, and serve at once. *Serves 4.*

Chicken in a Lemon Cream Sauce

Cheryl Scott

¼ cup butter
4 boneless, skinless chicken breasts
2 tablespoons dry white wine
½ teaspoon grated lemon peel
2 tablespoons lemon juice
¼ teaspoon salt
⅛ teaspoon white pepper
1 cup heavy cream
⅓ cup grated Parmesan cheese
1 cup sliced mushrooms
Red grapes and lemon peel for garnish

1. In a large skillet, melt butter over medium heat. Add chicken. Cook, turning, about 10 minutes or until chicken is brown and tender. Remove chicken and place in an ovenproof serving dish. Discard butter from skillet.

2. Add wine, lemon peel and lemon juice to skillet; cook and stir over medium heat 1 minute. Stir in salt and white pepper.

3. Gradually pour in cream, stirring constantly, until hot; do not boil. Pour cream sauce over chicken. Sprinkle with cheese and mushrooms.

4. Broil chicken about 6-inches from heat source until lightly browned.

5. Garnish with grapes and lemon peel.

Serves 8.

Portsmouth Apricot Chicken

Susan Mooney

1 envelope onion soup mix
1 (6-ounce) bottle Russian salad dressing (dark red color)
1 (12-ounce) jar apricot preserves
6-8 boneless, split chicken breasts

1. Combine onion soup mix, dressing and preserves. Mix well.

2. Place chicken in a greased 13 x 9-inch baking dish and pour the mixture on top. Bake, covered, at 350° for 35 to 40 minutes.

Raspberry Chicken

Cindy Wolodkin

This goes very well with Spinach Strawberry Salad with Creamy Cashew Dressing (page 118).

2 whole boneless, skinless chicken breasts
2 tablespoons butter
¼ cup finely chopped onion
¼ cup raspberry vinegar
¼ cup chicken broth
¼ cup heavy cream
1 tablespoon canned crushed tomatoes
¼ cup frozen raspberries

1. Split and flatten the chicken breasts.

2. In a large skillet, melt the butter. Add the chicken and cook for 3 minutes on each side; remove and set aside. Add the onion to the drippings in the pan and cook until tender. Add the vinegar and cook, uncovered, until the syrup is reduced to 1 tablespoon.

3. Whisk in the chicken broth, heavy cream and crushed tomatoes; simmer for 1 minute.

4. Return the chicken to the skillet and simmer gently in the sauce, basting often until done, about 5 minutes.

5. Remove the chicken. Add the raspberries to the sauce and cook over low heat for 1 minute. Pour the sauce over the chicken and serve over cooked linguine.

Serves 4.

Rock Cornish Hens with Red Raisin Sauce

Barbara MH Daigneault

*Bob and I love this recipe. So easy to prepare
and the taste of the sauce is absolutely delicious.*

4 (1-pound) Rock Cornish hens
Salt and pepper
1 tablespoon flour
1 large oven cooking bag
2 tablespoons butter, melted

1. Remove giblets from the hens. Wash hens and pat dry. Sprinkle body cavity with salt and pepper.

2. Place flour in a cooking bag, shake well. Brush hens with butter and place in bag.

3. Place bag in a roasting pan and bake at 425° for 1 hour. Serve topped with Red Raisin Sauce.

Red Raisin Sauce

1 (10-ounce) jar red currant jelly
½ cup golden raisins
2 tablespoons butter
2 teaspoons lemon juice, freshly squeezed
¼ teaspoon ground allspice
1 (16-ounce) jar spiced crabapples, drained for garnish

1. In a 2-quart saucepan over medium-low heat, cook sauce ingredients, stirring occasionally, until blended, about 10 minutes.

2. Spoon over cooked hens and top with crabapples.

Serves 4.

Baked Chicken with Broccoli and Blue Cheese

Jean Nilsson

1 (10-ounce) package frozen broccoli spears, cooked
1 can cream of chicken soup
½ cup sour cream
¼ cup blue cheese
2 cups cooked chicken pieces (white meat)
½ cup bread crumbs
  Paprika

1. Layer cooked broccoli in the bottom of a greased casserole dish. Top with chicken pieces.

2. Combine soup, sour cream and blue cheese. Pour over chicken. Top with bread crumbs and paprika.

3. Bake at 350° for 40 minutes.

You may pour a little milk over the casserole for a creamier casserole.

Serves 4 to 6.

Baked Chicken Mushroom Casserole

Carolyn Shannon

⅓ cup flour
1 teaspoon salt
¼ teaspoon pepper
1 tablespoon paprika
1 package boneless chicken breast
⅓ cup margarine
1 can cream of mushroom soup
1 cup sour cream
1 (4-ounce) can sliced mushrooms (do not drain)
  Rice or rice pilaf for serving

1. Combine flour, salt, pepper and paprika in a plastic bag. Add chicken and shake well.

2. In a large skillet, melt the margarine and brown the chicken. Arrange chicken in a greased 9 x 9-inch baking dish.

3. In a medium bowl, combine soup, sour cream and mushrooms with liquid. Pour over chicken.

4. Bake, uncovered, at 350° for 45 minutes. Serve over hot rice or rice pilaf.

Serves 4.

Chicken and Apple Curry

Rita Dignan

*A friend, Barbara Lawson, gave this recipe to me. She compiled
a collection of her recipes and shared them with me. This chicken dish
is to be served with Apple Ginger Chutney (page 47).*

2 tablespoons olive oil

3 tablespoons unsalted butter, divided

3½ pounds chicken, cut into pieces

Salt to taste

2 celery stalks, chopped fine

1 onion, chopped fine

2 cloves garlic, minced

2 Granny Smith apples, peeled and chopped

1 red bell pepper, chopped

1 tablespoon curry powder

½ teaspoon cinnamon

½ teaspoon cumin

2 tablespoons flour

2 cups chicken broth

Pepper to taste

¼ cup parsley (optional)

3 cups cooked rice

1. In a Dutch oven, heat oil and 1 tablespoon butter over moderately high heat until foam subsides. Season the chicken with salt and brown on both sides. Transfer the chicken with a slotted spoon to a plate.

2. Pour off excess fat from the Dutch oven; add the remaining butter, celery, onion and garlic. Cook over moderately low heat, stirring occasionally, until the vegetables are tender. Add apples and cook for approximately 5 minutes, stirring occasionally. Add the bell pepper, curry, cinnamon and cumin; stir and cook for 1 minute. Stir in the flour and cook for 3 minutes. Add the broth and chicken with any juices that have accumulated and bring the liquid to a boil.

3. Cook the chicken mixture, covered, at a very low simmer for 15 to 20 minutes, or until the chicken is cooked through and tender. Transfer the chicken with a slotted spoon to a serving plate.

4. Boil the vegetable mixture for 3 to 5 minutes, or until it thickens slightly, and season the sauce with salt and pepper. Pour the sauce over the chicken and top with parsley. Serve the chicken with rice and Apple Ginger Chutney.

Serves 4.

Chicken with Mushrooms and Muenster Cheese

Jayne Swart

This has been a favorite of my family for 20 years.
It's the perfect "company" dish. It can be assembled ahead of time,
refrigerated and then baked just before serving.

6	boneless chicken breast halves
4	tablespoons butter
	Juice of 1 lemon
½	cup olive oil
½	cup dry white wine
1	(10-ounce) package fresh sliced mushrooms
6	slices Muenster cheese

1. In a skillet, sauté chicken in butter until chicken turns white. Add lemon juice and cook for 5 minutes on each side.

2. Transfer chicken and juices to an 11 x 9-inch baking dish. Pour olive oil and wine over chicken. Sprinkle with mushroom slices; top with cheese.

3. Bake, covered, at 350° for 45 minutes. Remove foil during the last 15 minutes of baking.

Serves 4 to 6.

Chicken à la Romano

Deborah Dutton

A friend gave me this recipe when I needed to
start watching my cholesterol. Delicious and healthy!

2	boneless, skinless chicken breasts, quartered
1	clove garlic, minced
⅓	cup parsley flakes
1	teaspoon dried oregano
1	(16-ounce) can whole tomatoes, cut in wedges
	Pinch of red pepper to taste
	Salt to taste (optional)
	Pepper to taste
¼	cup grated Parmesan cheese
¼	cup olive oil

1. Place chicken in a 9 x 9-inch greased baking dish. Cover with garlic, parsley, oregano, tomato wedges, red pepper, salt and pepper. Sprinkle with Parmesan cheese and drizzle olive oil over top.

2. Bake, uncovered, at 350° for 1 hour or until cooked through.

Serves 4.

Chicken William (Marsala)

Audrey Mingolla

2 small boneless, skinless chicken breasts, split

Flour with a dash of garlic powder for dredging

1 egg, lightly beaten with 1 tablespoon water

2 tablespoons vegetable oil

2 tablespoons butter

¼ cup chopped shallots

2 teaspoons lemon juice

½ cup sliced mushrooms

Tabasco Sauce to taste

Worcestershire sauce to taste

3 tablespoons sweet Marsala, warmed slightly

¼ cup chicken or veal stock, thickened with cornstarch

4 slices mozzarella cheese

1. Dredge chicken in flour and dip in egg. Heat oil in a frying pan until almost smoking. Add chicken, turning when brown. Reduce heat to medium and cook 5 minutes. Remove chicken from pan and keep warm. Drain oil from pan.

2. Add butter, shallots, lemon juice, mushrooms, Tabasco Sauce and Worcestershire sauce to taste. Carefully pour Marsala over all and flame. Add stock.

3. Return chicken to pan and place mozzarella on each piece. Simmer until tender and cheese melts.

Serves 4.

Chicken with Tomato-Basil Cream Sauce

Linda Nydam

This is a one of my husband Doug's favorite dishes.

4 boneless, skinless chicken halves, pounded thin
Salt and pepper to taste
3 tablespoons butter, divided
2 plum tomatoes, chopped
1 small onion, chopped
¼ teaspoon salt
¼ cup white wine or chicken broth
½ cup whipping or heavy cream
2 tablespoons fresh basil leaves strips for garnish

1. Season chicken with salt and pepper.

2. In large skillet over medium-high heat, melt 2 tablespoons of butter. Add chicken and cook until chicken is no longer pink inside, turning once. Remove chicken and set aside.

3. In the same skillet, melt remaining 1 tablespoon of butter. Add tomatoes, onion and salt; cook until tomatoes are tender, about 3 minutes.

4. Stir in wine and cook until wine evaporates. Stir in cream.

5. Reduce heat to low and return chicken to skillet. Simmer, uncovered, 4 minutes or until sauce is thickened and chicken is heated through. Garnish with basil.

Fresh basil tends to bruise and discolor easily. To avoid this, stack the leaves together and roll them up cigar style. With a sharp knife, cut the leaves crosswise into strips.

Chicken and Wild Rice Casserole with Dried Cranberries

Barbara MH Daigneault

Ann Achorn served this at a party several years ago and I didn't want to leave without having the recipe. The beauty being it's a one-dish meal and can be made a day ahead. It also multiplies easily. Any recipe from Ann is a jewel and you will know why when you make this one. Perfect for a cold winter's night.

1½ cups wild rice, rinsed well and drained

5 tablespoons unsalted butter, divided

¼ cup plus 1 tablespoon all-purpose flour

3½ cups chicken broth

2 tablespoons minced shallot

4 cups sliced mushrooms

1½ cups heavy cream

⅛ teaspoon freshly grated nutmeg

2 tablespoons fresh lemon juice

3 cups cooked, cubed chicken

1 cup dried cranberries

Salt and pepper to taste

Sour cream as an accompaniment

1. In a saucepan, combine the rice with 4½ cups water. Bring the water to a boil and simmer the rice for 45 minutes to 1 hour or until it is just tender.

2. In a heavy saucepan, melt 4 tablespoons butter over moderately low heat, add the flour and cook the roux, whisking for 3 minutes. Add the broth, bring the mixture to a boil and simmer whisking occasionally for 15 minutes.

3. While the sauce is simmering, in a skillet cook the shallot and the mushrooms in the remaining 1 tablespoon butter over moderate heat, stirring occasionally, until most of the liquid is evaporated. Add the mushroom mixture to the sauce and stir in the cream, nutmeg, lemon juice, chicken, cranberries, rice, salt and pepper to taste.

4. Transfer the mixture to a greased 13 x 9-inch baking dish. Bake, covered, in the middle of the oven at 400° for 20 minutes. Bake the casserole, uncovered, for 15 to 25

minutes or until most of the liquid is absorbed. Garnish with additional cranberries and serve it with sour cream.

You may use dried cherries in place of dried cranberries. To reheat the casserole, if making 1 day in advance, reheat at 350° for 15-20 minutes, or until it is heated through.

~~~

Heavenly Chicken Lasagne

Kathy Dugan

This recipe was first shared with me at one of our company "Dugan's Drug" picnics which we have annually at our home.

1	stick butter
½	cup flour
3	cups chicken broth
	Pepper to taste
3	cups chopped cooked chicken breast
8	ounces ricotta cheese
1	egg, slightly beaten
1	(16-ounce) package lasagne noodles, cooked
1	(10-ounce) package chopped broccoli, cooked and drained
16	ounces shredded mozzarella cheese

1. In a saucepan over low heat, melt butter. Add flour and stir until smooth. Add chicken broth and pepper and continue stirring over heat until broth thickens. Add chicken; remove from heat.

2. In a separate bowl, mix ricotta and egg until blended.

3. In a greased 13 x 9-inch pan, layer as follows: ½ chicken mixture, ⅓ noodles, ½ ricotta mix, broccoli, ½ mozzarella, ⅓ noodles, ½ chicken mix, ½ ricotta mix, ⅓ noodles and ½ mozzarella.

4. Cover with foil. Bake at 375° for 45 minutes. Remove the foil and bake an additional 15 minutes. Let stand for 10 minutes before serving.

You may use cottage cheese in place of ricotta. If using a glass or ceramic dish, turn oven temperature down to 350° to prevent burning.

Serves 8 to 10.

Sherried Chicken with Mushrooms and Artichokes

LaDona Coll

*This came from a Fort Lauderdale, Florida cookbook.
I like to make it for guests. We served this the first time Bob and Barbara
Daigneault came to visit us when we lived in Canada.*

6 whole, boneless, skinless chicken breasts, split
Salt and pepper to taste
Paprika to season
2 sticks butter, divided
2 (15-ounce) cans artichoke hearts, drained and sliced
1 pound fresh mushrooms, sliced
¼ teaspoon tarragon
6 tablespoons flour
1 cup sherry
3 cups chicken broth

1. Season chicken with salt, pepper and paprika.

2. In a frying pan, melt 1 stick of butter. Sauté the chicken until golden brown. Place in a greased 13 x 9-inch baking dish; add artichokes.

3. Sauté the mushrooms and tarragon in the remaining butter for 5 minutes. Sprinkle with flour; add sherry and chicken broth. Simmer 4 minutes and pour sauce over chicken and artichokes.

4. Bake, covered, at 350° for 45 minutes.

Serves 6.

Barbecued Baked Chicken

Joy Reece

This is a favorite of my children. It's easy and always delicious!

1 (2½ to 3-pound) chicken, cut into pieces
⅔ cup barbecue sauce
⅓ cup molasses
⅓ cup ketchup

1. On a charcoal or gas grill, brown chicken. Place chicken in a greased 13 x 9-inch roasting pan.

2. In a small bowl, combine remaining ingredients and pour over chicken. Bake, uncovered, at 325° for 45 to 60 minutes.

Serves 4.

Chicken Cordon Gold

Liz Shannon Charest

Proscuitto adds a wonderful flavor and makes this seem gourmet!

6-8 boneless, skinless chicken breasts

½ cup flour

1 teaspoon salt

1 teaspoon pepper

12-16 very thin slices prosciutto

2 (5-ounce) packages Boursin cheese with garlic and herbs

1 stick butter plus ½ tablespoon butter, divided

1 cup chicken broth

½ cup plus 2 tablespoons white wine, divided

½ pound fresh portobello mushrooms, sliced

Rice Pilaf or Saffron rice

1. Pound chicken breasts thin.

2. Combine flour, salt and pepper. Dredge meat in seasoned flour. Place a slice of prosciutto on each breast and spread with 1 to 2 tablespoons of Boursin cheese. Roll up and secure with toothpicks (usually 3 will do).

3. In a large skillet, brown chicken rolls in 4 tablespoons butter; add broth and ½ cup wine. Cover and simmer 30 to 35 minutes.

4. Before serving, sauté mushrooms in remaining butter and wine for 8 to 10 minutes. Add to chicken breasts. Serve over rice.

Remember to remove the toothpicks before serving.

Serves 4 to 6.

Chicken Paprikash

Barbara Roy

Great served with mashed potatoes.

1   (3½-pound) whole chicken
1   tablespoon butter, softened
1   clove garlic, crushed
2   jumbo onions, thinly sliced
½   teaspoon salt
1   tablespoon paprika
¼   cup water
¼   cup chicken broth
2   tablespoons sour cream

1. Rinse chicken and pat dry. Mix butter with garlic.

2. With fingertips, gently separate skin from meat on chicken breast and thighs. Spread garlic mixture under skin.

3. In a small roasting pan, combine onions, salt, paprika and ¼ cup water. Place chicken, breast-side up, on top of onions.

4. Roast at 450° for 1 hour, stirring onions after 30 minutes.

5. Place chicken on platter when done and let stand for 10 minutes.

6. Skim and discard grease from pan. Add chicken broth and heat to boiling over medium heat, stirring onions. Stir in sour cream until heated through. Pour sauce over chicken and serve immediately.

Serves 4.

Greek Chicken with Capers and Raisins in Feta Sauce

Barbara MH Daigneault

I am a great fan of Cooking Light. Everyone I have made it for has requested this recipe. I find these items are a staple in most homes, so it's an easy "what should I make for dinner tonight" meal. The sweetness of the raisins and the salt from the feta and capers create a balanced harmony that is very pleasing.

4   boneless, skinless, chicken breast halves
2   tablespoons all-purpose flour
1   teaspoon dried oregano
1   tablespoon olive oil
1   cup thinly sliced onion
1½ cups fat-free, less-sodium chicken broth
⅓   cup golden raisins
2   tablespoons lemon juice
2   tablespoons capers
¼   cup crumbled feta cheese
4   thin lemon slices

1. Pound chicken breasts to ¼-inch thick.

2. Combine flour and oregano in a shallow dish; dredge chicken in flour mixture.

3. In a large nonstick skillet over medium-high heat, heat oil. Add chicken and cook 5 minutes on each side. Remove the chicken from pan and keep warm. Add onions to pan and sauté for 2 minutes. Stir in broth, raisins and lemon juice and cook for 3 minutes, scraping pan to loosen browned bits.

4. Return chicken to pan. Cover, reduce heat and simmer 10 minutes or until chicken is done. Remove the chicken once again from pan and keep warm.

5. Add capers and cheese to pan, stirring with a whisk. Top each chicken breast with ¼ cup sauce and 1 lemon slice.

Serves 4.

Pollo all'Arrabiata (Enraged Chicken!)

Carol Botty

This recipe originated from Florence's Restaurant in Boston's North End. You can dress it up by adding capers or a small amount of sliced Sicilian or kalamata olives.

2 tablespoons olive oil
1 large onion, finely chopped
2 cloves garlic, crushed
1 (2½ to 3-pound) free range chicken, cut in pieces
1 cup Chianti or robust red wine
½ hot chili pepper, slightly crushed
 Salt and pepper to taste
4-5 tomatoes, peeled, seeded and coarsely chopped

1. In a large, heavy saucepan over medium heat, heat oil and sauté onion and garlic until golden but not brown. Add chicken pieces and brown well on all sides.

2. Add wine, chili pepper, salt and pepper. Cook over low heat, turning frequently until wine is half evaporated.

3. Add tomatoes; cover and cook for approximately 20 minutes or until chicken is tender.

You may also use veal in place of chicken.

Serves 4.

Crunchy Chicken

Janet Dumas

My son Patrick loves this meal so much that he learned how to make it himself.

1 cup Ritz cracker crumbs
½ cup grated Parmesan cheese
1 stick butter, melted
1 package boneless, skinless chicken breasts
1 can cream of chicken soup
½ cup water
1 (4-ounce) can mushrooms, drained
1 cup sour cream

1. In a shallow bowl, combine cracker crumbs, Parmesan cheese and butter. Roll (dry) chicken in crumb mixture, reserving any leftover mixture. Place in a greased 13 x 9-inch baking dish.

2. In a medium bowl, combine soup, water, mushrooms and sour cream. Pour over chicken and top with remaining crumbs.

3. Bake, uncovered, at 350° for 1 hour.

Mediterranean Chicken Sauté

Bette Keene

I made this recipe up one evening in an attempt to liven up chicken breasts. Since then, it has become a favorite quick but flavorful supper. Any leftovers can be served as a salad the next day.

1½ pounds boneless, skinless chicken breasts, cut into strips
½ cup bottled Italian salad dressing
¼ cup olive oil
1 onion, sliced thin
1 green bell pepper, sliced thin
1 red bell pepper, sliced thin
1 (6-ounce) jar artichoke hearts
½ cup sun-dried tomatoes
¼ cup sliced black olives
Chopped garlic to taste
Juice of ½ lemon
Fresh or dried basil to taste
Salt and pepper to taste
½ cup crumbled feta cheese

1. Marinate chicken in salad dressing about 1 hour.

2. In a large skillet, heat the oil and sauté onions and peppers until soft. Remove from pan and set aside.

3. In the same pan, brown chicken on both sides. Return onions and peppers to pan; add artichokes and sun-dried tomatoes. Cook until the chicken is done. Add olives and garlic; continue cooking until heated.

4. Remove from heat; add lemon juice, basil, salt and pepper to taste. Place in a serving dish. Sprinkle with feta cheese. Serve over pasta or couscous.

May be made with shrimp.

Serves 4.

Chicken Scampi

Nancy C. Corey

½ cup butter
¼ cup olive oil
¼ cup finely chopped onion
1 tablespoon minced garlic
  Juice of 1 lemon (about
    3 tablespoons)
2 pounds boneless, skinless
  chicken breast, cut into
  ½-inch pieces
1 teaspoon salt
½ teaspoon pepper
¼ cup minced fresh parsley
2 medium chopped tomatoes
  Buttered noodles or rice

1. In a large skillet, heat butter and oil. Sauté onions and garlic. Add lemon juice, chicken, salt, pepper and parsley. Cook, stirring constantly, for 5 to 8 minutes or until chicken is cooked through.

2. Add tomatoes and heat through. Serve over noodles or rice.

Serves 4 to 6.

Mexican Chicken

Leeni Gravlin-Dunn

This is a great casserole to use up leftovers. The recipe is from the 1970's, when we used mushroom soup in everything.

1 green bell pepper, diced
1 medium onion, diced
1 precooked chicken, cut into
  small pieces
6 (6-inch) soft corn or flour
  tortillas
1½ teaspoons chili powder
1 (14½-ounce) can whole
  tomatoes
1 can cream of mushroom soup
1 can golden mushroom soup
2 cups Mexican flavored
  shredded cheese

1. In a medium bowl, mix pepper, onion and chicken; spread into a lightly greased 13 x 9-inch casserole dish. Layer chicken mixture with tortillas.

2. In a separate bowl, combine chili powder, tomatoes and soups. Spread on top of casserole. Cover with shredded cheese.

3. Bake at 350° for 30 to 45 minutes.

You may substitute any type of meat/ poultry and vegetables.

Serves 6 to 8.

Grilled Chicken Breasts with Chimichurri Sauce

Pauline Reid

Legend has it that the word chimichurri derives from the days when British laborers were working in Argentina. When they saw bowls of the aromatic sauce, they said, "Give me curry," which over the years became the word chimichurri.

Chimichurri Sauce

10 garlic cloves, peeled
1   bunch flat-leaf parsley, stemmed
¾   cup olive oil
¼   cup white balsamic vinegar
¼   cup water or chicken broth
¾   teaspoon dried oregano
¾   teaspoon dried basil
¼   teaspoon red pepper flakes
    Salt and freshly ground pepper to taste

1. In a food processor, puree the garlic. Add the parsley and process until finely chopped. Add the oil, vinegar, water and seasonings. Process to blend. Taste and adjust the seasonings. It should be very flavorful and spicy.

White wine vinegar may be used in place of balsamic vinegar. The sauce can be made up to 5 days ahead, covered and refrigerated. Remove from the refrigerator 30 minutes before serving. You may simmer the sauce for 10 minutes for a milder flavor.

Marinade

3   tablespoons Chimichurri sauce
2   tablespoons olive oil
3   whole chicken breasts, halved, boned and flattened

1. In a small bowl, combine all the marinade ingredients and stir until smooth. Put the chicken breasts in a food storage bag and pour in the marinade. Turn the chicken in the bag to coat it evenly. Close the bag and refrigerate for at least 30 minutes or up to 4 hours.

2. Prepare a barbecue grill for medium heat grilling. Remove the chicken from the marinade and grill for 7 to 10 minutes on each side or until cooked through.

3. Place on a platter and serve with the sauce on the side.

Try this with grilled flank steak or veal chops.
Serves 4 to 6.

Grilled Tuscan Chicken

Rebecca Smith

4   boneless, skinless chicken
    breasts, halved
1   teaspoon coarse salt
1   teaspoon cracked black
    peppercorn
½-1 teaspoon hot red pepper
    flakes
1   tablespoon chopped garlic
1   tablespoon chopped fresh
    rosemary
    Juice of 1 lemon
¼   cup extra-virgin olive oil
4   bricks, wrapped in aluminum
    foil

1. Wash and pat dry trimmed chicken breasts. Sprinkle the breasts on both sides with salt, cracked pepper and red pepper flakes. Sprinkle the breasts with garlic and rosemary, patting on with your fingers. Arrange breasts in a glass-baking dish.

3. Pour the lemon juice and oil over them and let marinate in refrigerator, covered, for 30 minutes to 1 hour, turning several times.

4. Prepare a grill for direct grilling and preheat to high. Use soaked wood chips for smoke. When ready to cook, brush and oil the grill grates. If using a charcoal grill, toss the wood chips on the coals.

5. Arrange the chicken breasts on the hot grates, all facing the same direction, at a 45-degree angle to the bars of the grate. Place a brick on top of each. Grill the breasts until cooked, 4 to 6 minutes per side, rotating the breasts 90 degrees after 2 minutes on each side to create an attractive cross-hatch of grill marks. Transfer the breasts to plates or a platter and serve at once.

Japanese Chicken

Jean Morse

1 egg, slightly beaten
1 cup flour
1-3 pounds boneless, skinless chicken breasts
2 sticks butter
3 tablespoons soy sauce
3 tablespoons water
1 cup sugar
½ cup vinegar

1. In a shallow bowl, beat egg slightly.

2. In another shallow bowl, place the flour. Dip chicken breasts in egg, then flour and shaking off excess.

3. In a large skillet, melt butter and sauté chicken until brown and crisp. Place chicken in a shallow roasting pan.

4. In a small saucepan, combine the remainder ingredients and heat to dissolve sugar. Spoon sauce over chicken. Bake, uncovered, at 350° for 30 minutes.

Turkey and Celery Loaf

From the Kitchen of Shirley Johnson
submitted by Pamela Gurney Farnum

1 pound ground turkey
½ cup dry bread crumbs
1 egg, slightly beaten
2 celery stalks, sliced
½ cup chopped onion
½ teaspoon rosemary
⅓ cup apple juice

1. In a large bowl, combine all ingredients.

2. Transfer to a greased loaf pan. Bake, uncovered in the center of oven, at 350° for 35-40 minutes. Let stand for 10 minutes before slicing.

Serves 6.

Maryland Fried Chicken

Joan E. Churn

In 1956, I received my first Joy of Cooking Cookbook as a young bride. My children loved this recipe. I serve this with wide noodles.

1   cup flour
    Salt and pepper to taste
    Paprika to taste
1   (3½-pound) package whole
    chicken, cut up
1   egg
½   cup milk
1   cup bread crumbs
1   stick butter
½   cup chicken broth
    Cooked wide noodles

1. In a large food storage bag, combine flour, salt, pepper and paprika. Place chicken in bag and shake to coat evenly.

2. In a shallow dish, combine egg and milk. Dip chicken in egg mixture. Roll chicken in bread crumbs.

3. Melt butter in a Dutch oven, add the chicken and fry until golden brown, about ½ hour.

4. Pour ½ cup broth in pan with chicken. Bake, covered, at 350° for 30 minutes. Serve with noodles.

You may make your own chicken broth by boiling giblets.

Serves 6.

Oriental Turkey Burgers

Joanne K. DiStefano

1   pound ground turkey
¼   cup chopped green onion
¼   cup dry bread crumbs
2   tablespoons hoisin sauce
1   teaspoon ground ginger
¼   teaspoon low sodium soy
    sauce
¼   teaspoon ground red pepper
    Hamburger rolls

1. In a large bowl, combine first 7 ingredients. Mix well. Shape into four ½-inch thick patties.

2. Prepare grill or broiler. Place patties on grill rack or broiler pan, coated with cooking spray. Cook 5 minutes on each side or until done. Serve on hamburger rolls.

Serves 4.

Thai Turkey

Cindy King

This is also excellent made with chicken!

1	tablespoon vegetable oil
3	green onions, thinly sliced
1	medium red bell pepper, sliced into 2-inch matchstick-thin strips
	Thai Sauce
3	cups coarsely shredded cooked turkey
	Rice
	Chopped fresh cilantro for garnish
	Sliced green onions for garnish

1. In a large skillet, heat oil over high heat. Add green onions and pepper. Cook until tender and golden, stirring frequently.

2. Stir in Thai Sauce and turkey and cook, stirring to coat turkey well, until heated through. Serve over rice. Garnish with cilantro and green onions.

Thai Sauce

1	clove garlic, minced
2	tablespoons soy sauce
1	tablespoon chopped fresh cilantro
1	tablespoon honey
1½	teaspoons curry powder
1	teaspoon Asian sesame oil
½	teaspoon cornstarch
¼	teaspoon crushed red pepper
⅓	cup water

1. In a small bowl, mix garlic, soy sauce and cilantro. Add remaining ingredients. Mix well. Set aside.

Bohemian Style Duck

Dolores Swatik

I found this method of cooking to be fast and clean and so easy to pour off the grease. The ducks comes out very moist.

1-3 ducks
1 tablespoon sea salt
1-2 tablespoons caraway seeds
Oven cooking bag

1. Wash ducks. Using a fork, pierce each duck several times to allow excess grease to escape. Rub the meat with sea salt and caraway seeds. Place ducks in an oven-cooking bag.

2. Bake at 325° for 2-3 hours. Towards the end of cooking, open the bag and allow ducks to brown. Pour off excess grease and cut up with kitchen scissors and serve.

Teriyaki Finger Steaks

Cheryl Bedard

A huge hit at cookouts! Everyone always asks for the recipe.

2 pounds boneless sirloin steak (flank)
½ cup soy sauce
¼ cup vinegar
2 tablespoons brown sugar
2 tablespoons minced onion
1 tablespoon vegetable oil
1 clove garlic, minced
½ teaspoon ground ginger
⅛ teaspoon pepper

1. Slice steak lengthwise into ½-inch strips. Place in a large glass bowl. Combine all remaining ingredients and pour over meat and toss gently. Cover and refrigerate for 2 to 3 hours.

2. Drain, discarding marinade. Loosely thread meat strips onto skewers.

3. Grill over medium-high heat, turning often, for 7 to 10 minutes or until meat reaches desired doneness.

If using wooden skewers, make sure to soak the skewers for at least 1 hour in water to prevent burning. You can even marinate on the skewers overnight to prepare ahead.

Serves 6.

Tenderloin Steaks with Cranberry-Port Sauce and Gorgonzola Cheese

Susan Koopman

I found this recipe in a cooking magazine. It is easy, elegant and delicious. Serve with potatoes, salad and red wine!

4 tablespoons butter, divided
2 large cloves garlic, sliced
1 large shallot, sliced
1¼ cups canned beef broth, divided
1 cup ruby port
¼ cup dried cranberries
4 (6-ounce) beef tenderloins, about 1-inch thick
 Salt and pepper to taste
½ teaspoon minced fresh rosemary
½ cup crumbled Gorgonzola cheese

1. In a medium saucepan over medium high heat, melt 2 tablespoons butter. Add garlic and shallot, 1 cup beef broth, port wine and cranberries. Boil liquid until reduced to ½ cup, about 8 minutes. Set sauce aside.

2. In a large skillet over medium high heat, melt remaining 2 tablespoons butter and sprinkle steaks with salt and pepper. Add steaks to skillet and cook to desired doneness. Transfer steaks to plate, cover loosely with foil.

3. Add rosemary, sauce and remaining ¼ cup broth to skillet. Boil 1 minute, scraping brown bits into sauce. Season with salt and pepper. Spoon sauce over steaks. Top each steak with Gorgonzola cheese.

For medium-rare steaks, cook about 5 minutes per side.

Serves 4.

Italian Stuffed Flank Steak

Beth Willoughby

This is a wonderful company or special holiday recipe.
It makes for an attractive buffet item. I serve this with Risotto Porcini Casserole
(page 250), freshly tossed spring greens and crusty bread.

8   ounces fresh spinach, trimmed and well rinsed
½   cup dried bread crumbs
½   cup grated Parmesan cheese
¼   cup olive oil
2   cloves garlic
1   (1½-pound) flank steak, butterflied
    Salt and freshly ground pepper to taste
4   ounces thinly sliced prosciutto
3   red bell peppers, roasted and cut in half
1   fresh hot cherry pepper, cored, seeded and minced

1. In a saucepan, place the spinach with just the water that clings to the leaves. Cover and cook over medium heat until wilted, about 5 minutes. Drain in a colander and press out the excess moisture with the back of a spoon.

2. In a food processor, combine the spinach, bread crumbs, Parmesan, olive oil and garlic and puree until thick and smooth. Transfer to a bowl.

3. Open the steak on a work surface and season with salt and pepper. Arrange the prosciutto in one layer on the steak. Top with a layer of the roasted peppers. Spread with spinach mixture and sprinkle with the minced cherry pepper. Starting with a long side, roll the steak up jelly-roll style. Tie with string at 2-inch intervals and brush with a little olive oil. Season with salt and pepper.

4. Place the steak in a shallow baking pan. Bake at 350° for 40 minutes for medium-rare. Cool slightly or to room temperature before slicing and serving.

To roast red peppers: halve peppers, remove seeds and membranes. Flatten peppers with palm of hand. Place on a piece of foil, skin side up and broil until skins are well charred. Transfer peppers while still hot to a paper bag and let stand for 15 minutes. Remove from bag and the charred skins will remove easily. Well-drained, jar roasted peppers can also be used.

Serves 4 to 6.

Yankee Pot Roast

Debbi Abbott Holmgren

This is my Mom's recipe. A hearty and "down home" meal, especially good during the cooler weather. This can also be started in a crockpot in the morning and cooked all day. This is a great meal because the meat, potatoes, vegetables and gravy are all cooked together.

1 envelope Lipton dry "beefy onion" soup mix
1 (3 to 4-pound) bottom round or rump roast
  Gravy Master
1 can cream of mushroom soup
½ cup water
  Potatoes, carrots, baby onions, fresh mushrooms, peeled and cut up

1. Cut 2 large pieces of heavy-duty aluminum foil and spray the top piece with cooking spray. Place ½ package of the dry soup mix on top of the foil.

2. Rub the roast generously with Gravy Master and place on top of the dry soup. Place the other ½ package of dry soup mix on top of the roast. Spoon the can of soup over the top; add the water and vegetables.

3. Fold the foil tightly to make a bag, making sure the edges are tightly sealed.

4. Place foil bag in a roasting pan. Bake at 250° for 4 to 5 hours.

Make sure the foil is tightly sealed or all the juices will spill out of packet.

Serves 6 to 8.

Beef Wellington for Two with Potted Mushrooms

Eileen Pastner

Beef Wellington for Two

½ teaspoons coarsely ground
　　 pepper
½ teaspoon salt
¼ teaspoon crumbled dried
　　 thyme leaves
2 (6-ounce) tournedos of beef
1 teaspoon Dijon mustard
1 tablespoon unsalted butter
¼ cup Potted Mushrooms
1 sheet frozen puff pastry,
　　 10 x 8-inches, ⅛-inch thick,
　　 thawed
1 egg
1 teaspoon milk

1. In a small bowl, combine the pepper, salt and thyme. Rub the tournedos on all sides with the mustard and sprinkle the spice mixture over them.

2. In a small skillet, melt the butter, sear the tournedos on all sides, about 5 minutes. Cool to room temperature. Arrange the tournedos on a small baking sheet and cover them with the potted mushrooms.

3. Cut out two 4 to 5-inch circles of pastry. Drape each over one of the tournedos and pinch the edges in four or five places to enclose the tournedos.

4. Blend the egg and milk and brush this glaze over the pastry. Decorate the tops with cutouts made from pastry trimmings, if desired.

5. Bake at 425° for 15 minutes for medium-rare. Serve immediately.

Serves 2.

Potted Mushrooms

5 tablespoons unsalted butter, divided
⅓ cup minced shallots
⅓ cup minced leeks, white part only
2 cloves garlic, minced
8 ounces cultivated mushrooms, finely chopped
2 teaspoons fresh thyme leaves
10 ounces fresh shiitake mushrooms, stems removed (reserve for another use), finely chopped
1 tablespoon finely snipped fresh chives
½ teaspoon salt
  Freshly ground pepper to taste
  Toast points, for serving

1. In a 10-inch skillet, melt 2 tablespoons of butter. Stir in the shallots, leeks and garlic; cook over low heat until translucent. Add the cultivated mushrooms and thyme; cook stirring occasionally until the mushroom liquid has evaporated and the mixture is just moist, 10 minutes.

2. Transfer the mixture to a bowl. Add the remaining 3 tablespoons butter to the skillet and stir in the shiitake mushrooms. Cook, stirring until they are just beginning to stick to the pan.

3. Pour off any juices that have accumulated in the bowl and add the shiitakes to the mushroom mixture. Stir well and season with the chives, salt and pepper. Serve with toast points

Yields 2 cups.

Beef Barbecue

Anne Conley

4 pounds beef stew meat
1 (28-ounce) can crushed
  tomatoes
1 quart water
½ teaspoon chili powder
1 cup ketchup
½ cup vinegar
½ cup Worcestershire sauce
4 cloves garlic, minced
  Salt and pepper to taste
  Dash Tabasco Sauce

1. Place all ingredients in a large Dutch oven, bring to a simmer and cook on low heat, uncovered, for about 6 hours or until meat falls apart.

2. Serve over mashed potatoes, rice or bulkie rolls.

This can also be cooked in a crockpot.

Serves 15.

Moist Meat Loaf

Linda Zolla

I always hated meatloaf until I had dinner at a friend's home and had to eat it. This recipe was wonderful and I have been making it for 39 years.

1 pound hamburger
½ pound ground pork
2 eggs, beaten
½ teaspoon salt
¾ teaspoon garlic salt
1 teaspoon pepper
1 large carrot, grated
1 large onion, chopped
4 slices bread, moistened with
  milk
1 large tomato, sliced

1. In a large bowl, combine first 6 ingredients; mix well. Add carrot, onion and bread.

2. Fold into a loaf pan, top with tomatoes.

3. Bake covered at 325° for 1 hour. Remove cover, bake an additional 30 to 40 minutes at 350° or until browned.

Serves 4 to 6.

Swedish Meatballs

From the Kitchen of Ethel Linder
submitted by her children Ken and Marie Linder

A favorite recipe of mother's we all enjoyed often. Tastes even better the next day.

4	slices bread, cubed
1	onion, cut into pieces
½	cup warm water
1	teaspoon pepper
½	teaspoon salt
	Dash of ground allspice (optional)
2	pounds hamburger

1. In a blender, combine above ingredients, except for hamburger.

2. Mix into hamburger and roll into 1-inch balls.

3. Brown in frying pan and continue to simmer in a small amount of water for 20 to 30 minutes.

You may also use a combination of half hamburger and half ground pork.

Stuffed Bell Peppers

Dorothy F. Graham

This recipe is from a former neighbor.
I treasure it and always think of her when using it.

4	medium green bell peppers
1	pound ground beef
2	cups cooked rice
¼	cup onion
1½	teaspoons salt
⅛	teaspoon pepper
1	(15-ounce) can tomato sauce
1	cup shredded Cheddar cheese

1. Cut a thin slice from the top of each pepper and seed. Boil approximately 5 to 10 minutes until slightly cooked.

2. In a large bowl, combine beef, rice, onions, salt, pepper and half of the sauce. Pile into peppers and top with cheese.

3. Arrange in an 8 x 8-inch shallow baking dish. Pour remaining sauce over peppers. Bake, covered, at 350° for 1 hour.

Serves 4.

Golomleki (Stuffed Cabbage)

Lee Wenc

1 head cabbage
1 cup rice, uncooked
2 pounds hamburger
¾ teaspoons salt
¼ teaspoon pepper
1 (18-ounce) can tomato sauce
1 can water

1. Boil cabbage about 15 minutes.

2. Meanwhile, cook rice according to package directions and set aside to cool.

3. In a large bowl, combine rice, hamburger, salt and pepper.

4. When cabbage is cooked, remove and separate the leaves. With the core end of the leaf near you, hollow side up, place rice mixture at the bottom of the leaf, leaving a 1-inch margin at either side. Start rolling and fold the sides in.

5. Place the stuffed cabbage in a covered roasting pan. Pour tomato sauce and 1 can of water over top. Bake, covered, at 350° for 3½ hours.

Zucchini Boats

Karen Melia

This was one of the first "meals" I prepared as a new bride.
A friend I met, while my husband was in law school, shared this recipe with
me. This quick dinner can be prepared in just 20 minutes.

4 medium zucchini squash
1 pound hamburger
1 onion, diced
1 (6-ounce) can tomato paste
½ cup grated Parmesan cheese
 Grated Cheddar cheese
  (optional)

1. Halve squash lengthwise and scoop out pulp. Boil for 15 minutes.

2. While squash cooks, in a large skillet, sauté hamburger and onion until cooked thoroughly. Add tomato paste and Parmesan cheese.

3. Fill squash boats with meat filling. Top with additional grated Parmesan or Cheddar cheese. Serve immediately.

Serves 4.

Sausage Casserole

Linda Erickson

1 pound sweet Italian sausage
1 pound hot sausage
2 pounds of potatoes
  (your choice)
1 large red bell pepper
1 large sweet onion
1 small tomato
2 tablespoons garlic salt
2 tablespoons minced garlic
2 tablespoons dried oregano
2 tablespoons dried sweet basil
2 tablespoons dried parsley
 Hot crusty bread

1. Cut sausage into bite-size pieces and brown in a non-stick skillet. Pour sausage and drippings into a casserole dish.

2. Add chopped, bite-size potatoes, red pepper, onion and tomato. Add seasonings and blend well.

3. Bake, uncovered, at 375° for 1 hour or until potatoes are done. Stir occasionally so juices and seasonings can blend. Serve with hot crusty bread.

Adjust seasonings according to your taste.

Serves 8.

Smoked Pork Chops with Maple Baked Apples

Jan Battema

This is excellent served with Glazed Brussels Sprouts (page 224)
and Spicy Sweet Potato Wedges (page 234).

4   (1-inch thick) smoked pork
      chops
1   large Rome apple, cut into
      8 pieces and cored
¼   cup raisins
1   tablespoon butter
2   onions, sliced
1   teaspoon chopped fresh thyme
¼   teaspoon pepper
½   cup chicken broth
2   tablespoons maple syrup
1   tablespoon all-purpose flour

1. In a large non-stick skillet, over medium-high heat, brown pork chops about 8 to 10 minutes. Remove and place in a 13 x 9-inch baking dish; add apple pieces and raisins.

2. In the same skillet, add butter, onions, thyme and pepper and cook until onions are browned and tender, about 15 minutes. Transfer to baking dish.

3. In a separate bowl, combine chicken broth, syrup and flour; add to baking dish.

4. Bake at 400° for 30 minutes or until sauce is bubbling.

Serves 4.

New Orleans Bourbon Soaked Pork Roast

Barbara MH Daigneault

Outstanding! I have never had a more flavorful pork roast. This recipe came from Carol Labossiere, a friend of the family who lives in Florida.

2 cups brown sugar
2 vanilla beans, sliced lengthwise
½ cup apple cider vinegar
1 fresh basil leaf
  Zest from 1 orange
1 cup bourbon
1 (7-pound) pork rib roast

1. Mix all ingredients together, except the pork roast. Simmer until well blended, remove from heat and let cool.

2. Place pork roast in a large food storage bag and pour marinade over meat. Marinate 48 hours, turning bag several times.

3. Remove from marinade and place in a greased roasting pan. Bake at 350° for 1 hour, turn heat to 325° and continue cooking an additional 1¾-2½ hours, or until thermometer reaches 170°.

Have the butcher cut the meat out and tie bone back in. This will make for a moister roast.

Serves 6.

Roast Double Loin of Pork with Port Wine Sauce

Barbara MH Daigneault

This seems long and complicated, but it really isn't and it is so worth the flavor. Perfect for a formal Christmas dinner party served with Scalloped Potatoes with Gouda and Fennel (page 233) and freshly steamed asparagus.

Spice Mixture

2   dried sage leaves
1   teaspoon black peppercorns
1   small bay leaf
¼   teaspoon whole allspice berries
¼   teaspoon dried thyme
1½ tablespoons salt

1. Grind all ingredients, except salt, in a spice grinder to a fine powder. Pour into a small bowl and add the salt. Rub the spice mixture all over the pork loins.

2. Align the loins with the fat sides out and with the tapered end of one against the widest end of the other. Tie the roast at 1-inch intervals with kitchen string and refrigerate for 24 to 48 hours.

Sauce

3   tablespoons vegetable oil
     Reserved pork bones
2   carrots, cut into 1-inch pieces
1   large onion, chopped
3   tablespoons all-purpose flour
4   cups hot chicken stock or
     canned broth
½   cup dry white wine
2   tomatoes, chopped
2   celery stalks, chopped
3   large garlic cloves, smashed
     Pinch of rosemary leaves
½   cup loosely packed parsley
     stems
     Salt and pepper to taste
2-3 tablespoons dry port

1. Heat the oil in a large stainless steel skillet; add the reserved pork bones brown over high heat, tossing frequently, 3 to 5 minutes. Add the carrots and onion; continue stirring until the vegetables are lightly colored.

2. Stir in the flour. Toss and cook over moderate heat to brown the flour, about 2 minutes. Remove from heat and let cool for several minutes.

3. Gradually stir in the hot chicken stock to blend with the flour. Add the wine, tomatoes, celery and garlic and bring to a simmer over moderately high heat, skimming as

necessary. Add the rosemary and parsley, cover loosely and simmer for about 2 hours.

4. Strain the sauce base, pressing hard on the solids to release the flavorful juices. Season with salt and pepper. Let cool, then cover and refrigerate until you are ready to make the sauce.

Meat

2	(2 to 2½-pound) centercut boneless pork loins
1	onion, coarsely chopped
1	carrot, coarsely chopped
2	garlic cloves, smashed

1. Arrange the pork in a roasting pan, fattiest side up. Roast in the middle of the oven at 350° for 1½ hours, basting the meat every 30 minutes with the fat that has accumulated in the pan.

2. Add the onion, carrot and garlic to the pan and continue roasting the pork, basting occasionally, for 30 to 45 minutes longer until the internal temperature reaches 160°.

3. Transfer the roast to a carving board and cover loosely with foil.

4. Spoon the fat, not the roasting juices out of the pan. Set pan aside until ready to make the sauce.

5. Skim the solidified fat from the surface of the chilled sauce base. Add the sauce base to the roasting pan and bring to a simmer, scraping up the browned bits from the bottom and mashing the roasted vegetables.

6. Strain the sauce into a small pan, pressing hard to extract all the juices. Season with salt and pepper, add the port and bring to a simmer, skimming any fat from the surface.

7. To serve, untie the roast and using a sharp knife carve the pork straight down into less than ¼-inch thick; the slices will separate as you serve them. Top with Port Wine Sauce.

Ask the butcher to chop up the bones removed from the pork loins to make the sauce.

Serves 8.

Medallions of Pork with Pear Sauce

Eileen Pastner

2 tablespoons vegetable oil

4 (½-inch thick) boneless pork
   loin chops
   Dried rubbed sage
   Salt and pepper
   All-purpose flour

2 pears, peeled, cored and thinly
   sliced (about 1 pound)

⅓ cup dry white wine

2 tablespoons sugar

2 tablespoons chopped
   crystallized ginger

1. Heat oil in a heavy large skillet over medium heat. Season pork with dried sage, salt and pepper. Coat pork with flour; shake off excess. Add pork to skillet and sauté until brown, about 3 minutes per side. Transfer to platter. Drain fat from skillet.

2. Add pears and sauté over medium heat 2 minutes. Stir in wine, sugar and ginger, scraping up any browned bits. Increase heat to high and boil until pears are tender and syrup is thick, about 5 minutes.

3. Return pork and any accumulated juices to skillet; simmer just until cooked through, about 1 minute. Season to taste with salt and pepper. Arrange pork on plates. Spoon the sauce over pork and serve.

Serves 4.

Marinated Grilled Pork Tenderloin

Lisa Sarmento

Summertime grilling can't be any easier! Great for a crowd.

Pork Marinade

3   cloves garlic, crushed
1   cup chopped onion
½   cup lemon juice, freshly
      squeezed
½   cup soy sauce
½   cup vegetable oil
⅛   cup sugar
3   tablespoons fresh chopped
      cilantro
      Splash of Tabasco Sauce
3   pork tenderloins (8 to 12
      ounces each)

1. In a large food storage bag, combine all ingredients, except the pork. Mix well. Add the tenderloins and marinate overnight.

2. Grill over medium-high heat, basting frequently with marinade. Cook for about 30 to 45 minutes, depending on desired doneness.

3. Bring remaining marinade to a boil and cook for 5 minutes. Spoon over sliced meat.

This also can be made with pork chops.

Pork Tenderloins with a Tangy Mustard Sauce

Nancy Winn

Pork Marinade

¼ cup bourbon
2 tablespoons brown sugar
¼ cup soy sauce
½ cup water
2 pork tenderloins
    (8 to 12 ounces each)

1. Combine all ingredients, except tenderloins, and mix well. Marinade tenderloins for at least 4 hours or overnight (making sure to make enough marinade to cover).

2. Grill tenderloins on low heat until golden brown and just a little pink inside.

3. Slice 1-inch thick and serve with a dollop of Tangy Mustard Sauce on the side.

Tangy Mustard Sauce

⅓ cup sour cream
⅓ cup mayonnaise
1 tablespoon dry mustard
1 tablespoon finely chopped
    green onion
1½ teaspoons balsamic vinegar
Salt to taste

1. Combine all ingredients and chill until ready to serve.

Pork Tenderloins with a Creamed Mustard Sauce

Cheryl Alderman

I have served this many times to family and friends.
Everyone always asks for the recipe. It's very easy.

Pork Marinade

2   tablespoons vegetable oil
2   tablespoons coarse grained
     mustard
½   teaspoon salt
½   teaspoon ground pepper
2   pork tenderloins
     (8 to 12 ounces each)
¼   cup chicken broth or dry white
     wine (optional)

1. Combine first 4 ingredients. Rub over pork. Place in a food storage bag and marinate at least 12 hours.

2. Grill over medium heat for about 25 minutes. Baste often with chicken broth or white wine.

3. Slice into 1-inch thick pieces and serve with Creamed Mustard Sauce.

Creamed Mustard Sauce

1¾ cups whipping cream
¼   cup coarse grained mustard
¼   teaspoon salt
⅛   teaspoon pepper

1. In a small saucepan over medium heat, cook the cream until reduced to 1¼ cups, about 20 minutes. Do not boil.

2. Stir in remaining ingredients and cook for 1 minute.

This can also be baked at 450° for 15 minutes, then reduce temperature to 400° and bake an additional 15 minutes. Meat thermometer should register 160°.

Serves 4.

Balsamic Molasses Bacon Pork Loin with Baby Spinach

Cheryl Bedard

This recipe was passed around my old neighborhood in Rutland, Massachusetts. It is a favorite of mine and great with Merlot wine.

1   (2 to 3-pound) boneless pork loin
2-3 tablespoons olive oil
     Salt and pepper to taste
½   pound bacon, cut into ½-inch pieces
2   cloves garlic, chopped
½   tablespoon dried rosemary
½   cup balsamic vinegar
½   cup molasses
     Fresh baby spinach

1. Trim fat from the pork loin.

2. In a large Dutch oven, sauté pork in olive oil. Season with salt and pepper. Cook until meat is lightly browned, 5 minutes.

3. Bake at 325°, in same pan, for 35 minutes or until meat thermometer registers 160°.

4. When the pork is cooked remove from pan and pour juice from the pan over the meat. Let rest for 10 to 15 minutes.

5. Return pan to stove and cook bacon until brown. Pour off and discard all but 2 tablespoons of bacon grease. Return pan with bacon to stove. Sauté garlic until brown. Add rosemary, balsamic vinegar, molasses, salt and pepper. Simmer on low heat until mixture gels, 15 minutes.

6. Cut pork loin in ¾ inch slices and arrange 2 to 3 pieces on a dinner plate. Drizzle above mixture over the pork and also use as a dressing on a side of fresh baby spinach.

Serves 2 to 4.

Pork Tenderloins with Ginger Maple Sauce

Joanne K. DiStefano

Guests always enjoy this recipe and it is easy to prepare.

2 teaspoons chili powder
1¼ teaspoons salt
1 teaspoon ground pepper
1 teaspoon ground cinnamon
2 pork tenderloins (8 to 12 ounces each)
2 tablespoons butter
1 cup chopped onion
2 tablespoons freshly grated gingerroot
1 cup chicken broth
½ cup maple syrup

1. In a small bowl, combine first 4 ingredients. Rub over tenderloins.

2. In a large skillet, brown tenderloins on all sides, about 6 minutes.

3. Transfer to a broiler pan, coated with cooking spray. Bake at 375° for 25 minutes or until thermometer registers 155°. Let stand 10 minutes before slicing.

4. While the pork is baking, melt butter in a medium saucepan over medium high heat. Add the onion and cook for 10 minutes or until golden brown, stirring frequently. Add ginger and cook for 4 minutes. Stir in broth and syrup, scraping pan to loosen browned bits. Bring broth mixture to a boil and cook until reduced to ¾ cup, about 10 minutes.

5. Cut pork into ¼-inch slices and serve with sauce on the side.

Serves 6.

Pan-Roasted Pork Loin with Leeks

Barbara MH Daigneault

Leeks and pork are a wonderful combination. The aroma in the house is welcoming when dinner guests walk through the door.

4	large leeks (about 2¼ pounds)
½	cup water
3	teaspoons butter, divided
½	teaspoon salt, divided
½	teaspoon pepper, divided
1	(2-pound) boneless pork loin
½	cup dry white wine
	Chopped fresh parsley (optional)

1. Remove roots and tough upper leaves from leeks. Cut each leek in half lengthwise. Cut each half crosswise into ½-inch thick slices (you should have about 6 cups). Soak in cold water to loosen dirt, rinse and drain.

2. In a Dutch oven or deep sauté pan, combine the sliced leeks, water, 1 teaspoon butter, ¼ teaspoon salt and ¼ teaspoon pepper. Cook over medium-high heat for 10 minutes or until the leeks have wilted. Pour into a bowl.

3. Heat remaining 2 teaspoons of butter in pan over medium-high heat. Add pork and cook 5 minutes, browning on all sides. Add remaining salt, pepper and wine. Cook for 15 seconds, scraping pan to loosen browned bits.

4. Return leek mixture to pan. Cover; reduce heat and simmer 1½ hours or until pork is tender.

5. Remove pork from pan and increase heat to reduce leek sauce if it is too watery. Cut pork into ¼-inch thick slices. Serve with leek mixture and garnish with parsley if desired.

Serves 6.

Spinach and Roasted Red Pepper Stuffed Pork Tenderloin with Arugula Sauce

Anne Conley

Pork Tenderloin

2   pork tenderloins
     (8 to 12 ounces each)
1   (10-ounce) package fresh
     spinach, cooked
2   red bell peppers, roasted
¼   cup pine nuts
2   ounces fontina cheese
½   cup flour
3   eggs
½   cup fresh bread crumbs
2   tablespoons olive oil

1. Split tenderloins almost through. Flatten out and pound thin.

2. Top with cooked spinach, roasted peppers, pine nuts and cheese. Roll up and dip in flour.

3. Brush with egg wash (whisk together 3 eggs and 2 tablespoons water) and roll in bread crumbs.

4. In a Dutch oven, heat the oil and brown pork on all sides. Finish baking in oven at 350° for approximately 15 minutes.

5. Slice into ¼-inch thick slices and serve with Arugula Sauce, topped with additional cornichons.

To roast red peppers see Note under Italian Stuffed Flank Steak (page 162).

Arugula Sauce

¼   cup pine nuts
¼   cup cornichons
½   cup olive oil
¼   cup Parmesan cheese

1. Combine first 3 ingredients in a food processor. Gradually add olive oil and Parmesan cheese, blending constantly.

Cornichons are tiny sweet gherkin pickles.

Serves 4.

Sweet and Sour Pork Skillet

Carolyn Brigham

1 pound boneless pork, cut into ¾-inch cubes

1 tablespoon vegetable oil

1 (20-ounce) can pineapple chunks, drained (reserve liquid)

¼ cup apple cider vinegar

1½ teaspoons salt

¼ teaspoon garlic powder

2 tablespoons sugar

1 cup white rice (not minute rice)

1 medium green bell pepper, cut into cubes

1 medium tomato, cut into cubes

1 medium onion, sliced

1. In a 10-inch skillet, brown pork in oil, drain off excess fat. Combine reserved pineapple juice and water to equal 2½ cups. Add to skillet with vinegar, salt, garlic and sugar. Bring this mixture to a boil. Lower heat to a simmer, covered, for 20 minutes.

2. Uncover and stir in rice. Cover and cook about 25 minutes or until liquid is absorbed and pork is tender.

3. Add pineapple, green peppers, tomatoes and onion. Heat thoroughly.

Sliced water chestnuts or bamboo shoots can be added.

Serves 6.

Scalloped Ham with Potatoes

From the Kitchen of Faith Kimball Putnam Hebert
submitted by her daughter Barbara MH Daigneault

My husband Bob would always ask my mother to make this for him. He still refers to it as "Mom's" Scalloped Ham and Potatoes. This is a great dish served with fresh green beans and a little horseradish on the side.

3 all-purpose potatoes, peeled and sliced ¼-inch thick

6 boneless ham steaks, cut in half (about 3 pounds)

1 tablespoons flour

2 tablespoons finely chopped onion

10 Ritz crackers

1-2 cups milk

½ cup Cheddar cheese

1. In an 11 x 9-inch greased baking dish, place half of the potatoes. Place ham slices on top of potatoes and sprinkle with flour and onion. Add remaining potatoes.

2. Crumble crackers over entire casserole; add enough milk to come half way up the sides of the baking dish. Top with cheese.

3. Bake covered at 425° for 1 hour and 15 minutes or until potatoes are tender.

You may use a combination of all-purpose and sweet potatoes.

Serves 6.

Fruited Pork

Linda Sinacola

2 pounds lean pork, cut into cubes
2-4 tablespoons flour
3 tablespoon cooking oil
1 cup orange juice
2 tablespoons lemon juice
1 tablespoon Worcestershire sauce
3 tablespoons packed brown sugar
1 teaspoon salt
¼ teaspoon pepper
1 tablespoon cornstarch
¼ cup water
⅓ cup raisins
1 (11-ounce) can Mandarin orange segments, drained

1. Dredge meat in flour. Heat oil in a large skillet and brown meat on all sides. Transfer to a 2-quart casserole dish. Discard any fat in frying pan. Pour orange and lemon juices into pan. Add Worcestershire sauce, sugar, salt and pepper.

2. In a small bowl, combine cornstarch with water; mix well. Pour into juice, stirring constantly and bring to a boil. Pour over meat. Add raisins and oranges; stir lightly.

3. Bake, covered, at 350° for 1½ to 2 hours or until meat is cooked through and very tender.

Serves 6.

Veal Piccata

Cheryl Scott

Easy and yummy! The secret of this dish is to sauté the scaloppine gently. Overdoing may dry them out and make them tough. Add some capers for a little color.

2¾ pounds veal scaloppine
Flour, for dredging
4 tablespoons butter, divided
1 clove garlic, minced
¼ cup dry vermouth
1 tablespoon lemon juice

1. Dredge veal in flour. In a large skillet, melt 3 tablespoons butter. Add garlic and cook slightly. Add veal and cook 1 to 2 minutes per side; remove to dish.

2. Add remaining butter, vermouth and lemon juice to pan. Simmer for 1 minute and pour over veal.

Serves 6.

Cream Glazed Mushrooms with Sautéed Ham

Barbara MH Daigneault

My friend, Gail Leighton, always made great dinners for Bob and I, as we visited her and her husband Donald. Whether they lived in the Northeast, Mid-West or on the pacific coast, she always entertained with class and style.

6   large mushrooms, thinly sliced
2   teaspoons fresh chopped tarragon or ½ teaspoon dried
1   cup whipping cream
2   tablespoons butter
2   slices ham

1. In a heavy saucepan, place mushrooms, sprinkle with tarragon and add cream; bring to a boil. Reduce heat and simmer until cream is thick and brown, approximately 30 minutes.

2. During the last 10 minutes of cooking, in a large skillet, melt butter over medium heat. Add ham and cook on both sides until lightly browned and heated through. Arrange on plates and top with cream glazed mushrooms.

Serves 2.

Veal Scaloppine

Barbara Mosher

This is one our favorite recipes, however, not one of the Blue Jays!

4   veal steaks
2   medium onions, chopped
1   green bell pepper, chopped
2   tablespoons oil
1   (14.5-ounce) can whole tomatoes
1   (8-ounce) can tomato sauce
½   teaspoon dried rosemary
1   cup sherry
     Salt and pepper to taste

1. In a large skillet, sauté veal, onions and pepper in oil. Add tomatoes and tomato sauce. Simmer covered for 45 minutes.

2. Add sherry, salt and pepper and continue to simmer for 10 minutes. Serve over noodles or rice.

Serves 4.

Braised Lamb Shanks with Cranberries and Apricots

Cynthia C. Windle

Approximately 11 years ago, I received this recipe from Capriel's Café in Portland, Oregon. For a complete dinner, I have added the apricots and vegetables. My family and friends have enjoyed this hearty dinner, especially during the winter season.

4	medium to large lamb shanks
½	cup flour
2	tablespoons olive oil
6	whole garlic cloves
¾	cup dried cranberries
8	dried apricots, cut into quarters
1	bay leaf
½	teaspoon dried thyme
1	sprig fresh rosemary
	Salt and freshly ground pepper to taste
¼	cup chopped fresh parsley
2½	cups chicken stock
1	(14½-ounce) can stewed tomatoes
4	pearl onions
20	baby carrots
2	whole shallots
6	ounces whole fresh mushrooms
8	small red skinned potatoes

1. Remove fat from lamb shanks, dredge lamb in flour, pat and shake off excess. Sauté lamb in olive oil and garlic and brown both sides over medium heat. Remove lamb and garlic, discarding oil and place in a Dutch oven.

2. Add cranberries, apricots, bay leaf, thyme, rosemary, salt, pepper, parsley, chicken stock and stewed tomatoes to the Dutch oven.

3. Bake, covered, at 350° for 1½ hours.

4. At that point, turn shanks and add the onions, carrots, shallots, mushrooms and potatoes. If necessary, add more chicken stock. Continue cooking for approximately 1½ hours or until lamb and vegetables are tender.

Serves 4.

Roasted Racks of Lamb

Ann Bouvier Achorn

I doubt you will find a more elegant recipe for that special dinner that is this simple to prepare. For even further ease on cleanup, I place the racks, one at a time, on a parchment or wax paper-lined work surface, then proceed with the mustard and crumb mixture.

3 cups fresh bread crumbs

2 tablespoons fresh thyme or 2 teaspoons dried

1 tablespoon fresh rosemary or 1 teaspoon dried

½ cup finely chopped fresh parsley

4 cloves garlic, minced

¾ cup olive oil, divided

6 (1½-pound) racks of lamb
Salt and freshly ground pepper to taste

¾ cup Dijon mustard (approximately)
Fresh sprigs of rosemary or thyme for garnish

1. To form crumb topping, in a small mixing bowl, combine bread crumbs, thyme, rosemary, parsley, garlic and ½ cup olive oil. Mix well, adding more olive oil, if necessary, to sufficiently moisten all ingredients.

2. Wrap exposed bones with aluminum foil to prevent burning during roasting.

3. Coat the racks, except the bones, liberally with the Dijon mustard and then divide crumb mixture into six portions and press one portion evenly over the mustard on each rack.

4. Put racks in pan and roast at 400° for 25 minutes (for medium-rare) or until meat thermometer registers an internal temperature of 122°. Remove racks from oven and let stand for 10 minutes.

5. To serve, remove foil from bones and slice racks into individual chops. Arrange 4 overlapping chops on each plate. Garnish with fresh sprigs of rosemary or thyme, if desired.

Make sure the racks each have 8 chops and ask the butcher to "French" the bones (i.e., strip the fat and gristle from the final 3-inches of each bone).

Serves 12.

Lamb Barbacoa

Anne Conley

Growing up in Australia, we frequently had lamb.
This is a recipe my mom received from one of our Aussie friends.
"Lamb on the Barb-ee" is a favorite in our family and I hope you enjoy!

1	cup water
1	cup port wine
½	cup olive oil
1	tablespoon salt
1	teaspoon freshly ground pepper
⅛	teaspoon marjoram
⅛	teaspoon dry mustard
8-10	drops Tabasco Sauce
2	medium tomatoes, diced
1	medium green bell pepper, diced
1	medium onion, sliced
½	cup coarsely chopped fresh parsley
3	cloves garlic, minced
1	(6-pound) leg of lamb, butterflied

1. In a large bowl, combine ingredients, except lamb; mix well. Place lamb in a shallow pan and pour marinade over top. Marinate 24 hours, basting frequently.

2. Take lamb out of marinade and lay flat on preheated grill, approximately 325°. Grill for 45 minutes, basting with marinade juice.

Reserve some marinade, before pouring onto lamb, to serve on the side as a relish.

Grilled Salmon with a Brown Sugar Mustard Glaze

Barbara MH Daigneault

Bob and I never ate salmon, until we came across this recipe. It is absolutely scrumptious as the brown sugar and ginger glaze caramelizes on the fish. We generally serve this with brown rice and steamed asparagus. A very colorful plate and it's an easy clean-up, just toss out the aluminum foil when cooked.

1   tablespoon brown sugar
1   tablespoon honey
2   teaspoons unsalted butter
2   tablespoons Dijon mustard
1   tablespoon soy sauce
1   tablespoon olive oil
2   tablespoons grated fresh gingerroot
4   salmon fillets, skin on (about 2 pounds)
     Lemon wedges for garnish

1. In a microwave safe bowl, melt brown sugar, honey and butter. Blend in mustard, soy sauce, olive oil and fresh ginger.

2. Wash and pat dry fillets. Place, skin side down, on a large sheet of greased heavy aluminum foil. Fold up edges to make a pan, so glaze won't drip out. Coat each piece of salmon with glaze.

3. Grill salmon indirectly over medium heat until the edges begin to brown, about 25 to 30 minutes.

4. Slide a spatula between the skin and flesh and remove the salmon to individual plates. Serve immediately with lemon wedge.

I ask the gentlemen at the fish market to slice me 4 fillets, about 1½-inch wide and 1-inch thick. Generally this measures out to about 2 pounds. Having it cut into 4 pieces, allows you to slid the fish off the skin after cooking and serve immediately onto the dinner plates.

Serves 4.

Mustard and Dill Steamed Salmon

Linda Carr

1 tablespoon olive oil
1 tablespoon sherry or white wine
1 tablespoon brown or deli mustard
1 teaspoon dried dill
1 (1-pound) salmon fillet

1. Whisk together all ingredients, except the salmon. Marinate the salmon in the refrigerator for 10 to 15 minutes.

2. Steam fish until just done, about 10 to 15 minutes.

I use a bed of vegetables (asparagus or green beans) to lay fish on and steam. They take about the same time to cook and absorb the flavor of the marinade. You can also use a regular steamer to cook the fish.

Serves 2.

Salmon à la Sicily

Michael Daigneault

Any type of fish will work with this sauce.

2 cups canned tomatoes
1 cup water
1 large onion, thinly sliced
3 cloves garlic, minced
1½ teaspoons sugar
3 tablespoons butter
3 tablespoons flour
¾ teaspoon salt
¼ teaspoon pepper
2 pounds salmon fillets, skinless

1. In a medium saucepan, cook tomatoes, water, onion, garlic and sugar for 20 minutes.

2. In a small bowl, melt the butter; blend in flour and stir into tomato mixture. Add salt and pepper and cook about 10 minutes, stirring constantly.

3. Place fish in a lightly greased 11 x 9-inch baking dish and pour sauce over top. Bake at 350° for 35 minutes or until fish flakes easily. Baste often.

If keeping the skin on fish make sure to bake skin side down.

Serves 4 to 6.

Alaska Salmon Bake
with Pecan Crunch Coating

Cynthia C. Windle

*Twenty-three years ago, Terry and I spent our honeymoon in
Alaska where our love for salmon began. This recipe originated in Juneau, Alaska.
My family enjoys eating this elegant dish as well as our dinner guests.*

2   tablespoons Dijon mustard
2   tablespoons melted butter
4   teaspoons honey
¼   cup bread crumbs
¼   cup finely chopped pecans or
      walnuts
2   teaspoons chopped fresh
      parsley
4   (4 to 6-ounce) Alaska salmon
      fillets
      Salt and pepper to taste
      Lemon wedges

1. In a small bowl, mix together mustard, butter and honey. Set aside.

2. In another small bowl, mix together bread crumbs, pecans and parsley. Set aside.

3. Season each fillet with salt and pepper. Place on a lightly greased baking sheet or broiling pan. Brush each fillet with mustard-honey mixture. Pat bread crumb mixture on top of each fillet.

4. Bake at 450° for 10 minutes per inch of thickness, measure at thickest part or until salmon just flakes when tested with a fork. Serve with a lemon wedge.

Serves 4.

Salmon Coulibiac

Mary A. Green

I love to serve this on very special occasions.

Béchamel Sauce (White Sauce)

2   tablespoons unsalted butter
½   cup flour
1   cup milk
¼   peeled onion (do not chop)
1   clove
1   bay leaf
   Salt and pepper to taste

1. In a small saucepan over medium heat, melt butter. Stir in flour and cook for 5 minutes until the roux is fragrant but not darkened. Remove from heat.

2. In a separate saucepan, heat the milk, onion, clove and bay leaf. Simmer gently, about 15 minutes, to infuse flavors. Discard the onion, clove and bay leaf.

3. Slowly add the hot milk to the roux, stirring constantly. Reduce heat to low. Simmer for 30 minutes.

4. Strain through a fine-mesh sieve. Season with salt and pepper.

Stuffing

2	tablespoons olive oil
¼	cup chopped onion
¼	cup chopped mushrooms
½	cup Béchamel Sauce
2	cups spinach, blanched and chopped
1	hard-boiled egg, chopped
8	ounces cooked fillets of sole, flaked
¼	cup cooked wild rice
½	teaspoon chopped fresh dill
½	teaspoon chopped fresh thyme
¼	teaspoon grated lemon rind
	Salt and pepper to taste
1	(12-ounce) sheet puff pastry
1½	pounds skinless salmon fillets
1	egg, beaten

1. In a medium skillet, heat olive oil over medium heat until hot. Add onion and mushrooms; cook until the onion is tender. Stir next 8 ingredients. Season with salt and pepper. Continue cooking until stuffing is dry; cool slightly.

2. On a floured board, roll out puff pastry to twice the width of the salmon and 2 inches longer and about ⅛-inch thick.

3. Spread half the stuffing down the center of pastry. Place salmon on top, folding tail down under. Spread rest of stuffing over salmon. Fold pastry over salmon and pinch seams to seal well.

4. Place seam down on a greased baking sheet. Brush with beaten egg. Prick pastry with fork. Bake at 400° for 20 minutes until pastry is golden. Spoon remaining Béchamel Sauce over pastry before serving.

Serves 6.

Baked Haddock with Tahini Sauce

Paula A. Salem

This is an old time family recipe. My mother would make this dish on holidays. It can be served cold as an appetizer with pieces of pita bread or as a main course. Serve with rice pilaf and a tossed salad.

Tahini Sauce

6 tablespoons tahini (sesame paste)
1 clove garlic, crushed
½ teaspoon salt
Juice of 1 lemon
6 tablespoons water

1. Blend all ingredients thoroughly.

Baked Haddock

3 pounds haddock fillets
5 tablespoons oil, divided
2 tablespoon lemon juice
1 clove garlic, crushed
½ teaspoon salt
3 medium onions, sliced into thin wedges
½ cup almonds, walnuts or pine nuts (optional)
Chopped fresh parsley for garnish

1. Marinate fish with 2 tablespoons oil, lemon juice, garlic and salt. Wrap in aluminum foil with opening on top.

2. Place in a baking pan. Bake at 350° for 30 minutes.

3. Remove fish from foil and place on a serving platter.

4. Sauté onion in remaining 3 tablespoons of oil. Sauté until a dark brown color. Pour Tahini Sauce over baked fish on serving platter. Garnish with sautéed onion mixture. Top with parsley.

You can also brown ½ cup almonds, walnuts or pine nuts and add to browned onions. This can also be made with chicken.

Serves 6 to 8.

Baked Stuffed Sole

Paula Beauregard

8	skinless fillets of sole
	Salt and pepper to taste
6	tablespoons butter, divided
½	cup finely chopped onion
⅓	cup chopped green bell pepper
⅓	cup chopped celery
¼	cup dry white wine
½	pint clams
1-1½	cups bread crumbs
1	egg, slightly beaten
¼	cup finely chopped fresh parsley
	Juice of 1 lemon
¼	teaspoon paprika

1. Sprinkle the sole with salt and pepper.

2. In a skillet, melt 2 tablespoons of butter; add onion, pepper and celery. Cook, stirring constantly, until liquid evaporates. Add wine and cook for 1 minute, add clams.

3. Remove from heat; add bread crumbs, eggs and parsley.

4. Spoon filling on top of fish. Cover with a second fillet. Place filled fillets in a greased 11 x 9-inch baking dish.

5. In a small saucepan, melt remaining 4 tablespoons butter and add lemon juice. Pour over the filled fillets. Sprinkle with paprika.

6. Bake, uncovered, at 450° for 10 minutes.

Serves 4.

Sicilian Tuna Steaks with Couscous

Carrie Daigneault

*This simple dish is prepared in a foil
oven bag and takes less than 5 minutes to put together.*

1 regular-size foil oven bag

¼ cup fat-free, less-sodium
chicken broth

2 tablespoons chopped fresh
parsley

2 tablespoons chopped pitted
green olives

1 tablespoon raisins

1 tablespoon capers

2 tablespoons dry white wine

1 tablespoon balsamic vinegar

1 teaspoon sugar

2 teaspoons olive oil

¼ teaspoon salt

⅛ teaspoon black pepper

1 (14½-ounce) can Italian-style
stewed tomatoes (do not
drain)

½ cup uncooked couscous

2 (5-ounce) tuna steaks
(about ¾-inch thick)

1 tablespoon pine nuts, toasted

1 tablespoon chopped fresh
parsley

1. Coat inside of oven bag with cooking spray. Place the bag on a large shallow baking pan.

2. In a large bowl, combine chicken broth and next 11 ingredients and stir in couscous. Place couscous mixture in prepared oven bag.

3. Place tuna on couscous mixture. Fold edge of bag over to seal.

4. Bake at 450° for 20 minutes or until fish is medium rare or desired degree on doneness.

5. Cut open the bag with a sharp knife and peel back foil. Sprinkle with the toasted pine nuts and 1 tablespoon parsley.

Serves 2.

Chardonnay Cilantro Grilled Swordfish

Kimberli Daigneault

This recipe is so wonderful. Placing all ingredients in a storage bag makes for a real easy cleanup. The blend of herbs and seasonings are outstanding. This will become your favorite grilled swordfish recipe.

1 tablespoon olive oil
2 tablespoons freshly squeezed lime juice
½ cup Chardonnay wine
1 tablespoon dry mustard
1 teaspoon mustard seeds
1 tablespoon chili powder
1 teaspoon pepper
4 tablespoons finely chopped fresh cilantro
1 pound swordfish steaks (1 to 1½-inch thick)

1. Combine all ingredients in a large food storage bag. Shake to mix well. Add swordfish steaks and marinate at least 2 hours, turning bag often.

2. Grill over direct high heat about 5 minutes per side.

Serves 4.

Baked Grouper with Chunky Tomato Basil Caper Sauce

Leigh Hebert

I am a vegetarian and my fiancé, Dave Gates, is not. We always compromise on what to have for dinner and it ends up being seafood. This recipe provides a great way to kick your seafood dishes up a notch.

3½ cups chopped seeded
    tomatoes (about 4 medium)
¼ cup chopped green onion
¼ cup dry white wine
1 tablespoon chopped fresh basil
1 teaspoon capers
1 teaspoon bottled minced garlic
1 teaspoon freshly squeezed
    lemon juice
½ teaspoon salt
¼ teaspoon crushed red pepper
¼ teaspoon black pepper
2 teaspoons olive oil
4 (6-ounce) grouper fillets

1. In a medium bowl, combine first 10 ingredients and mix well.

2. Heat oil in a large Dutch oven. Place fish, skin side up, in the pan and cook for 2 minutes.

3. Turn fish over and top with tomato mixture; bring to a boil.

4. Place pan in oven and bake at 425° for 8 minutes or until fish flakes easily when tested with a fork.

5. Serve fillets with ½ cup tomato mixture on top.

Can also be made with chicken, mahi mahi, shrimp, tilapia and red snapper.

Serves 4.

Lobster Thermidor

Barbara MH Daigneault

This is a standard for New Year's eve at our home. We love this recipe. Once the lobsters are prepared, it is so easy to put together. Simply serve with steamed asparagus and a little rice. Yummy! The lobsters and sauce can be prepared early in the day and placed in the refrigerator until ready to assemble.

4	(1½-pound) lobsters, cooked
3	tablespoons butter
2	tablespoons flour, adjust accordingly
½	teaspoon salt
⅛	teaspoon ground nutmeg
⅛	teaspoon paprika
¾	cup half & half
¾	cup lowfat milk
3	tablespoons sherry
½	cup shredded Cheddar cheese
	Parsley for garnish

1. Remove lobster meat from shells. Slice meat from each lobster into chunks and place in individual lightly greased casserole dishes, balancing the portions.

2. In a 3-quart saucepan over medium heat, melt the butter. Blend in flour, salt, nutmeg and paprika to form a roux. Whisk in the half & half, milk and sherry. Cook, stirring constantly, until thickened.

3. Spoon sauce evenly over lobster meat. Top with Cheddar cheese. Broil until mixture is hot and golden brown. Serve in the casserole dish to keep warm.

Traditionally a Lobster Thermidor would be served out of the lobster shell. To do so, leave the antennae, head and tail intact when removing the meat. Wash and drain the lobster shells. Spoon the meat back into the shells and follow instructions above.

Serves 4.

Lobster with Ginger and Gewürztraminer

Barbara MH Daigneault

Gewürztraminer is a white wine known for its crisp and spicy characteristics. This lobster dish is fabulous. You will not believe the flavors that all blend together for a harmonious symphony on the palate. Most of this can be prepared 1 day in advance.

2 (1½-pound) lobsters
3½ cups water
2 tablespoons sugar, divided
1 (2½ x 1¼-inch) piece peeled fresh gingerroot, cut into matchstick-size strips
1½ cups Gewürztraminer wine
2 tablespoons olive oil
4 tablespoons butter, divided
1 pound fresh spinach
 Salt and pepper to taste
1 tablespoon fresh lime juice
1½ teaspoons minced lime peel, green part only

1. Bring a large pot of water to boil over high heat. Plunge lobsters into water and cover. Boil 5 minutes. Transfer lobsters to bowl of cold water to stop cooking.

2. In a saucepan over medium-high heat, bring water, 1 tablespoon of sugar and ginger to a boil. Boil until ginger is tender and liquid is almost evaporated, about 45 minutes.

3. Add wine and boil until liquid is reduced to 2 tablespoons, about 15 minutes. Remove from heat.

4. Meanwhile, drain lobsters, remove meat and set aside. (Can be prepared 1 day ahead. Cover ginger reduction and lobster meat separately and then refrigerate.)

5. Place lobster meat on a broiler pan and brush with olive oil. Broil until cooked thoroughly.

6. Meanwhile, melt 2 tablespoons butter in a large skillet over medium heat. Add spinach and sprinkle with remaining sugar. Sauté spinach until wilted, about 4 minutes. Season with salt and pepper.

7. Heat ginger reduction sauce in small saucepan over medium heat. Gradually, whisk in remaining 2 tablespoons butter. Whisk in lime juice and peel. Season with salt and pepper.

8. Place a bed of spinach on each dinner plate and arrange lobster meat on top. Drizzle sauce over lobster and serve.

Serves 2.

Barbecued Chilean Sea Bass with Orange Sauce

Susan Koopman

1-1½ pounds Chilean sea bass
¾ cup orange juice
3 tablespoons tomato paste
2 tablespoons vegetable oil
2 tablespoons vinegar
1 tablespoon brown sugar
2 cloves garlic, minced
1 teaspoon grated orange zest
1 teaspoon ground ginger
½ teaspoon dried hot red pepper flakes

1. Rinse the sea bass with cold water and pat dry. Set the fish in a lightly greased shallow dish.

2. In a small bowl, combine remaining ingredients; mix well. Pour over the fish, turning the fish to evenly coat. Cover and marinate in the refrigerator for 1 to 3 hours.

3. Preheat a grill or broiler. Grill or broil the fish about 4-inches from the heat, until well browned on one side, 3 to 5 minutes. Brush the marinade and cook on the other side until fish is no longer opaque in the center, about 5 minutes longer.

Serves 4.

Lobster Risotto

Jim Burke

In place of lobster, this recipe was also made with scallops, clams and shrimp and was called "Seafood Risotto" when served to our dinner guests.

Risotto

4	tablespoons butter, divided
16	ounces risotto (Arborio rice)
3	cups chicken stock or water
1	cup white wine
½	onion, finely diced
½	bunch finely chopped fresh thyme
	Salt and pepper to taste

1. In a large skillet, sauté the onion with 2 tablespoons butter until translucent.

2. Add risotto and stir to coat with butter. Pour in the white wine and stir, deglazing the pan by scraping up any bits that adhere to the pan.

3. Reduce the white wine to about ¼ cup and add the chicken stock or water, stirring continuously. Cook until tender and add thyme and remaining butter. Season to taste.

Lobster Sauce

2	(1-pound) lobsters, boiled 6 to 8 minutes
1	onion, chopped
3	carrots, chopped
½	stalk celery, chopped
½	cup sherry
½	cup brandy
4	ounces tomato paste
1	cup cream
½	bunch finely chopped fresh thyme

1. Chop off the lobster heads and put them in a pan to sauté with the onions, carrots and celery. Remove the rest of the lobster meat from the shells and set aside.

2. Deglaze the pan by adding the sherry and brandy and scraping up any bits that adhere to the pan. Boil off the alcohol and reduce the liquid by half.

3. Add tomato paste, cream and thyme. Boil and reduce by half. Season to taste.

4. Strain sauce through a fine mesh strainer to remove the lobster shells. This should result in a smooth, clean sauce.

5. Chop the reserved lobster meat and in a pot, mix risotto, lobster and sauce. Bring to a simmer and serve immediately.

Serves 4 to 6.

Basil Shrimp with Feta and Orzo

Carrie Daigneault

1	regular-size foil oven bag
½	cup uncooked orzo
2	teaspoons olive oil, divided
1	cup diced tomato
¾	cup sliced green onions
½	cup crumbled feta cheese
½	teaspoon grated lemon rind
1	tablespoon fresh lemon juice
¼	teaspoon salt
¼	teaspoon black pepper
¾	pound large shrimp, peeled and deveined
¼	cup chopped fresh basil

1. Coat inside of oven bag with cooking spray. Place the bag on a large shallow baking pan.

2. Cook the pasta in boiling water for 5 minutes, omitting salt and fat. Drain.

3. Place pasta in a large bowl. Stir in 1 teaspoon oil and next 7 ingredients.

4. Place the orzo mixture in prepared oven bag. Combine shrimp and basil. Arrange shrimp mixture on orzo mixture.

5. Fold edge of bag over to seal. Bake at 450° for 25 minutes or until the shrimp are done.

6. Cut open bag. Drizzle with 1 teaspoon oil and serve.

Serves 2.

Baked Stuffed Shrimp

Susan B. Ekstrom

*This recipe came from a very good friend of the family.
I often recall my parents saying she could open the refrigerator and make something excellent out of whatever was in there. My dad used to make it and I thought
it was just as good, if not better, than any restaurant version and easy too.*

30 medium or large shrimp,
      peeled and deveined
1   (4-ounce) package Ritz
      crackers (1 sleeve), crumbled
1   stick butter
1   tablespoon cooking sherry
      Juice of 1 lemon (optional)

1. Slice shrimp to open flat and lay on a greased cookie sheet.

2. Combine remaining ingredients to form stuffing. Place stuffing on each shrimp.

3. Bake at 400° for 15 to 20 minutes.

Serves 6 to 7.

Caribbean Shrimp Packets

Gerry Massad

4   sheets 12 x 18-inch heavy duty
      foil
1   (15½-ounce) can pineapple
      chunks, drained
1½ pounds large shrimp, peeled
      and deveined
1   medium red bell pepper,
      seeded and chopped
1   medium jalapeño pepper,
      seeded and finely chopped
1   tablespoon freshly grated
      gingerroot
1   tablespoon seafood seasoning
1   stick butter, cut into 16-pieces
¼   cup packed light brown sugar
1½ tablespoons lemon juice
      Rice pilaf

1. Preheat gas grill to medium-high.

2. Arrange ¼ can of pineapple in center of each piece of foil. Arrange raw shrimp in an even layer over pineapple.

3. In a medium bowl, combine both peppers, ginger and seafood seasoning; sprinkle over shrimp. Top with 4 pieces of butter on each and sprinkle with brown sugar. Drizzle with lemon juice.

4. Double fold tops and ends of foils to seal packets, leaving room for heat circulation inside.

5. Grill for 8 to 10 minutes covered or bake on a cookie sheet at 450° for 12 to 14 minutes. Serve over rice pilaf.

Serves 4.

Mediterranean Shrimp

Carmen O'Brien

1 pound large or jumbo shrimp, leave tails on, peeled and deveined
2 teaspoons olive oil
1 teaspoon lime juice
1 tablespoon finely minced garlic
1 teaspoon chopped dried rosemary
1 teaspoon chopped dried thyme
¼ teaspoon black pepper
¼ teaspoon cayenne pepper
¼ teaspoon salt
Fresh lime slices for garnish

1. In a large bowl, combine all ingredients, except limes. Marinate at room temperature for 1 hour.

2. Heat a dry skillet on medium-high heat. When skillet is hot, lay shrimp in pan. Cook shrimp 3 minutes per side, brushing them with marinade before turning. Garnish with lime slices.

Adjust cayenne pepper to your liking.

Serves 4.

Basic Baked Scallops

From the Kitchen of Faith Kimball Putnam Hebert
submitted by her daughters Jane, Barbara and Diane

*Mom always made Baked Scallops.
This is such a basic recipe, but the flavor is delicious.*

½ pound scallops
2 tablespoons freshly squeezed lemon juice
¼ cup white wine
Salt and pepper to taste
10 Ritz crackers
1 tablespoon butter
Lemon wedges

1. Place scallops in a lightly greased baking dish. Drizzle with lemon juice, white wine, salt and pepper.

2. Crumble crackers on top. Dot with butter.

3. Bake at 350° for 20 minutes.

Serves 2.

Giglio's Camperie

Eileen Botty

When in Florence, we went to Giglio's Restaurant and had this dish.
We liked it so well, we returned the next night. When the chef heard this
he came out to meet us and seeing we were from America, he gave me the
recipe if I promised never to cook it in Italy.

10-15	large shrimp, peeled and deveined
4	tablespoons butter, divided
¼	cup flour
2	tablespoons olive oil
	Salt and pepper to taste
	Worcestershire sauce to taste
	Tabasco Sauce to taste
1	snifter of Cognac to flame
1	tablespoon lobster butter
	Semi-whipped cream

1. Dip shrimp in 2 tablespoons of melted butter and lightly flour.

2. In a large skillet, heat remaining 2 tablespoons butter and olive oil and braise shrimp to color.

3. Add spices. Add cognac and ignite flame; tip pan and burn off cognac. Add lobster butter and mix thoroughly. Add 8 dollops of whipped cream to pan. Stir.

4. Just before serving add 2 more dollops. Serve.

You may use lobster concentrate in place of lobster butter.

Serves 4.

Thai Shrimp and Sesame Noodles

Beth Willoughby

This is nice with sliced cucumbers that have been chilled in rice wine with a hint of sugar. This is also great with boneless chicken.

1   pound medium shrimp, peeled and deveined
1   (8-ounce) bottle light Italian dressing, divided
2   tablespoons chunky peanut butter
1   tablespoon soy sauce
1   tablespoon honey
1   teaspoon peeled, grated gingerroot
½   teaspoon crushed red pepper
2   tablespoons salad oil
1   tablespoon sesame oil
1-2 medium carrots, shredded
½-1 cup sliced scallions
2   tablespoons chopped fresh cilantro
1   (8-ounce) package capellini or angel hair pasta, cooked
    Fresh cilantro for garnish

1. Marinate shrimp in ½ cup dressing. Cover and refrigerate for at least 1 hour.

2. Whisk peanut butter, soy sauce, honey, gingerroot, red pepper and remaining dressing.

3. In a medium skillet, heat oils over high heat, stir-fry carrots and cook for 1 minute. Add drained shrimp and scallions; cook until shrimp turns opaque.

3. In a large bowl, toss warm pasta in peanut butter mixture; add shrimp mixture and cilantro. Garnish with additional cilantro.

If you are in a hurry, just buy the cooked and peeled shrimp and eliminate the first step.

Serves 4.

Seared Sesame Scallops

Cheryl Scott

These scallops are yummy served over Pea and Mint Couscous (page 244).

3 tablespoons sesame seeds
1½ teaspoons kosher salt
⅛ teaspoon freshly ground
    pepper
12 large sea scallops (about 10
    ounces)
1½ tablespoons vegetable oil
    Lemon wedges for garnish

1. In a small bowl, stir together sesame seeds, salt and pepper. Dip flat sides of each scallop in sesame mixture.

2. In a 12-inch nonstick skillet, heat oil over moderately high heat until hot but not smoking and sauté scallops on flat sides until sesame seeds are golden and scallops are just cooked through, about 4 minutes total.

3. Serve with lemon wedge.

Serves 2.

Alta Eaton's Oyster Casserole

Alta M. Eaton

This is a good recipe for a pot luck dinner. It is also a recipe that came from Maude MacLaren and was served many times to the "Hikers" of which she was a member.

2 cups cooked macaroni or
    noodles
½ teaspoon garlic salt or powder
1 cup thin sliced cheese
1 (8-ounce) can oysters
1 (13-ounce) can evaporated
    milk
2 cups whole milk
10 Ritz crackers

1. In a large bowl, stir together macaroni, garlic salt, cheese and oysters.

2. Combine evaporated and whole milk; add to noodle mixture. Pour into a greased glass loaf pan.

3. Cover top with crumbled Ritz crackers.

4. Bake, uncovered, at 350° for 35 minutes or until set.

Serves 6.

Deviled Seafood Casserole

Penny Thompson

This dish is served as a buffet item on Christmas Eve. It has been a tradition in my home for many years. Serve with Cocktail Cheese Wafers (page 16).

2 pounds haddock fillets
1 stick butter
4-5 tablespoons flour
1 cup evaporated milk or cream
1½ cups milk
1 tablespoon lemon juice
1 tablespoon Worcestershire sauce
4 tablespoons ketchup
1 tablespoon horseradish
1 clove garlic, minced
1 teaspoon prepared mustard
1 teaspoon soy sauce
½ teaspoon salt
4 tablespoons fresh chopped parsley
½ cup sherry
1 pound lobster meat, chopped
½ pound scallops
Fine bread crumbs
2 tablespoons butter

1. Steam haddock over boiling water for approximately 20 minutes until fish is white and flaky. Cool and separate fish into small pieces.

2. In a large skillet, melt butter and blend in flour. Heat evaporated milk and additional 1½ cups milk. Pour slowly into flour mixture stirring constantly. Cook until thick.

3. Add lemon juice, Worcestershire sauce, ketchup, horseradish, garlic, mustard, soy sauce, salt, parsley and sherry. Mix thoroughly.

4. Add lobster meat, haddock, scallops; toss well.

5. Pour into greased casserole. Sprinkle top with bread crumbs, dot with butter.

6. Bake at 400° for 30 minutes.

You may also steam fish in microwave.

Serves 10.

Soy-Ginger Grilled Scallops

Cheryl Scott

¼ cup freshly squeezed lime juice (about 3 limes)

2 tablespoons low-sodium soy sauce

2 tablespoons rice-wine vinegar

2 tablespoon peanut oil

1 tablespoon freshly grated gingerroot

8½ ounces soba noodles (Asian noodles)

1 pound fresh spinach, stems removed, leaves cut into ½-inch wide strips

1 bunch scallions, white and pale-green parts only, thinly sliced diagonally

1 pound shiitake or white mushrooms, stems removed

1½ pounds sea scallops (16 large)

1. In a bowl, whisk together lime juice, soy sauce, vinegar, peanut oil and ginger; set aside.

2. Bring a medium saucepan of water to a boil and cook noodles until al dente, about 8 minutes.

3. Place spinach in a colander in the sink and drain noodles over spinach. Transfer the spinach and noodles to a bowl and add 6 tablespoons ginger mixture and the scallions. Toss to combine and set aside.

4. Place remaining ginger mixture in a large bowl. Add mushrooms and scallops. Toss to coat.

5. Place mushrooms on a very hot grill, smooth sides up and cook until lightly browned. Turn over and continue cooking until soft. Remove from grill and slice into ¼-inch wide strips.

6. Add to noodle salad and place on a serving platter.

7. Place scallops on grill and cook until opaque and firm, turning once halfway though cooking. Transfer to the serving platter with the noodles and serve.

Serves 4.

Easy and Elegant Lobster Tortellini

Anne Sweeney

*This tortellini casserole can also be made with
a combination of scallops, crabmeat and lobster.*

1	pound cheese tortellini, cooked and cooled
4	tablespoons butter
2	teaspoons Spanish paprika
4	tablespoons all-purpose flour
3	cups milk, heated
½	cup sherry
½	teaspoon salt
½	teaspoon pepper
8	ounces shredded Monterey Jack cheese
4	ounces chopped lobster meat

1. Cook tortellini according to package directions and set aside.

2. In a medium saucepan, melt butter and stir in paprika. Add flour and stir until thickened.

3. Turn heat to high and stir in heated milk with a whisk until smooth and boiling. Add sherry, salt and pepper; stir in lobster meat and reduce heat.

4. Place the cooled tortellini in a greased casserole dish. Pour the lobster sauce over the tortellini; top with cheese.

5. Bake at 350° for 20 minutes.

Spanish paprika can be found in specialty markets. If it is not available, regular paprika will do.

Serves 6 to 8.

Pasta with Spinach and White Beans

Linda Hendrikse

This is a family favorite and is very easy to make.

1 tablespoon olive oil
1 cup finely chopped onion
¾ cup finely chopped celery
3 cloves garlic, minced
1 bay leaf
3¼ cups chicken broth
1 (15-ounce) can small white beans, drained
1 (6-ounce) can tomato paste
⅛ teaspoon dry red pepper
½ cup uncooked elbow macaroni
2 cubes chicken bouillon
2 cups fresh chopped spinach
Freshly grated Parmesan cheese for garnish

1. Sauté first 5 ingredients until tender. Add chicken broth, beans, tomato paste and red pepper.

2. Bring to a boil and add macaroni and bouillon cubes. Reduce heat and cook until tender.

3. Remove bay leaf.

4. Add spinach just before serving and let wilt. Top with Parmesan cheese.

Small white beans are also called habichuelas blancas. Adjust dry red pepper to desired spiciness.

Penne Pasta with Spinach, Shrimp, Tomatoes and Basil

Kimberli Daigneault

12 ounces penne pasta

2 tablespoons olive oil

1 pound medium shrimp, peeled and deveined

Salt and pepper to taste

3 cloves garlic, minced

5 large plum tomatoes, cut into thin wedges

6 tablespoons chopped fresh basil, divided

3 tablespoons fresh lemon juice

2 teaspoons grated lemon peel

6 cups packed baby spinach leaves (6-ounces)

1. In a large pot of boiling water, cook pasta until just tender, but firm to bite.

2. Before draining, reserve 1 cup pasta cooking water. Drain pasta and return to pot; cover to keep warm.

3. Meanwhile, in a large skillet over medium high heat, heat oil. Sprinkle shrimp with salt and pepper. Add shrimp and garlic to skillet and sauté 2 minutes.

4. Add tomatoes, 4 tablespoons basil, lemon juice and lemon peel. Sauté until shrimp are cooked, about 3 minutes.

5. Add spinach leaves to hot pasta and toss until it wilts. Add shrimp mixture and toss to blend. Add enough reserved pasta liquid to moisten. Season with salt and pepper. Sprinkle with remaining 2 tablespoons basil and serve.

Serves 6.

Fettuccine Gorgonzola with Sun-Dried Tomatoes

Linda Nydam

1 (8-ounce) box spinach or tri-color fettuccine
1 cup low-fat cottage cheese
½ cup plain nonfat yogurt
½ cup crumbled Gorgonzola cheese
⅛ teaspoon white pepper
2 cups rehydrated sun-dried tomatoes, cut into strips

1. Cook pasta according to package directions. Drain well. Cover to keep warm.

2. In a food processor, combine cottage cheese and yogurt and process until smooth.

3. Transfer to a medium saucepan and heat over low heat.

4. Add Gorgonzola and white pepper; stir until cheese is melted.

5. In a large bowl, combine cooked pasta and tomatoes. Pour cheese mixture over pasta and mix well. Serve immediately.

Serves 4.

Artichoke and Pasta Dish

Jack Strouse

1 tablespoon olive oil
½ teaspoon red pepper flakes
1 tablespoon minced garlic
2 (8½-ounce) cans artichoke hearts
1 tablespoon capers
1 (48-ounce) can low fat chicken stock
1 (15-ounce) can cannellini beans
1 (10-ounce) bag baby spinach
  Zest of 1 lemon
  Juice of ½ lemon
  Salt and pepper to taste
1 tablespoon cornstarch
¼ cup water
1 pound cooked pasta

1. In a skillet, heat oil. Add red pepper flakes and cook until sizzled. Add garlic and cook until it changes color. Add artichokes and capers and sauté for 3 to 4 minutes.

2. Add chicken stock, lemon zest and lemon juice. Reduce stock to taste. Add beans.

3. Make slurry by combining cornstarch and water in a small bowl. Pour slurry into sauce to thicken.

4. Add the spinach and cook until wilted. Add cooked pasta. Toss and serve.

Cajun Chicken Pasta

April Brown

My husband never tires of this recipe and if he could have his way, he would have it for dinner once a week.

¼ pound linguine

2 boneless, skinless chicken breasts, cut into 1-inch pieces

2 teaspoons Cajun seasoning

2 tablespoons butter

1 green bell pepper, finely chopped

½ red bell pepper, finely chopped

4 fresh mushrooms, sliced

1 green onion, minced

1½ cups heavy cream

¼ teaspoon salt

¼ teaspoon dried basil

¼ teaspoon lemon pepper

⅛ teaspoon garlic powder

⅛ teaspoon pepper

2 tablespoons grated Parmesan cheese

1. Cook pasta according to package directions until al dente; drain.

2. Place chicken and Cajun seasoning in a bowl and toss to coat.

3. In a large skillet over medium heat, sauté chicken in butter until tender, about 5 to 7 minutes. Add green and red bell peppers, mushrooms and onions and cook for 2 to 3 minutes.

4. Reduce heat and add heavy cream, basil, lemon pepper, salt, garlic powder and pepper; heat through.

5. In a large pasta bowl, toss linguine with sauce. If desired, sprinkle with Parmesan cheese. Serve warm.

For a lower fat version, omit butter and use vegetable spray on the skillet. Also, use light cream instead of heavy cream. For extra spicy, double the Cajun seasoning.

Serves 2 to 4.

Spaghetti Pie

Kathy Averka

Serve this one-dish meal with a salad and warm garlic bread.

Your favorite spaghetti sauce (with or without meat)
1 pound spaghetti
4 tablespoons butter, melted
3 eggs
½ cup grated Parmesan cheese, divided
1 (8-ounce) package cream cheese
1 (2-pound) container ricotta cheese
2 cups shredded mozzarella cheese

1. Prepare spaghetti sauce.

2. Cook spaghetti according to package directions and drain.

3. Place spaghetti in a 13 x 9-inch glass dish. Mix butter in with spaghetti.

4. Beat eggs and ¼ cup of Parmesan cheese. Mix well with spaghetti.

5. Layer cream cheese and ricotta on top of spaghetti. Top with spaghetti sauce.

6. Sprinkle with mozzarella cheese and remaining Parmesan cheese.

7. Bake at 350° for 35 to 40 minutes. Let stand for 10 minutes and cut into squares.

Four-Cheese Vegetable Lasagne

Sue Hebert

12 uncooked lasagna noodles
2 teaspoons vegetable oil
2 cups chopped broccoli
1½ cups thinly sliced carrots
1 cup sliced green onion
½ cup chopped red bell pepper
3 cloves garlic, minced
½ cup all-purpose flour
3 cups 1% milk
½ cup grated Parmesan cheese, divided
¼ teaspoon salt
¼ teaspoon pepper
1 (10-ounce) package frozen chopped spinach, thawed, drained and squeezed dry
1½ cups 1% low-fat cottage cheese
1 cup shredded part-skim mozzarella cheese
½ cup shredded Swiss cheese
Freshly ground pepper (optional)

1. Cook lasagna noodles, omitting salt and fat. Drain and set aside.

2. In a Dutch oven, coated with cooking spray over medium-high heat, heat oil until hot. Add broccoli and next 4 ingredients and sauté 7 minutes; set aside.

3. Place flour in a medium saucepan. Gradually add milk stirring with a whisk until blended. Bring to a boil over medium heat and cook 5 minutes or until thick, stirring constantly. Add ¼ cup Parmesan cheese, salt and pepper; cook for 1 minute, stirring constantly. Remove from heat.

4. Stir in spinach, reserving ½ cup mixture for top layer of casserole and set aside.

5. Combine cottage cheese, mozzarella and Swiss cheese; stir well.

6. Spread ½ cup spinach mixture in bottom of a lightly greased 13 x 9-inch baking dish. Arrange 4 lasagna noodles over spinach mixture in dish. Top with ½ of cottage cheese mixture, ½ of broccoli mixture and ½ of remaining spinach mixture. Repeat layers ending with noodles. Spread reserved ½ cup spinach mixture over noodles, sprinkle with ¼ cup Parmesan cheese.

7. Bake, covered, at 375° for 35 minutes. Let stand 10 minutes before serving. Sprinkle with pepper, if desired.

Serves 9.

~~~

Potato Gnocchi with Spinach and Yellow Squash

Carrie Daigneault

1   (1-pound) package vacuum-packed potato gnocchi
1   tablespoon olive oil
1   yellow squash, quartered lengthwise and thinly sliced
1½ teaspoons bottled minced garlic
1   (10-ounce) package fresh spinach, torn
¼   cup fat-free milk
¼   teaspoon freshly ground pepper
⅛   teaspoon salt
½   cup shredded Gouda cheese

1. Cook gnocchi in boiling water according to package directions.

2. While gnocchi cooks, heat oil in a large skillet over medium heat. Add squash and sauté 4 minutes or until crisp-tender. Add garlic and sauté 1 minute. Add spinach; cover and cook 2 minutes or just until spinach wilts.

2. Reduce heat to low and stir in milk, pepper and salt.

3. Add gnocchi and cheese. Stir gently. Serve immediately.

You may use grated sharp provolone cheese in place of Gouda.

Serves 4.

Macaroni and Cheese

From the Kitchen of Mary W. King Luther
submitted by her daughter-in-law Barbara King

On the back of Mary Luther's recipe card it reads,
"This is my mother's recipe - (Marion West)".

¾ pound elbow macaroni
1 (10-ounce) package extra
    sharp white cheese
1-2 cups milk
¼ cup bread crumbs
4 tablespoons butter

1. Cook macaroni according to package directions; drain.

2. Cut cheese into small pieces.

3. Put macaroni and cheese in a greased 2-quart casserole dish. Add milk to about ½ full.

4. Sprinkle with bread crumbs on top. Dot with butter.

5. Bake, uncovered, at 375° for 40 minutes.

Light Fettuccine Alfredo

Jane KH Walsh

*Rich flavor without the fat! My sister Barbara shared
this recipe with me several years ago and it is a favorite. It is quick, easy
and tasty. Cataumet Shrimp for Two (page 30) is a nice prelude to this fine Fettuccini Alfredo. As a side dish, serve with a fresh sliced tomato, chopped fresh basil,
crumbled feta cheese and a little drizzle of olive oil on top. Sliced grilled chicken is
also a tasty accompaniment. Bon appetite!*

1   tablespoon butter

1-2 small cloves garlic, minced

1   tablespoon all-purpose flour

1⅓ cups skim milk

2   tablespoons light cream cheese

1¼ cups grated Parmesan cheese,
    divided

4   cups hot cooked fettuccini,
    cooked without salt or fat

2   teaspoons chopped fresh
    parsley
    Freshly ground pepper

1. In a saucepan over medium heat, melt the butter; add garlic and sauté 1 minute. Stir in flour.

2. Gradually add milk, stirring with a whisk until blended. Cook 8 minutes or until thickened and bubbly, stirring constantly.

3. Stir in cream cheese, and cook 2 minutes. Add 1 cup of Parmesan cheese, stirring constantly until it melts.

4. Pour over hot cooked fettuccine; toss well to coat. Top with remaining ¼ cup Parmesan cheese, fresh parsley and pepper.

Serves 4.

Italian Macaroni and Cheese

Patricia M. Morse

A different twist on Macaroni and Cheese.

1 (8-ounce) package macaroni
8 ounces cheese, cubed
1 (5-ounce) can evaporated milk
1 teaspoon dry mustard
1 (16-ounce) can stewed Italian
   tomatoes
½ cup dry bread crumbs
2 tablespoons butter, melted
2 tablespoons grated Parmesan
   cheese

1. Cook macaroni according to package directions. Set aside.

2. In a medium bowl, combine cheese, evaporated milk and dry mustard. Microwave on high 2 to 3 minutes until cheese melts, stirring every minute.

3. Add macaroni to cheese mixture and mix well.

4. In a lightly greased, 2-quart casserole dish, layer ½ of the macaroni and cheese mixture. Cover with stewed tomatoes, then remainder of macaroni and cheese.

5. In a small bowl, combine bread crumbs, butter and Parmesan cheese; mix well. Sprinkle over casserole.

6. Bake at 350° for 30 minutes.

Hot pepper cheese works great too!

Serves 4.

Vegetables & Side Dishes

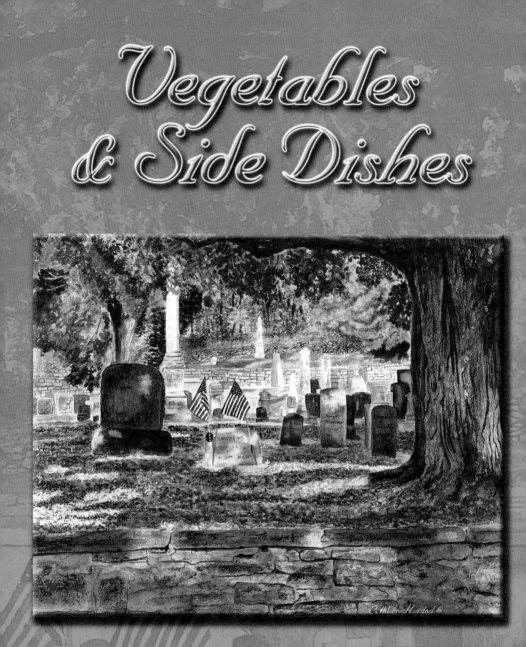

Harvest Time

The West Sutton Cemetery, West Sutton Road

This was the original cemetery for the Stephen and Huidah Waters (Waters Farm) family. Tombstones date back to the late 1700's. You will notice the stones in the background are a lighter shade, this is where the Waters family rests. Around 1915, the Waters family deeded the cemetery over to the Town. As Cathleen painted this, she reflected on the many seasons of life in this quiet corner of the world.

Vegetables and Side Dishes

Roasted Asparagus
with Balsamic Browned Butter

Barbara MH Daigneault

A nice light twist for asparagus and so easy to prepare.

2 pounds asparagus spears, trimmed
¼ teaspoon kosher salt
⅛ teaspoon pepper
2 tablespoons butter
2 teaspoons low-sodium soy sauce
1 teaspoon balsamic vinegar

1. Arrange asparagus in a single layer on a greased baking sheet. Sprinkle with salt and pepper. Bake at 400° for 12 minutes or until tender.

2. In a small skillet, melt butter over medium heat and cook for 3 minutes or until lightly browned, shaking pan occasionally.

3. Remove from heat; stir in soy sauce and vinegar. Drizzle over asparagus, tossing well to coat. Serve immediately.

Serves 8.

Harvard Beets

Janet A. Whittier

This recipe came from The Hillside Club Bicentennial Cookbook and was submitted by Kay Leonard. When beets are plentiful in the summer from our garden, I make a large batch and freeze in small containers for use during the winter months.

1 cup sugar
1½ teaspoons cornstarch
¼ cup vinegar
¼ cup water
12 small beets, cooked and cut into slices or cubes
2 tablespoons butter

1. Mix sugar and cornstarch. Add vinegar and water and boil for 5 minutes.

2. Add beets and let stand over low heat for 30 minutes.

3. Just before serving, bring to a boiling point and add butter.

Green Beans with Toasted Pecans and Blue Cheese

Beth Willoughby

This can be doubled or tripled and makes a wonderful buffet item. Adds a special touch to burgers and really compliments a good steak! I am always asked for this recipe.

¾ pound green beans
½ cup pecans
2 teaspoons olive oil, divided
½ teaspoon salt
¼ teaspoon Dijon mustard
1 teaspoon cider vinegar
2 teaspoons finely chopped shallots
1½ ounces blue cheese

1. Blanche green beans for 3 minutes. Drain and transfer to ice water to stop cooking and keep color.

2. Sauté pecans in 1½ teaspoons of olive oil with salt. Remove excess oil and chop. Set aside.

3. Combine mustard, vinegar, shallots and remaining ½ teaspoons of oil. Toss cooled beans with dressing.

4. Put in serving dish and top with toasted nuts and blue cheese.

Serves 2.

Glazed Brussels Sprouts

Jan Battema

These compliment Spicy Sweet Potato Wedges (page 234) and Smoked Pork Chops with Maple Baked Apples (page 170).

2 (10-ounce) packages Brussels sprouts
3 tablespoons melted butter
3 tablespoons white wine
2 teaspoons sugar
¼ teaspoon salt
Worcestershire sauce to taste

1. Cook Brussels sprouts and cut in half.

2. Toss with remaining ingredients.

3. Transfer to a 13 x 9-inch pan. Roast at 450° for 20 minutes, shaking pan occasionally.

Serves 6.

Lemon Broccoli Crunch

Carol Botty

Delicious stuffed in pita bread for a sandwich or served over couscous.

1   large bunch broccoli florets, steamed until tender (about 3 to 4 cups)

1   (15-ounce) can chick peas, drained

¼   cup lemon juice, freshly squeezed

3   tablespoons extra-virgin olive oil

Grated rind of 1 lemon

¼-½ teaspoon lemon pepper seasoning

1. In a large serving bowl, toss broccoli and chick peas together.

2. In a separate covered jar, mix in remaining ingredients. Shake well and toss with broccoli mixture.

Dressing keeps in refrigerator for 1 week.

Serves 4 to 6.

Braised Red Cabbage and Apples

Barbara MH Daigneault

This is an excellent side dish served with pork.

1   small head red cabbage, quartered, cored and thinly sliced

2   tablespoons butter

3   tablespoons finely chopped onions

1   large green apple, peeled, cored and cut into matchsticks

3   tablespoons red wine vinegar

2   tablespoons honey

1   teaspoon salt

⅛   cup caraway seeds

1. Immerse cabbage briefly in cold water. Drain well and set aside.

2. In a large Dutch oven, melt butter and sauté onions over medium-low heat until golden. Add cabbage, apple, vinegar, honey, salt and caraway seeds.

3. Cover the pan and cook over medium-low heat until cabbage is very soft, about 1 to 1½ hours. Add boiling water if needed during cooking.

Serves 4.

Sweet Carrot Soufflé

April Brown

2 pounds carrots, chopped
1 stick butter, melted
1 cup sugar
3 tablespoons all-purpose flour
1 teaspoon baking powder
1 teaspoon vanilla
3 eggs, beaten
1 teaspoon confectioners' sugar
  for dusting

1. In a large pot, boil carrots in salted water and cook until tender, about 15 minutes. Drain and mash.

2. Add remaining ingredients, except for confectioners' sugar and mix well.

3. Transfer to a 2-quart greased casserole dish. Sprinkle with confectioners' sugar. Bake, uncovered, at 350° for 30 minutes.

Serves 8.

Orange Glazed Carrots

Kathleen M. Handfield

This glaze was intended to be served with pork tenderloin, however, I thought this would taste great with carrots. I tried it and loved it.

1 (16-ounce) package baby
  carrots, cooked
⅔ cup sugar
1 tablespoon cornstarch
½ teaspoon salt
½ teaspoon cinnamon
1 tablespoon freshly grated
  orange rind
1 cup orange juice
  Dash of ground cloves

1. In a small saucepan, combine all ingredients, except the carrots and cook over medium heat until thickened, stirring with a whisk.

2. Place carrots in a serving dish and pour glaze over carrots.

Serves 6 to 8.

Zippy Carrots

Susan B. Ekstrom

This sauce added to carrots gives them a special touch. Excellent and easy to prepare. Guests will think you went out of your way to make this!

1 pound carrots, sliced and cooked
2 tablespoons butter, melted
¼ cup brown sugar
2 tablespoons Dijon mustard
¼ teaspoon salt (optional)
Fresh chopped parsley for garnish

1. In a small bowl, melt the butter in a microwave.

2. Combine remaining ingredients and pour over hot cooked carrots. Garnish with parsley.

Serves 4.

Creamy Corn Pudding

Mary Lou Peterson

Excellent with ham or served on a buffet.

1 (14¾-ounce) can cream style corn
2 tablespoons flour
2 tablespoons sugar
½ teaspoon salt
⅛ teaspoon pepper
2 eggs, beaten
1 cup milk
2 tablespoons butter

1. Mix all ingredients, except butter and pour into a greased 2-quart casserole dish. Dot with butter.

2. Bake, uncovered, at 350° for 1 hour.

Serves 6 to 8.

Christmas Cauliflower Casserole

Cathleen Haddad

Red, white and green! Great for Christmas dinner!

1   large head cauliflower, cut into florets
4   tablespoons butter
1   (8-ounce) package sliced mushrooms
¼   cup diced green bell pepper
⅓   cup all-purpose flour
2   cups whole milk
1   cup shredded Swiss cheese
2   tablespoons diced pimientos
1   teaspoon salt
    Paprika (optional)

1. Steam the cauliflower until crisp-tender. Drain and rinse under cold water to stop the cooking process. Set aside to drain well.

2. In a large skillet, melt the butter and sauté the mushrooms until the liquid is released and begins to evaporate. When the liquid is mostly evaporated, add the peppers. Sauté 2 minutes longer or until slightly cooked.

3. Add flour and coat all mushrooms and peppers. Gradually add the milk and bring it to a boil. Boil for 2 minutes, stirring constantly. Be careful the milk doesn't burn on the bottom with the flour.

4. Remove from heat and stir in the cheese until melted. Add pimientos and salt.

5. Place ½ the cauliflower in a greased 2½-quart baking dish. Top with half the cheese sauce. Repeat the layers.

6. Bake, uncovered, at 325° for 25 minutes or until bubbly. Sprinkle with paprika if desired.

When steaming the cauliflower, watch it closely. If it overcooks then your casserole will be mushy.

Corn and Cheese Casserole

Bette Keene

About 10 years ago my friend, MaryBeth, brought this dish to a cookout at my home. Everyone loved it and she shared the recipe. Since that time, I have served it many times at group gatherings. It is always a big hit.

1 stick butter
¼ cup chopped green bell pepper
¼ cup chopped red bell pepper
1 small onion, chopped
2 eggs, beaten
1 (15¼-ounce) can corn niblets, drained
1 (14¾-ounce) can cream style corn
1 (8½-ounce) package cornbread mix
2 cups sour cream
2 cups grated white Cheddar cheese, divided

1. In a small saucepan, melt butter and sauté peppers and onions until tender.

2. In a medium bowl, mix eggs with both cans of corn and add cornbread mix.

3. Add onions, peppers and butter. Pour into a greased 13 x 9-inch baking dish.

4. Mix sour cream and 1 cup of Cheddar cheese. Spread on top of the corn mixture. Sprinkle with remaining cheese.

5. Bake, uncovered, at 375° for 40 minutes.

This dish reheats well in the microwave.

Serves 12.

Grilled Eggplant and Tomato Gratin

Kim Hunkeler

A summer favorite!

2 large tomatoes, sliced thin
½ teaspoon salt
2 medium eggplant, sliced ½-inch thick
Olive oil
¾ teaspoon dried basil
¾ teaspoon dried oregano
2 cloves garlic, minced
½ cup heavy cream
1½ cups shredded fontina cheese

1. Place tomato slices on a paper towel and sprinkle with salt. Let stand for 30 minutes.

2. Coat eggplant slices with olive oil. Grill over medium heat, 5 minutes each side.

3. Coat a large shallow baking dish with olive oil. Alternately layer tomatoes and eggplant. Sprinkle with herbs and garlic. Pour cream over top and sprinkle with fontina cheese.

4. Bake at 350° for 35 to 45 minutes and cheese is golden brown.

Scalloped Potatoes and Carrots

Helen Silun Ordung

4 cups thinly sliced potatoes
3 cups thinly sliced carrots
4 tablespoons butter
½ cup chopped onion
2 tablespoons flour
3 cups milk
2 teaspoons salt
¼ teaspoon dried dill weed
⅓ cup chopped fresh parsley

1. In a greased 13 x 9-inch baking dish, alternate layering potatoes and carrots.

2. In a medium saucepan, melt butter and sauté onion until tender. Add flour and cook for 1 minute.

3. Gradually add milk, salt, dill weed and parsley and cook until slightly thickened. Pour over potato mixture.

4. Bake, covered, at 350° for 30 minutes. Remove the cover and bake for an additional hour.

Serves 8.

Grilled Veggies in Foil

Carol Botty

*This is a staple in the summer. Any leftovers are usually mixed with
lots of tomatoes and cooked ziti or farfalle for a pasta veggie fresco the next day.*

1   medium eggplant, peeled, cut
    into bite-size pieces
½   pound mushrooms, washed,
    cut into bite-size pieces
1   medium zucchini, cut into bite-
    size pieces
1   red bell pepper, cut into strips
1   yellow bell pepper, cut into
    strips
½   cup sun-dried tomatoes,
    chopped
1-2 cloves garlic, pressed
¼   cup olive oil
1   teaspoon salt

1. In a large bowl, combine all
ingredients. Mix well. Marinate for
2 to 3 hours.

2. Spoon vegetables and any liquid
into a large sheet of heavy
aluminum foil. Close by pinching
foil edges together to make a
packet.

3. Place on hot grill for 45 minutes.

4. Open foil and vegetables should
be tender and juicy.

*Add any "sturdy" veggie you desire and
also add fresh herbs after grilling. This
can also be baked in the oven at 350° for
45 minutes.*

Serves 4 to 6.

Mushroom Casserole

From the Kitchen of Irma B. Whitney
submitted by her daughter Karen Melia

7   slices buttered bread, divided
2   tablespoons butter
1   pound fresh mushrooms,
    coarsely chopped
½   cup chopped celery
½   cup chopped green bell pepper
½   cup finely chopped onion
½   cup mayonnaise
¾   teaspoon salt
¼   teaspoon ground pepper
2   eggs, slightly beaten
1½ cups milk
1   can cream of mushroom soup

1. Cut 3 slices of bread into 1-inch squares and layer in a greased 2½-quart casserole dish.

2. Melt butter in a large skillet and sauté mushrooms.

3. In a medium bowl, combine celery, peppers, onions, mayonnaise, salt and pepper. Add mushrooms and mix well. Pour over bread squares.

4. Layer 2 more slices of cubed bread on top of mushroom mixture.

5. Mix eggs with milk and pour over casserole. Refrigerate overnight.

6. When ready to bake, pour soup over casserole and cover with remaining cubes of bread.

7. Bake at 320° for 50 minutes or 310° for 1 hour and 10 minutes. Serve hot.

Serves 6 to 8.

Scalloped Potatoes with Gouda and Fennel

Barbara MH Daigneault

Everyone will want to know what the secret ingredient is in this recipe.
It's fennel. I have served this at countless dinner parties and guests always want
this recipe. This recipe is delicious served with Roast Double Loin
of Pork with Port Wine Sauce (page 172).

1   cup whipping cream
1   cup half & half
1   medium fennel bulb, trimmed, halved and thinly sliced
1   teaspoon fennel seeds, crushed
1   pound russet potatoes, peeled and thinly sliced
1   pound sweet potatoes, peeled and thinly sliced
2   cups shredded and firmly packed Gouda

1. In a large skillet, combine cream, half & half, fennel, fennel seeds and potatoes. Bring mixture to boil over high heat, stirring frequently to separate potato slices. Boil 5 minutes. Season generously with salt and pepper.

2. Transfer half of potato mixture to a greased 8 x 8-inch glass baking dish. Sprinkle with half the Gouda.

3. Top with remaining potato mixture. Firmly press mixture down.

4. Sprinkle remaining Gouda over top.

5. Bake, covered, at 400° for about 40 minutes or until potatoes are tender. Uncover and bake until top is golden brown, about 10 minutes longer. Let stand for 10 minutes before serving.

Serves 6.

Butternut Squash Casserole

Mary K. Connor

This is a Thanksgiving favorite. It almost tastes too good not to serve as a dessert.

3   pounds butternut squash, peeled and cut
1   stick plus 2 tablespoons unsalted butter, melted
¾   cup milk
2   tablespoons flour
½   teaspoon cinnamon
½   teaspoon cloves
½   teaspoon nutmeg
1   cup sugar
3   eggs
½   cup vanilla wafer crumbs (about 15)
¼   cup packed dark brown sugar

1. Cook squashes until very tender and drain.

2. In a large mixing bowl, beat squash, 1 stick of melted butter, milk, flour, spices, granulated sugar and eggs until smooth.

3. Pour into an 8 x 8-inch greased baking dish. Bake at 350° for 50 minutes.

4. Mix remaining 2 tablespoons butter with wafer crumbs and brown sugar and spread on top of squash and bake until just set, about 15 to 25 minutes.

Serves 8.

Spicy Sweet Potato Wedges

Jan Battema

This recipe is perfect with Glazed Brussels Sprouts (page 224) and Smoked Pork Chops with Maple Baked Apples (page 170).

2   pounds sweet potatoes, cut into ½-inch wide wedges (do not peel)
1   tablespoon vegetable oil
1   teaspoon sugar
1   teaspoon chili powder
¾   teaspoon salt
2   tablespoons maple syrup
1   teaspoon cider vinegar

1. In a large bowl, toss potatoes with vegetable oil, sugar, chili powder and salt. Spread on a lightly greased baking sheet.

2. Roast at 475° for 15 to 20 minutes, shaking once during cooking.

3. Drizzle with maple syrup mixed with cider vinegar.

Serves 4.

Sweet Potato and Apple Casserole

Kathy Dugan

A thoughtful friend of mine first made this for an early Thanksgiving dinner she decided to have for a mutual friend of ours who was quickly losing her battle with cancer. This recipe has since become a tradition at our family Thanksgiving table to truly remind us what a gift life itself is.

2 pounds sweet potatoes, peeled, cut into ¼-inch slices

2 pounds Golden Delicious or McIntosh apples, peeled, cored, cut into ¼-inch slices

6 tablespoons firmly packed light brown sugar, divided

6 tablespoons butter, divided

½ cup apple cider or apple brandy

Golden raisins sprinkled throughout (optional)

1. Gently boil sweet potato slices in salted water until tender but not falling apart (about 5 minutes). Drain and set aside.

2. Grease an 8-cup soufflé or deep baking dish. Arrange a layer of sliced apples over the bottom of the dish.

3. Sprinkle with 1 tablespoon of brown sugar and dot with 1 tablespoon of butter.

4. Cover the apple layer with a layer of sweet potato slices and sprinkle with the sugar and butter. Raisins can be sprinkled throughout if desired.

5. Continue layering until all ingredients are used, ending with a layer of apples.

6. Drizzle the cider over the top. Cover tightly with foil. Bake at 350° for 1 hour and 20 minutes or until apples are very soft.

This dish can be made a few hours ahead of time, but not too soon that apples will brown.

Serves 8 to 10.

Sweet Potato Tipsy

Cathleen Haddad

The combination of brown sugar and sherry gives this dish a special taste.
This is a great accompaniment for a fall dinner on a cool crisp evening.

8   sweet potatoes, peeled
2   pinches salt
7   tablespoons butter, divided
½   cup half & half
¼   cup dry sherry
3   tablespoons brown sugar

1. Boil potatoes in salted water for 30 to 40 minutes or until soft. Drain and coarsely mash with a fork.

2. In a large bowl, combine 5 tablespoons of butter and remaining ingredients along with potatoes and beat with mixer for 2 minutes.

3. Transfer mixture to a greased baking dish. Dot with remaining butter.

4. Bake, uncovered, at 350° for 30 minutes or until golden brown.

Can be prepared ahead of time.

Serves 6 to 8.

Three Cheese Spinach Casserole

Anne Conley

3   eggs
3   (10-ounce) packages frozen chopped spinach, thawed and well-drained
4   tablespoons butter, melted
    Salt and pepper to taste
1   tablespoon flour
4   ounces American cheese, shredded
4   ounces Cheddar cheese, shredded
1   (16-ounce) container small curd cottage cheese

1. Beat eggs and stir in spinach, butter, salt and pepper.

2. Sprinkle in flour and stir. Blend 3 cheeses and stir into spinach.

3. Pour into a greased 2-quart casserole. Bake at 350° for 1 hour.

Serves 6 to 8.

Maple Glazed Yams with Pecan Topping

Karen Thibodeau

4 pounds yams, peeled, cut into
   ¼-inch slices
   Salt to taste
½ cup pure maple syrup
1 stick chilled butter, cut into
   ½-inch pieces, divided
⅓ cup all-purpose flour
⅓ cup firmly packed brown sugar
½ cup coarsely chopped pecans

1. Bring a large pot of salted water to a boil. Add yams. Cook until water returns to simmer (about 4 minutes). Drain and rinse under cold water.

2. Arrange yams in a greased 13 x 9-inch baking dish, overlapping slightly. Season with salt. Pour syrup over yams. Dot with 3 tablespoons of butter.

3. Bake, covered, at 400° for 25 minutes or until yams are almost tender.

4. In a medium bowl, combine flour and brown sugar. Add remaining 5 tablespoons of butter. Rub with fingers until resembles coarse meal.

5. Mix in pecans. Sprinkle pecan mixture over yams.

6. Bake an additional 20 minutes or until yams are tender.

Can be made 2 hours in advance. Cover and let stand at room temperature. Reheat, uncovered, at 375° for 20 minutes.

Serves 12.

Cheesy Summer Squash Casserole

Cindy King

Our family lived across the street from Miss Louise Ray on the Sutton Town Common. She would send this casserole over on occasion during the summer months. She could see I had my hands full with 3 toddlers. Wow, what an old fashioned neighbor. I think of her whenever I make it.

3 cups summer squash, cooked and drained well	1. Mix first 6 ingredients together.
½ cup mayonnaise	2. Pour into a greased 8 x 8-inch baking dish. Top with cheese and bread crumbs. Drizzle with butter.
½ cup chopped onion	
1 egg, slightly beaten	
1 teaspoon sugar	3. Bake at 350° for 30 minutes.
Salt and pepper to taste	
1 cup grated mozzarella cheese	*Can add pre-cooked chicken if desired.*
½ cup bread crumbs	
4 tablespoons butter, melted	*Serves 4 to 6.*

Summertime Summer Squash Bake

Lynn Murphy O'Neal

Always a hit at the "Summer Party" at the farm!

2 pounds summer squash	1. Parboil squash and onion in salted water. Drain well.
½ cup chopped onion	
1 cup shredded carrot	2. Mix with carrots, sour cream and soup.
1 cup sour cream	
1 can cream of chicken soup	3. Mix butter with stuffing mix.
2 sticks butter, melted	
1 package stuffing mix	4. Line an 11 x 9-inch baking dish with buttered stuffing and reserve some for the top. Add squash mixture and top with remainder of crumbs.
	5. Bake, uncovered, at 350° for 20 to 25 minutes.
	Serves 8 to 10.

Mediterranean Vegetables

Priscilla DiLeo

¼ cup olive oil
8 sprigs thyme, minced
4 cloves garlic, pressed
¼ teaspoon salt
¼ teaspoon pepper
2 small summer squash, cut into ½-inch slices
2 small zucchini squash, cut into ½-inch slices
1 medium eggplant, cut into bite-size pieces
2 medium red onions, thinly sliced
4 medium tomatoes, cut into quarters
Grated Parmesan cheese (optional)

1. Mix first 5 ingredients and pour ⅓ of mixture into an 11 x 9-inch baking dish.

2. Layer squashes, eggplant, onions and tomatoes in baking dish. Pour the remainder of oil mixture over vegetables. Top with Parmesan cheese if desired.

3. Bake, covered, at 350° for 30 to 40 minutes or until vegetables are crunchy, but softened.

Excellent leftover as the veggies have had time to mellow in the juices. Can be prepared in advance and can be served either hot or cold.

Serves 8.

Garlicky Parmesan Squash

Dorothy F. Graham

A member of my quilting group gave this recipe to me. Easy to prepare and delicious if you like garlic.

¼ cup flour
Salt and pepper to taste
2 medium summer squash, cut into cubes
⅓ cup Parmesan cheese
¼ cup olive oil
1 clove garlic, minced

1. In a large plastic bag, combine flour, salt and pepper. Add squash and shake to coat evenly.

2. Place in a greased 9 x 9-inch pan and top with Parmesan cheese, oil and garlic.

3. Bake, uncovered, at 450° for 45 minutes.

Serves 4.

Zucchini Casserole

Jennifer Quinn

*Don't let the zucchini fool you. It's not fat free! This casserole is
perfect at outdoor barbecues or as a side dish. It's one of my favorites.*

6   cups cubed zucchini
1   cup onion (optional)
1   package stove top chicken
     flavored stuffing
2   sticks butter, melted
1   cup sour cream
1   can cream of chicken soup

1. Boil zucchini and onions for
5 minutes or until almost tender.
Drain and set aside.

2. Combine stuffing and butter. Set
aside.

3. Combine sour cream and
chicken soup. Set aside.

4. In a greased 13 x 9-inch baking
dish, alternate layers of zucchini
mixture with stuffing mixture.
Reserve a little stuffing for topping.

5. Pour sour cream mixture over
casserole and top with remaining
crumbs.

6. Bake at 350° for 25 to 35 minutes.

Yummy Zucchini Pie

Cheryl Scott

1	stick butter
1	small onion, thinly sliced
2-3	medium zucchini, thinly sliced
½	cup chopped fresh parsley
½	teaspoon salt
½	teaspoon pepper
¼	teaspoon garlic powder
¼	teaspoon basil
¼	teaspoon oregano
2	eggs, slightly beaten
8	ounces shredded mozzarella or Muenster cheese
1	package Pillsbury crescent crust
2	tablespoons Dijon mustard

1. In a large saucepan, melt butter and sauté onion and zucchini until tender.

2. In a separate bowl, combine parsley, salt, pepper, garlic powder, basil and oregano. Add eggs and cheese.

3. Combine zucchini and cheese mixture. Set aside.

4. Spread crescent crust into a greased pie plate. Spread crust with Dijon mustard. Pour mixture into prepared crust.

5. Bake at 375° for 18 to 20 minutes. Let stand 10 minutes before slicing.

Tomato Cheese Pie

Nancy A. Johnson

This is an old family recipe. The amount of tomato and onion can vary according to availability of fresh tomatoes. Always serve in the fall when tomatoes are plentiful.

1	cup Bisquick
¼	cup milk
3	large tomatoes, seeded and cut into chunks
1	medium onion, coarsely chopped
1	cup shredded mozzarella cheese
½	cup mayonnaise
2	tablespoons sugar
1	tablespoon minced fresh parsley

1. Combine Bisquick and milk. Spread into a greased pie plate.

2. Place tomatoes and onions on top of Bisquick mixture.

3. Combine remaining ingredients and spread over tomatoes and onions.

4. Bake, uncovered, at 375° for 30 minutes.

Serves 8.

Roasted New Potatoes with Spring Herb Pesto

Ann Bouvier Achorn

1½ cups chopped fresh parsley

⅔ cup chopped fresh chives

3 tablespoons chopped fresh rosemary

6 tablespoons olive oil, divided

3 cloves garlic, minced

2 tablespoons lemon juice, freshly squeezed

1 teaspoon grated lemon peel

1 teaspoon salt

5 pounds red skin new potatoes, halved lengthwise

Freshly ground pepper to taste

1. In a food processor, blend fresh herbs with 2 tablespoons olive oil, garlic, lemon juice, lemon peel and salt to a coarse puree. Set pesto aside.

2. In a large bowl, toss potatoes with remaining oil. Sprinkle with pepper.

3. Arrange potatoes cut side down, on a rimmed baking sheet. Roast at 400° about 30 to 40 minutes or until golden brown and tender.

4. Using a spatula, transfer potatoes to a large bowl. Add pesto and toss to coat. Serve immediately.

Pesto can be made one day ahead. Cover and refrigerate. Bring to room temperature before using.

Serves 12.

Cheesy Company Potatoes

Arlene Uppstrom

I received this recipe from a toile painting class student.
I first served this at a Memorial Day family gathering and it has
become a family favorite for large parties.

2 cups sour cream
2 cups grated Cheddar cheese
1 can cream of mushroom soup
4 tablespoons butter, melted
½ cup chopped onion
1 (2-pound) package frozen hash browns, thawed
½ cup buttered bread crumbs

1. In a large bowl, combine sour cream and cheese. Add soup, butter and onion. Mix well.

2. Add hash browns and toss to cover evenly.

3. Pour into a greased 13 x 9-inch baking dish. Top with bread crumbs.

4. Bake, uncovered, at 350° for 40 to 45 minutes or until bubbly.

This dish can be prepared ahead of time. Use approximately 2 tablespoons of melted butter to moisten bread crumbs.

Serves 10 to 12.

P.E.I. Potatoes

Barbara O'Connor

I first had this recipe at a family party. It is a great addition for a buffet. This dish requires very little preparation. Best of all, everyone loves it!

1	can cream of celery soup
2	cups sour cream
1	cup grated Parmesan cheese
1	teaspoon minced onion
	Dash of milk
3	cups frozen hash brown (do not thaw)
1	cup crushed corn flakes

1. In a large bowl, combine soup, sour cream, cheese and onion. Add milk.

2. Fold in hash browns.

3. Pour into a greased 13 x 9-inch baking dish. Sprinkle with corn flakes.

4. Bake, uncovered, at 350° for 1 hour.

This dish can be prepared ahead of time.

Serves 10 to 12.

Pea and Mint Couscous

Cheryl Scott

This is a great dish to serve with Seared Sesame Scallops (page 208). Simply place the scallops on top of this dish and it's a meal altogether.

⅔	cup water
½	teaspoon salt
½	cup frozen peas
⅔	cup couscous
1	tablespoon chopped fresh mint leaves
2	teaspoons lemon juice, freshly squeezed
	Salt and pepper to taste

1. In a small saucepan, bring water to a boil with salt. Add peas and return water to a boil. Stir in couscous and cover pan. Immediately remove pan from heat and let couscous stand, covered, 5 minutes.

2. Fluff couscous with a fork and stir in mint, lemon juice, salt and pepper to taste.

Serves 2.

Red Bliss Potato Puff

Beth Hyder

Our family loves this potato dish anytime. It is great to serve on holiday's because it is such a great "make ahead of time" dish.

5 pounds red bliss potatoes, with or without skins
8 ounces sour cream
6 ounces cream cheese
2 sticks butter, softened
   Salt to taste
   Garlic cloves, Parmesan cheese and chives to taste (optional)

1. Boil potatoes until cooked thoroughly. Drain.

2. In a large mixing bowl, combine potatoes, butter, sour cream, cream cheese and salt. Mix on low speed.

3. Add any optional ingredients as well. Once blended, mix on a higher speed for 2 minutes.

4. Pour into a greased casserole dish. Bake, covered, at 350° for 1 to 1½ hours.

Any potato would work well, except for new white. This recipe can be served immediately or it's even better the next day. If you choose to have it the next day, it usually takes the full time to reheat after being refrigerated. When heated through, the edges will be golden brown.

Serves 10 to 12.

Kugali (Lithuanian Potato Casserole)

Barbara Morris

My grandmother from Lithuania always made Kugali during the cold winter months. This was shared amongst our relatives when our family grew up in Worcester, Massachusetts living in a three decker.

9 large potatoes, peeled and grated
1 small onion, chopped
1 (3 x 3-inch) piece of salt pork
1 cup scalded milk
½ cup flour
3-4 eggs, beaten
Salt and pepper to taste
Sour cream for topping

1. Grate potatoes and set aside.

2. In a small saucepan, sauté onion and salt pork until onions are tender.

3. In a large bowl, combine potatoes and remaining ingredients.

4. Pour into a greased 13 x 9-inch casserole dish. Bake, uncovered, at 350° for 1¼-hours or until browned.

5. Cut into squares and serve with a dollop of sour cream.

Serves 8 to 10.

Macadamia and Pineapple Rice Pilaf

Jim Burke

This pilaf goes very well with roast pork and with shrimp. A colorful Hawaiian rice.

1	tablespoon unsalted butter
1½	cups long-grain white rice
2	teaspoons minced garlic
¼	cup diced red bell pepper
¼	cup diced yellow bell pepper
3	cups chicken stock
½	cup golden raisins
½	cup chopped roasted macadamia nuts (preferably unsalted)
1	sage leaf
½	teaspoon salt
⅓	cup chopped fresh coriander
1	cup diced pineapple

1. In a Dutch oven, melt butter and add rice. Stir for a few seconds, until the butter coats the rice.

2. Add garlic and stir for a few seconds, but not long enough to let the rice change color. Add the peppers and cook for a few seconds, again not long enough to let the peppers change color.

3. Add the stock and bring the mixture gently to a boil. Add the raisins, nuts, sage and salt. Cover.

4. Bake at 375° for 18 to 20 minutes. Remove from oven and let stand for 10 minutes.

5. Add coriander and pineapple. Serve at once.

This doubles, even triples well for large gatherings. If using salted macadamia nuts, you won't have to add the salt.

Serves 4.

Risotto with Butternut Squash

Jim Burke

This is a fabulous vegetarian dish. The key to cooking risotto is not cooking it too fast. By doing this you allow the Arborio rice to absorb the liquid and it will be a creamy mixture.

1	ounce dried porcini mushrooms
1½	cups hot water
4	cups seeded and diced butternut squash
6	cups vegetable stock
2	tablespoons olive oil
1	large onion, chopped
	Salt and pepper to taste
2	cups Arborio rice
2	sprigs fresh thyme
¾	cup grated Parmesan cheese

1. In a medium bowl, soak the mushrooms in hot water for 10 minutes. Use a slotted spoon to remove the mushrooms, then strain the liquid through a sieve and reserve. Chop the mushrooms into small pieces, discarding any hard pieces and stems.

2. In a medium saucepan, bring the stock to a simmer and set it aside over medium heat.

3. In a large saucepan, heat the oil over medium heat and cook the onion, stirring often, until softened. Add the squash, salt and pepper and continue cooking, stirring occasionally, for 10 minutes or until the squash is tender.

4. Add the rice and cook, stirring for about 2 minutes. Stir in 1 cup of hot stock and cook, stirring until the rice absorbs the stock. Use a ladle to continue adding stock, about ½ cup at a time, stirring each addition into the rice and waiting until it is absorbed before adding more.

5. After you've added about 3 cups of stock, add the mushrooms, thyme and the reserved mushroom-

soaking liquid, ½ cup at a time, stirring until the liquid is absorbed. Then continue adding the remaining stock.

6. Taste the rice after 18 minutes. When it is done, the risotto is very creamy and the rice is tender, with a slight chewy center. If it is not done, keep adding more liquid until the risotto is cooked. Taste for seasoning.

7. To serve, ladle risotto into large shallow bowls. Sprinkle with Parmesan cheese and serve at once.

About 2 pounds of butternut squash yields 4 cups.

Serves 4.

Armenian Rice Pilaf

Nancy Lee Sarkisian

*This is a traditional Armenian recipe and couldn't be simpler to make.
This recipe has been handed down by word of mouth from grandmother to grandchild.*

4	tablespoons butter
½	cup vermicelli
1	cup long-grain white rice
5	chicken bouillon cubes
2½	cups water
	Pepper to taste

1. In a large shallow saucepan, melt butter. Break vermicelli into pieces and fry in the butter until slightly browned, stirring constantly.

2. Add rice and stir. Add bouillon, water and season with pepper.

3. Mix well and bring to a boil. Lower heat and simmer, covered, for 15 to 20 minutes until broth is absorbed and rice is fluffy.

You may also use 2½ cups of canned chicken broth.

Serves 6.

Risotto Porcini Casserole

Jim Burke

This is great as a main course or served with fish or lamb.

2	ounces dried porcini
1	stick butter, divided
2	bunches scallions, chopped
3	carrots, peeled and minced
2	cups Arborio rice
½	cup dry white wine
4-5	cups beef broth
1	pound fresh cultivated mushrooms, wiped clean and sliced
3	cloves garlic, minced
¾	cup chopped fresh parsley
	Salt and freshly ground pepper to taste
2	cups grated Parmesan cheese
1	cup heavy or whipping cream
2	eggs
	Pinch of ground nutmeg

1. In a small bowl, place porcinis and add hot water to cover. Let stand 30 minutes.

2. In a 10 to 12-inch skillet over medium heat, melt 4 tablespoons of butter. Add the scallions and carrots and sauté for 10 minutes. Add the rice and cook, stirring to coat with the butter and vegetables, for 1 minute.

3. Drain the porcinis, strain the liquid through cheesecloth and pour it over the rice. Add the wine and enough of the stock to completely cover the rice.

4. Simmer, covered, over low heat, adding more stock as needed, until the rice is tender but still firm, about 30 minutes.

5. While the rice is cooking, melt the remaining 4 tablespoons butter in a medium skillet over medium heat. Add the porcini and cultivated mushrooms and sauté for 10 minutes.

6. Stir in the garlic and parsley and simmer, uncovered, for 10 minutes. Season with salt and pepper to taste.

7. Spread half the rice in the bottom of a greased 2-quart baking dish. Top with all the mushrooms. Sprinkle with 1 cup Parmesan and top with remaining rice.

8. Whisk the cream, eggs and nutmeg together and pour evenly over the rice. Sprinkle with the remaining 1 cup Parmesan cheese.

9. Bake at 350° about 30 minutes or until the top is puffed and brown. Let cool several minutes before serving.

Chicken or vegetable broth can be used in place of beef broth

Serves 8.

Edith Barnett's Baked Beans

Eileen Botty

This goes back 4 generations in my family and was always served on Saturday night, usually with Steamed Brown Bread (page 56).

2 cups dried navy beans, soaked overnight	1. Drain beans and add fresh water to cover.
½ pound salt pork	2. Bring to a boil and shut off. Drain.
¼ teaspoon dry mustard	
½ tablespoon brown sugar	3. Cut salt pork and put in the bottom of a crockpot or bean pot. Add mustard, brown sugar and molasses. Stir well.
3 tablespoons molasses	
1 medium onion	
Rind from salt pork, cut up	4. Place onion in middle of beans and top with pork rind. Cover with boiling water.
	5. Cover pot and bake at 250° for 6 to 8 hours.

Serves 4 to 6.

Vegetable Basmati Pilaf with Cashews

Cheryl Bedard

Cinnamon and cloves spike this vibrantly colored Indian dish, creating a wonderfully aromatic blend of flavors. Serve this with Balsamic Molasses Bacon Pork Loin (page 178).

½ cup raw cashews, toasted
2 tablespoons unsalted butter
1 tablespoon vegetable oil
1 medium onion, finely diced
1 clove garlic, minced
½ teaspoon minced fresh gingerroot
½ teaspoon turmeric
⅛ teaspoon cayenne pepper
1 cinnamon stick
2 cloves
1 bay leaf
1 cup white basmati rice
1 pound green beans, cut into 1-inch lengths
1 carrot, very thinly diced
⅓ cup raisins
½ teaspoon salt
1¾ cups boiling water

1. In a large skillet, over medium heat, melt the butter and oil. Add the onion, garlic, ginger and sauté 2 minutes.

2. Mix in the turmeric, cayenne, cinnamon stick, cloves and bay leaf and cook for 1 minute longer, stirring constantly.

3. Mix in the rice and toss to coat.

4. Pour the mixture into a greased 2-quart baking dish.

5. Stir in the green beans, carrot, raisins, cashews and salt. (You can prepare the dish to this point up to 4 hours in advance and refrigerating it.)

6. Pour in the boiling water and tightly cover the casserole.

7. Bake at 400° for 40 minutes or until all of the liquid is absorbed.

8. Remove the cinnamon stick and bay leaf, fluff with a fork, and let stand covered for 5 minutes before serving.

Raw cashews can be found at any natural foods store. A 10-ounce package of frozen cut green beans can be used in place of fresh.

Serves 3 to 4.

Desserts

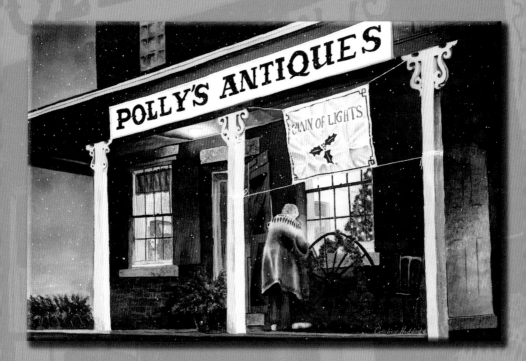

Finishing Touches

Polly's Antiques, Boston Road

At the end of a long day, as the snow begins to fall, Polly is putting finishing touches on an antique wagon wheel before the Chain of Lights celebration. The Brick Block was built in 1839. These bricks were made from a clay field and fired in a kiln on location 1.4 miles west on Boston Road. This building in years past has been a grocery store, general store with a post office, a dance hall and a penny candy store. Around 1964, Polly Putnam Shaw purchased the Brick Block and operated her antique store from there. Currently, her daughter Linda Sinacola displays her original paintings in the building called the Brick Block Art Gallery.

Desserts

Desserts

Almond Cream Cake

Audrey Mingolla

Delicious and so simple to make!

Cake

1 cup heavy cream
1½ cups flour
1 cup sugar
2 teaspoons baking powder
⅛ teaspoon salt
2 eggs
1 teaspoon almond extract

1. In a large bowl, beat cream to stiff peaks.

2. Combine dry ingredients. Add to whipped cream, along with eggs and extract.

3. Line the bottom of an 8-inch springform pan with wax paper. Grease and flour paper and pan. Pour cake into prepared pan. Bake at 350° for 25 minutes.

Topping

2½ tablespoons butter
1½ tablespoons cream
⅓ cup sugar
⅓ cup blanched sliced almonds
1 tablespoon flour

1. In a small saucepan, melt butter and combine cream, sugar and almonds.

2. Add flour and stir over heat, blending well.

3. Spoon over warm cake, just when done, not cooled at all.

4. Place back in oven for 5 to 8 minutes.

5. Cool thoroughly.

Serves 8 to 10.

Fresh Apple Nobby Cake

Ruth S. Putnam

Serve this hot or cold with ice cream or whipped topping.

1	cup granulated sugar
2	tablespoons shortening
1	egg
1	teaspoon vanilla
1	cup flour
1	teaspoon baking soda
½	teaspoon salt
½	teaspoon cinnamon
½	teaspoon nutmeg
3	cups peeled and diced apples

1. In a large bowl, cream sugar, shortening and egg together until light and fluffy.

2. Add vanilla and sifted dry ingredients; mix well.

3. Stir in diced apples and pour into a greased 8 x 8-inch pan.

4. Bake at 350° for 30 minutes.

Blueberry Cake

Jeanne Foster

2	sticks butter
2	cups sugar
3	eggs, beaten
½	cup milk
3	cups flour
1½	teaspoons baking powder
⅛	teaspoon salt
3	cups blueberries

1. In a large bowl, cream butter and sugar.

2. Add eggs, alternating with milk.

3. In a separate bowl, sift together dry ingredients. Add to sugar mixture.

4. Fold in blueberries and carefully pour into a Bundt pan. Sprinkle top of batter with additional sugar.

5. Bake at 350° for 1 hour and 20 minutes.

You can add more blueberries if desired.

Blueberry Lemon Pound Cake

Barbara MH Daigneault

My father, Rene P. Hebert, and I always picked fresh blueberries at Hill Side Farm in West Sutton, Massachusetts. The hint of lemon gives this pound cake a most refreshing taste on the palate. Great as a breakfast bread or served as dessert.

2 cups granulated sugar

1 stick light butter

½ (8-ounce) package ⅓ less fat cream cheese, softened

3 large eggs

1 large egg white

3 cups all-purpose flour, divided

2 cups fresh blueberries

1 teaspoon baking powder

½ teaspoon baking soda

½ teaspoon salt

8 ounces lemon low-fat yogurt

2 teaspoons vanilla extract

½ cup confectioners' sugar

4 teaspoons lemon juice

1. Beat first 3 ingredients at medium speed of a mixer until well-blended, about 5 minutes.

2. Add eggs and egg white, 1 at a time, beating well after each addition.

3. Lightly spoon flour into dry measuring cups. Level with a knife. Combine 2 tablespoons flour and blueberries in a small bowl and toss well. Combine remaining flour, baking powder, baking soda and salt.

4. Add flour mixture to sugar mixture alternately with yogurt, beginning and ending with flour mixture.

5. Fold in blueberry mixture and vanilla. Pour cake batter into a lightly greased 10-inch tube pan.

6. Bake at 350° for 1 hour and 10 minutes or until a wooden pick inserted in center comes out clean. Cool the cake in pan 10 minutes. Remove from pan.

7. Combine confectioners' sugar and lemon juice in a small bowl. Drizzle over warm cake. Cut with a serrated knife.

Yields 16 servings.

Turtle "B" Cake

Penny Thompson

My honey takes full credit for this fabulous cake. Even though I did the baking, he claims ownership as he bought me the cookbook. This makes a great birthday cake.

1   box German chocolate cake
    mix
1   (14-ounce) bag caramels
½   cup evaporated milk
¾   cup butter, melted
1   cup chocolate chips (white or
    milk chocolate)
2   cups chopped nuts, divided
    (optional)
    Whipped cream or ice cream
    for topping
    Fresh strawberries for garnish

1. Prepare cake mix according to package directions. Pour half the batter into a greased Bundt pan.

2. Bake at 350° for 15 minutes.

3. In a medium bowl, melt caramels with evaporated milk and butter. Stir constantly.

4. Pour over cake. Sprinkle with chocolate chips and 1 cup of nuts.

5. Pour remaining batter over filling. Sprinkle with remaining nuts.

6. Bake an additional 20 minutes.

7. Serve with a dollop of ice cream or sweetened whipped cream.

You may omit the chopped nuts and add additional chocolate chips.

Serves 8 to 10.

Chocolate Roll with Sinful Chocolate Sauce

Audrey Mingolla

This recipe came from Ruth Goldstein, a former member at Pleasant Valley Country Club, in Sutton, Massachusetts. My family still calls this "Mrs. Goldstein's Chocolate Jelly Roll".

Chocolate Cake

¼ cup cocoa
¾ cup flour
1 teaspoon baking powder
½ teaspoon salt
3 eggs
1 cup sugar
1 teaspoon vanilla
⅓ cup hot water
2 tablespoons confectioners' sugar

1. In a small bowl, sift together first 4 ingredients; mix well.

2. In a large mixing bowl, beat eggs at high speed until lemon colored. Gradually add sugar 1 tablespoon at a time; add vanilla. Reduce speed to low.

3. Add dry ingredients to egg mixture only until folded. Add water all at once. Beat to a smooth batter.

4. Grease a jelly roll pan (15½ x 10½-inches) and line bottom and sides of pan with wax paper. Grease wax paper. Pour batter into pan. Bang on counter to get air bubbles out.

5. Bake, with rack positioned in the center of oven, at 375° for 12 to 14 minutes.

6. Sift confectioners' sugar on cake while still hot. Place another piece of wax paper across top of cake and cover with a clean dish towel. Turn upside down onto a cooling rack. Peel off first piece of wax paper and dust this side with confectioners' sugar.

7. Roll cake up with towel, to prevent it from sticking to itself, the long way and cool.

8. When cool, unroll the cake, still leaving it on the towel and spread with the filling, making sure to fill with whipped cream almost to the ends.

9. Roll cake up, this time without the towel extra gently, being careful not to squeeze the filling out the ends.

10. Transfer to a good-sized serving platter. This cake freezes well wrapped in plastic wrap.

Filling

1   pint heavy cream
⅓   cup brown sugar
½   teaspoon instant coffee

1. Combine filling ingredients and chill for ½ hour.

2. Beat until whipped cream.

Chocolate Sauce

1   stick butter
2   unsweetened chocolate
      squares
1½ cups sugar
1   cup light cream
2   teaspoons vanilla

1. In a saucepan, combine first 4 ingredients.

2. Bring to a boil and let it bubble twice. Remove from heat and add 2 teaspoons vanilla. Cool.

If chocolate sauce is too thick, add a few drops of milk.

Chocolate-Hazelnut Cake

Eileen Pastner

Filling

½ cup whipping cream
1   tablespoon light corn syrup
8   ounces imported milk
    chocolate, finely chopped
½   cup hazelnuts, toasted and
    husked
2   teaspoons confectioners' sugar

1. In heavy small saucepan, bring cream and corn syrup to simmer.

2. Place chocolate in medium bowl. Pour hot cream mixture over and let stand 1 minute. Stir until chocolate melts and mixture is smooth; set aside.

3. Blend hazelnuts and sugar in processor until paste forms, stopping occasionally to scrape down sides.

4. Stir paste into chocolate mixture. Refrigerate until cool but still spreadable, about 2 hours.

Cake

1   cup sifted all-purpose flour
⅓   cup unsweetened cocoa
    powder
½   teaspoon salt
¼   teaspoon baking powder
¼   teaspoon baking soda
1½ tablespoons hot water
1   tablespoon instant espresso
    powder or instant coffee
    powder
½   cup buttermilk
1½ sticks unsalted butter, room
    temperature
1⅓ cups sugar
1   teaspoon vanilla extract
3   large eggs

1. Sift first 5 ingredients into a medium bowl.

2. In a small bowl, stir hot water and espresso powder until espresso dissolves. Mix in buttermilk.

3. In a large bowl, using an electric mixer beat the butter until light and fluffy. Gradually beat in sugar and vanilla. Add eggs 1 at a time, beating well after each addition.

4. Beat in dry ingredients alternately with buttermilk mixture in two additions each.

5. Butter a 9-inch diameter cake pan with 2-inch sides. Line bottom with parchment paper and dust with flour, tapping out excess. Pour batter into pan.

6. Bake at 350° for 45 minutes or until toothpick inserted into center comes out clean. Cool the cake in pan on rack 5 minutes. Turn out cake onto rack. Peel off parchment. Turn right side up onto another rack and cool.

7. Using a wooden spoon, beat filling until slightly softened and lightened in color, about 30 seconds.

8. Cut cake horizontally in half. Place 1 layer cut side up on platter. Slide waxed paper strips under edges of cake. Spread half of filling over cake. Top with second layer, cut side down. Spread remaining filling over top and sides of cake. Chill 10 minutes.

Glaze

6	ounces bittersweet (not unsweetened) or semisweet chocolate, chopped
1	stick unsalted butter, cut into pieces
1	tablespoon light corn syrup
12	whole hazelnuts, husked

1. In the top of a double boiler over simmering water, combine chocolate, butter and syrup. Stir until smooth. Remove from over water. Cool to lukewarm, stirring occasionally.

2. Pour glaze in pool over center of cake. Using icing spatula spread over top and sides of cake.

3. Arrange 12 nuts around top edge of cake. Remove waxed paper.

Can be made 1 day ahead. Cover with cake dome and chill. Let stand 1 hour at room temperature before serving.

Serves 12.

Fudge Cake for Chocolate Lovers

Rita E. Johnson

A dense, rich cake.

⅓ cup butter
⅓ cup margarine
1¾ cups sugar
2 eggs
1 teaspoon vanilla
2½ ounces baking chocolate, melted and cooled
2¼ cups all-purpose flour
1½ teaspoons baking soda
½ teaspoon salt
1½ cups ice water

1. In a large bowl, cream together butter, margarine and sugar.

2. Add eggs and vanilla, beating until light and fluffy. Beat 5 minutes. Blend in the cooled chocolate.

3. Sift together flour, soda and salt. Add to creamed mixture alternating with the ice water. Pour into two greased 8-inch or 9-inch layer pans.

4. Bake at 350° for 30 to 35 minutes, use a tester. Cool completely. Frost with dark chocolate icing.

Dump Cake

Penny Nunnemacher

1 (20-ounce) can cherry pie filling
1 (20-ounce) can crushed pineapple
1 box yellow cake mix
1 cup shredded coconut
1 cup chopped walnuts
2 sticks butter, melted

1. In a greased 11 x 9-inch glass baking dish, layer ingredients as listed above.

2. Drizzle melted butter over entire cake pan.

3. Bake at 350° for 1 hour and 15 minutes.

Serves 8.

Molten Chocolate Cakes with Cherry Sauce

Rebecca Smith

*I love this desert because you can prepare it ahead and so easy
and when you serve, it looks fabulous! You can serve these with ice cream,
cream, any fruit or chocolate sauce. Have fun and be creative!*

Cakes

5   ounces bittersweet or
    semisweet chocolate,
    chopped
1¼ sticks butter
3   large eggs
3   large egg yolks
1½ cups confectioners' sugar
½   cup flour

1. Melt chocolate and butter; cool.

2. Mix eggs, egg yolks, sugar and
flour and add to chocolate
mixture.

3. Grease 6 large muffin tins or
custard cups and fill.

4. Bake at 450° for 11 to 14 minutes.

*Batter can be made a day ahead. Place
batter in muffin tins, cover and chill until
ready to bake.*

Cherry Sauce

1   (16-ounce) bag frozen, dark,
    pitted sweet cherries
    (do not drain)
¾   cup sugar
¼   cup Kirsch, brandy or cherry
    brandy
¼   teaspoon cinnamon

1. In a saucepan, combine all
ingredients. Stir over medium heat
until sugar dissolves and sauce
thickens.

*These cherries can be found in most
health food stores.*

Serves 6.

Carrot Zucchini Cake with Pineapple Glaze

Nancy C. Corey

Cake

3 cups flour

½ cup sugar

2 teaspoons cinnamon

2 teaspoons baking soda

1 teaspoon baking powder

1 teaspoon salt

½ teaspoon ground ginger

1 (20-ounce) can crushed pineapple

1 cup packed light brown sugar

1 (8-ounce) container Eggbeaters (thawed)

⅔ cup salad oil

1 tablespoon vanilla extract

2 cups shredded carrots (3-4 large)

1 cup shredded zucchini (1 medium)

1 cup dark seedless raisins

1. In a large bowl, combine first 7 ingredients.

2. Drain pineapple well, reserving juice.

3. In a medium bowl, whisk together drained pineapple, brown sugar, Eggbeaters, salad oil and vanilla until smooth.

4. Stir pineapple mixture, carrots, zucchini and raisins into the flour mixture just until flour is moistened.

5. Pour batter into a greased Bundt pan. Bake at 350° for 1 hour and 5 minutes or until toothpick inserted into center of cake comes out clean. Cool the cake in pan on wire rack for 10 minutes. Remove cake from pan and cool completely on rack and glaze.

Pineapple Glaze

¾ cup confectioners' sugar

2½ teaspoons reserved pineapple juice

1. In a small bowl, mix sugar with pineapple juice to make a spreadable glaze. With a spoon, drizzle glaze over top of cake, allowing some to drip down the sides.

Serves 16.

Traditional Carrot Cake

Cheryl Bedard

*This recipe went around the pre-schoolers moms group that
I belonged to years ago in California. It is the best carrot cake I have had.*

2	cups sugar
4	eggs
1½	cups vegetable oil
2	cups flour
2	teaspoons baking soda
1	teaspoon cinnamon
1	teaspoon salt
3	cups grated carrot (about 3 large)
2	teaspoons vanilla extract

1. In a large bowl, beat together sugar, eggs and oil. In a separate bowl, sift together flour, baking soda, cinnamon and salt; add to moist mixture. Mix well.

2. Add carrots and vanilla; blend.

3. Pour into a greased and floured 13 x 9-inch pan. Bake at 350° for 30 to 40 minutes. Apply icing once cooled.

Icing

1	stick butter, softened
1	(8-ounce) package cream cheese, softened
1	(1-pound) box confectioners' sugar
1	teaspoon vanilla extract
1	cup chopped walnuts (optional)

1. Cream together butter and cream cheese.

2. Add remaining ingredients and mix well.

Marbled Cheesecake (Low Fat)

Barbara MH Daigneault

Low fat cheesecake and it tastes good? You bet! Wait until you try this one, it is sinfully delicious without the fat and calories, only 289 calories and 5 grams of fat.

Crust

1   cup chocolate wafer crumbs (about 18)

1   tablespoon unsalted butter, melted

1. In a small bowl, combine crumbs and butter. Mix well.

2. Press into bottom of an 8-inch springform pan. Wrap outside of pan with heavy-duty foil. Set aside.

Filling

3   (8-ounce) packages nonfat cream cheese, softened

1¼ cups granulated sugar

1   cup nonfat sour cream

1   tablespoon all-purpose flour

2   teaspoons vanilla extract

2   large eggs

2   (2-ounce) squares semisweet chocolate, melted

1. In a large bowl, using an electric mixer beat cream cheese and sugar on medium speed for 2 minutes.

2. Beat in sour cream, flour and vanilla. Add the eggs, 1 at a time, beating well after each addition.

3. Transfer 1½ cups of batter to a small bowl; stir in chocolate.

4. Spread half of vanilla batter over crust. Top with half of chocolate batter.

5. Spoon the remaining vanilla batter over chocolate batter. Top with remaining chocolate batter.

6. Using a knife, gently swirl batters together.

7. Place pan in a shallow roasting pan. Add enough boiling water to come half way up the sides of springform pan.

8. Bake at 325° for 1 hour and 15 minutes or until just set. Place pan on a wire rack and cool to room temperature. Cover and chill for 4 hours.

Serves 10.

Eggnog Bundt Cake

Carrie Daigneault

Cake
1   (18.25-ounce) pudding-added
     yellow cake mix
     Vegetable oil, according to
     package directions
     Eggs, according to package
     directions
1   teaspoon nutmeg
     Eggnog, substituted for water
     on package directions

1. Combine dry cake mix with required oil, eggs and nutmeg. Omit the water, adding the same amount of eggnog in its place; mix well.

2. Pour into a greased Bundt pan and bake according to package directions. Cool. Top with Eggnog Glaze.

Glaze
2   cups confectioners' sugar
2   tablespoons butter, softened
1   teaspoon vanilla extract
3   tablespoons eggnog

1. In a medium bowl, combine all ingredients, adding enough eggnog for desired consistency.

Serves 12.

Holiday Cake

Cathleen Haddad

This recipe was given to my mother from her aunt,
Sister Mary Zeno from the Order of the Sister's of Providence. Sister Mary Zeno
worked with foster children in North Carolina for many years. I make this cake
once a year because I love it so much and can't resist eating most of it myself,
just one sliver at a time. It's a dense cake and so easy to make.

4 cups flour, divided
2 cups chopped pecans
2½ cups white raisins
4 sticks butter
2 cups sugar
6 eggs
2 tablespoons lemon or almond
     extract

1. In small bowl, combine 1 cup of flour with pecans and raisins. Set aside.

2. In a large bowl using an electric mixer, cream butter and sugar; add eggs and extract.

3. Blend in remaining flour and nut mixture. Mix well.

4. Pour into a greased and floured Bundt pan. Bake at 325° for 1½ hours or until tested done.

Perfect Pineapple Cheesecake

Paula Carafotes

*This recipe originated from my sister-in-law Victoria Macrokanis
and has been enjoyed at our holiday tables for many years.*

Crust

1¼ cups graham cracker crumbs
2   tablespoons sugar
4   tablespoons butter, melted

1. Mix all ingredients and put in a 9-inch springform pan. Pack down with a spoon to form a crust.

2. Bake crust at 350° for 10 minutes. Remove from oven and set aside.

Filling

3   eggs
1   cup granulated sugar
2   (8-ounce) packages cream
     cheese, softened
1   teaspoon vanilla

1. Beat eggs and sugar; add cream cheese and vanilla; mix well. Make sure the mixture is smooth.

2. Pour into crust. Bake at 350° for 50 minutes or until center is firm to touch. Cool completely.

Do not use low fat cream cheese.

Pineapple Glaze

2   (8-ounce) cans pineapple
     chunks, drained and reserve
     liquid
½   cup sugar
2   tablespoons cornstarch
2-3 drops yellow food coloring

1. In a small saucepan, combine reserved pineapple juice, sugar, cornstarch and food coloring. Heat and stir until mixture thickens.

2. Remove from heat and stir in pineapple chunks. Cool thoroughly.

3. Pour over cooled cheesecake and refrigerate for at least 3 hours.

Ricotta Cheese Cake

Karen Thibodeau

This is not your traditional cheesecake. It is truly a cheese cake.

1 box yellow cake mix
2 pounds ricotta cheese
4 eggs
1 teaspoon vanilla
1 cup sugar

1. Prepare cake mix according to package directions. Pour cake mix into a greased 13 x 9-inch baking pan.

2. Combine remaining ingredients and mix well. Pour ricotta mixture over cake mix.

3. Bake, uncovered, at 350° for 1 hour and 30 minutes or until toothpick inserted in the center comes out clean.

Cheese will sink and cake will rise with baking.

Topsy Turvey Cake

Blanche Charest

*This can be made with any kind of cake mix and pie filling.
Try a spice cake with apple pie filling, yellow cake with raspberry pie filling or devil's food cake with cherry pie filling.*

1 box cake mix
1 (10½-ounce) package mini marshmallows
1 (21-ounce) can pie filling

1. Mix cake according to package directions.

2. In a greased 13 x 9-inch pan, cover bottom with marshmallows.

3. Put cake mix on top of marshmallows. Put pie filling on top of cake mix.

4. Bake at 350° for 40 to 45 minutes. The cherries will sink to the bottom and the marshmallows will float to the top. No need to frost.

Old-Fashioned Gingerbread

Deborah Dutton

This recipe has been in the family for generations. A typical comment after serving this is "this is the best gingerbread I have ever had!"

½   cup shortening
½   cup sugar
1   cup molasses
2   cups flour
½   teaspoon ground ginger
½   teaspoon cinnamon
1   cup boiling water
1   teaspoon baking soda
1   egg
    Homemade whipped cream

1. In a large bowl, beat together shortening, sugar and molasses.

2. Add flour, ginger and cinnamon. Mix well.

3. Dissolve 1 cup boiling water into baking soda. Add immediately to mixture and mix well.

4. Add egg and mix well.

5. Pour into a greased 9 x 9-inch glass baking dish. Bake at 325° for 50 minutes. Serve with homemade whipped cream.

Ida's Swedish Tea Cakes

Lillian Peterson

¾   cup sugar
2   eggs
⅔   cup flour
1½ teaspoons almond extract
1   stick butter, melted and cooled

1. In a large bowl, beat sugar and eggs until thick.

2. Add flour and almond extract. Add cooled butter.

3. Pour into a greased 8 x 8-inch baking dish. Bake at 350° for 25 minutes. Cool before cutting.

Hummingbird Cake

Diane Lavoie

An excellent cake for bake sales!

Cake

3   cups all-purpose flour
2   cups sugar
1   teaspoon cinnamon
1   teaspoon baking soda
½   teaspoon salt
1   (8-ounce) can crushed
    pineapple
1   cup cooking oil
3   large eggs, well beaten
2   cups chopped banana
    (3 bananas)
½   cup finely chopped walnuts or
    pecans
1½ teaspoons vanilla extract

1. In a large mixing bowl, stir together the flour, sugar, cinnamon, baking soda and salt.

2. Remove 2 tablespoons of the juice from the can of pineapple. Set aside for the glaze.

3. Add the pineapple with remaining juice, oil, eggs, banana, nuts and vanilla to the flour mixture. Stir until just blended (do not beat).

4. Pour batter into a generously greased 10-inch tube pan. Bake at 325° for about 1 hour and 10 minutes or until a wooden toothpick inserted near the center comes out clean. Cool in the pan for 15 minutes. Invert the cake onto a wire rack and remove the cake from the pan. Cool completely.

Glaze

1   tablespoon butter, melted
1   cup sifted confectioners' sugar

1. In a small bowl, combine the melted butter and sugar.

2. Add enough of the reserved pineapple juice to make a glaze of drizzling consistency.

3. Drizzle the glaze over the cooled cake.

Serves 12.

Irma's Fruitcake

From the Kitchen of Irma B. Whitney
submitted by her daughter Karen Melia

*This was a Christmas tradition for my mother, as it was with
her mother. Friends and relatives all received an Irma's Fruitcake and they were
truly a labor of her love, whether eaten or passed on. I miss them.*

1	pound golden raisins
½	pound seedless raisins
¼	pound currants
½	cup rum
1	pound mixed (candied) fruit
¼	pound chopped walnuts
¼	pound sliced almonds
2	cups flour, divided
¼	teaspoon ground mace
½	teaspoon cinnamon
½	teaspoon baking soda
1	stick butter
1	cup sugar
1	cup packed brown sugar
5	eggs, slightly beaten
1	tablespoon milk
1	teaspoon almond extract
	Rum or brandy for wrapping

1. The day before making, combine the raisins and currants with ½ cup rum; toss and let stand covered overnight.

2. On the baking day, line tube or angel food pan with greased brown paper.

3. Add candied fruits and nuts to raisin mixture and mix well.

4. Sift 1½ cups flour with spices and baking soda.

5. Mix ½ cup flour with fruits and nuts. Beat butter until light. Add sugar and brown sugar and beat until fluffy.

6. Beat in eggs, milk and almond extract.

7. Add flour and mix with fruit and nuts.

8. Turn into lined pan. Bake at 275° for 3 hours and 15 minutes.

To store: wrap cake in cheesecloth (or white sheet material) soaked with rum or brandy. Refrigerate overnight. To use loaf pans instead of tube pan, use 2 loaf pans. Bake approximately 1½ hours. Test with toothpick for doneness.

White Fruitcake

From the Kitchen of Emily Swindell
submitted by her daughter Janice Swindell

My mother made this recipe every Christmas. It was a very pretty and colorful fruitcake. One Christmas, when Mom was mixing the cake batter, Ed MacLaren came to see Dad about something. He saw what was in the mixing bowl and said "this looks like the morning after the night before". Leave it to Ed!

1½ cups sugar

2 sticks butter

4 eggs, separated, whites beaten separately

1 cup milk

4 cups flour

2 teaspoons baking powder

1½ cups chopped hickory nuts

½ pound glazed pineapple, cut very fine

½ pound glazed or candied cherries, cut very fine

1. In a large bowl, cream sugar and butter.

2. Add egg yolks, milk and beaten egg whites.

3. In a separate bowl, blend flour and baking powder.

4. Rub in fruit and nuts.

5. Add flour/fruit mixture to sugar mixture. Blend together.

6. Pour in two 8½ x 4½-inch metal loaf pans. Bake at 350° for 1 hour and 30 minutes.

Pudding Cake

Dawn Uppstrom

Cake

1   box yellow cake mix
1   cup water
4   eggs
1   (3-ounce) package instant chocolate pudding
1   cup oil

1. In a large bowl, mix together cake mix, water, eggs, pudding and oil. Beat with an electric mixer until smooth.

2. Pour into 2 greased and floured 9 x 9-inch metal cake pans. Bake at 350° for 28 to 30 minutes.

Frosting

1   (3-ounce) package instant chocolate pudding
1   (3-ounce) package instant vanilla pudding
1   pint all-purpose or whipping cream
2   cups milk

1. While cake is baking, whip pudding with cream and milk until thick enough to frost the cake. Frost cakes when completely cooled.

This can also be make in a Bundt pan.

Serves 15 to 20.

Neena's Spice Cake

Denise Harrison

This recipe was a favorite of my grandmothers. She made it every Thanksgiving and Christmas when I was growing up. It was a much-loved dessert by everyone.

2   cups flour
1   cup sugar
1½ sticks butter
1   teaspoon ground cloves
1   teaspoon cinnamon
1   egg
1   cup milk with 1 teaspoon baking soda added to sour

1. In a large bowl, combine flour, sugar and butter to form a crumb mixture. Reserve ½ cup of the crumbs for topping.

2. Add cloves, cinnamon, egg and sour milk to flour mixture; blend well.

3. Pour into a greased 8 x 8-inch baking dish. Sprinkle with reserved crumb mixture. Bake at 350° for 30 minutes.

Nutmeg Feather Cake

Betty Benjamin LeClaire

Quick, light and not too sweet.

1 stick butter
1½ cups sugar
½ teaspoon vanilla extract
3 eggs
2 cups flour
2 teaspoons ground nutmeg
1 teaspoon baking soda
1 teaspoon baking powder
¼ teaspoon salt
1 cup buttermilk
Confectioners' sugar for
dusting

1. In a large bowl, cream together butter, sugar, vanilla and eggs. Mix well.

2. Add dry ingredients to creamed mixture alternately with milk.

3. Pour into a greased and floured 12 x 9-inch metal baking pan. Bake at 350° for 35 to 40 minutes. When cooled, dust with confectioners' sugar.

In place of buttermilk, you may use 1 tablespoon of lemon juice or 1 tablespoon of apple cider vinegar plus whole milk to make 1 cup.

Rhubarb Cake

From the Kitchen of Barbara Gurney Weaver
submitted by her niece Pamela Gurney Farnum

1 package white Jiffy cake mix
3 cups rhubarb, cut into ½-inch
pieces
1¾ cups sugar
2 eggs
Whipped cream for topping

1. Prepare cake mix according to package directions.

2. Pour half of mixture into a greased 9 x 9-inch pan.

3. Combine remaining ingredients and pour over mixture in pan; top with remaining cake batter.

4. Bake at 350° for 30 minutes. Serve warm with whipped cream.

Old-Fashioned Buttermilk Pound Cake

Laila Helgerson

This is a favorite cake to be kept in the freezer for last minute desserts. Serve with ice cream and sauce or fresh fruit and whipped cream. It is also delicious just by itself.

1	stick butter
½	cup shortening
2	cups sugar
4	eggs
½	teaspoon baking soda
1	cup buttermilk
3	cups flour
½	teaspoon salt
2	teaspoons lemon extract
1	teaspoon almond extract

1. In a large bowl, cream butter and shortening.

2. Gradually add sugar, beating well at medium speed of electric mixer. Add eggs one at a time.

3. Dissolve soda in buttermilk.

4. Combine flour and salt; add to creamed mixture alternately with buttermilk, beginning and ending with flour mixture. Mix just until blended after each addition.

5. Stir in flavorings.

6. Pour batter into a greased and floured 10-inch tube pan, or two 9 x 5-inch loaf pans. Bake at 350° for 1 hour. If using bread pans, bake for 45 to 50 minutes.

One tablespoon lemon juice or vinegar added to regular milk can be substituted for buttermilk.

Pistachio Crumb Cake

Donna Marie Swart

This recipe was given to me from my best friend's sister and has been a hit at every party. Many people have asked me for this recipe and have made it. It's great because this cake freezes well. I am known as the "Pistachio Cake Lady"

Nut Mixture

¾ cup sugar
1 cup finely chopped walnuts or pecans
4 tablespoons cinnamon

1. In a small bowl, combine all ingredients. Mix well and set aside.

Batter

1 box yellow or butter cake mix
1 (3-ounce) box pistachio instant pudding
½ cup vegetable oil
1 tablespoon almond extract
8 ounces sour cream
4 eggs
 Confectioners' sugar for dusting

1. In a large bowl, combine all ingredients together with a wooden spoon; mix well.

2. Pour ½ of batter into a greased and floured Bundt pan. Spread ½ of the nut mixture on top, then the remaining batter and top with the remaining nut mixture.

3. Bake at 350° for 1 hour. Remove from pan and dust with confectioners' sugar.

Do not use an electric mixer to blend. Low fat or fat free sour cream can be used.

Serves 12 to 16.

Pumpkin Roll with Cream Cheese Filling

Debbie Costa

This dessert is a family favorite at Thanksgiving or Christmas. It is great for brunches and office functions, too. I usually bring extra copies of the recipe with me, since I always get several requests for it whenever I make it.

Pumpkin Roll

3 eggs
1 cup sugar
⅔ cup pumpkin (canned or fresh)
1 teaspoon baking soda
1 teaspoon cinnamon
¾ cup flour
  Confectioners' sugar for dusting

1. In a large bowl, beat together eggs and sugar.

2. Add next 4 ingredients and mix well.

3. Pour into a greased and floured jelly-roll pan (14 x 11 x 1-inch). Bake at 375° for approximately 15 minutes. Let cool a few minutes and then carefully lift out of the pan. Do not flip it over!

4. Place on a towel and sprinkle with confectioners' sugar. Then roll it up the long way with the towel. Let cool for a few more minutes while making the filling.

Cream Cheese Filling

1 (8-ounce) package cream cheese, softened
4 tablespoons butter
½ teaspoon vanilla extract
1 cup confectioners' sugar
½ cup chopped nuts (optional)

1. Combine all ingredients and mix until well blended.

2. Remove pumpkin roll from towel and evenly spread filling over top, leaving ½-inch from all sides.

3. Roll up again without the towel and wrap in aluminum foil. Chill for approximately 1 hour before slicing.

This can also be frozen until ready to serve. You may also use wax paper to roll the cake in place of a towel.

Pie Crust

Gretel Smith

I learned how to make pie crust from my mother, Albertine Putnam and my Home Economic teacher, Mrs. Agnes Davagian. However, it was my sister-in-law, Barbara Smith who taught me the secret of keeping it tender and flaky by increasing shortening to half the amount of the flour and using as little water as possible.

2 cups flour
1 teaspoon salt
1 cup shortening, divided
6-7 tablespoons ice water

1. Sift together flour and salt.

2. Add ½ of the shortening and blend until pieces are the size of small peas. Repeat with second half of shortening.

3. Add water one tablespoon at a time, blending with a fork until moistened enough to form a ball. Use as little water as necessary.

4. Roll out ½ of the ball on a lightly floured surface, rolling ball from the center out until large enough to fill a 9 to 10-inch pie plate.

5. Trim the edge even with edge of pie plate. Add favorite filling.

6. Do the same for the top crust, only trim ½-inch beyond edge of plate. Turn the crust under and flute edge. Be sure to vent top crust with slits.

7. To brown the top crust, sprinkle with sugar and dot with butter.

8. Depending on the filling, bake at 425° for 15 minutes. Reduce temperature to 375° and continue cooking until browned, about 30 to 40 minutes.

Cooking spray works well as a substitute for butter in browning the top crust.

Diane's Easy Apple Pie with Perfect Pie Crust

Diane Lavoie

Perfect Pie Crust

4   cups flour
1½ cups shortening
1   tablespoon sugar
2   teaspoons salt
1   tablespoon vinegar
1   egg
½   cup water

1. In a large bowl, combine first 4 ingredients with a fork.

2. In a separate bowl, combine liquids.

3. Combine the two mixtures.

4. Mold dough into a ball.

Dough can be left in refrigerator up to 3 days or can be frozen until ready to use.

Yields 2 (9-inch) pie crusts.

Filling

1   cup sugar
¼   teaspoon salt
2   tablespoons flour (approximately)
6   McIntosh or Cortland apples, peeled and sliced
1   tablespoon butter
1   teaspoon cinnamon (optional)

1. Sift dry ingredients and mix with apples.

2. Line pan with pastry; fill with apple mixture. Dot top with butter and cover with top crust. Slit top with holes as vents.

3. Bake at 450° for 15 minutes. Reduce heat to 350° and bake an additional 45 minutes or longer.

You may brush the top crust with milk or egg before baking. Also, may wrap edges with foil if browning too rapidly.

Zucchini "Apple" Pie

Cathleen Haddad

You truly will not believe this is actually made with zucchini, it tastes just like apple pie. You really have to try it to believe it. My husband's cousin, Joanne Murphy, gave this recipe to me years ago. It's a great way to use all those overgrown zucchini's in the garden.

4 cups sliced zucchini, cooked until tender crisp
2 tablespoons lemon juice
Dash of salt
1¼ cups sugar
1½ teaspoons cinnamon
1½ teaspoons cream of tartar
Dash of nutmeg
3 tablespoons flour
2 (9-inch) pie crusts
2 tablespoons butter

1. Peel and cut zucchini in quarters lengthwise, remove the seeds and slice crosswise.

2. In a large bowl, toss together zucchini, lemon juice and salt. In a separate large bowl, combine sugar, cinnamon, cream of tartar, nutmeg and flour.

3. Add the zucchini and mix well. It will be runny, but that's OK.

4. Pour the filling into a 9-inch pie crust and dot with butter. Add the top crust. Bake at 400° for 40 minutes or until golden brown.

Use big zucchinis, but still tender enough that you can pierce the skin easily with your thumbnail.

Butterscotch Pie

Becky (Lavalley) Vaundell

Every Thanksgiving and Christmas holiday, my mom would make her famous Butterscotch Pie. Her eleven children have carried on this tradition. Her children, grandchildren and great-grandchildren still treasure this special holiday treat.

1   cup light brown sugar
1   cup dark brown sugar
4   oversized tablespoons flour
4   tablespoons butter, melted
4   egg yolks, reserve whites in a
     separate bowl
4   cups evaporated milk
1   teaspoon vanilla
1   (8 or 9-inch) Pie Crust
     (see page 280)

1. In a 2-quart saucepan, combine the two sugars and flour.

2. Add melted butter and mix well.

3. Add egg yolks and stir.

4. Gradually stir in the evaporated milk. Cook over medium high heat, stirring constantly until it thickens.

5. Remove from heat and stir in vanilla. Pour into a cooked pie shell.

6. Beat egg whites until it peaks. Pour on top of pie filling.

7. Bake at 350° until it browns lightly. Refrigerate to cool and serve.

Coconut Custard Pie

From the Memories of Helen's Kitchen
submitted by their nephew Mark Bailey

As a young boy of twelve, I began working in my aunts' bakery, Helen's Kitchen in Millbury. Four sisters, known in town as the "Bailey Girls", began working at this establishment during high school when it was operated as Fischer's Grocery. Years later their friend Helen O'Brien purchased it and hence it received the name Helen's Kitchen which could be seen in gold and black letters on two large storefront windows for decades. When my aunts Gladys, Edith, Mamie and Alta, purchased it, the business retained the name of their good and loyal friend. A fifth sister Dorothy joined them at work in the bakery. I vividly recall the wonderful aromas of pastry as I opened the door and entered the front sales room ready for work at 7:00 a.m. on Saturday mornings. The "girls" would have already been working since 5:30 a.m. making tantalizing treats to fill the pastry cases. At first, I learned the ropes of a job that required much more effort than I had every imagined. Baking bread, peeling apples on an antique peeler that had longed for retirement fifty years earlier and baking pies and tarts in the same gas ovens still in use since the late 1800's. Saturdays brought lines of customers causing a continuous hustle-bustle as "the girls" catered to their requests. During the following six years I baked, washed pots, pans, floors and attended to any job asked of me. I look back with fond memories of a rare opportunity to experience a unique family business that was truly the end of a by-gone era. This is a favorite recipe taken from an old tin box that sat on the side-baking table of Helen's Kitchen. I hope you enjoy this as much as I do.

3 eggs	1. Combine all ingredients.
½ cup sugar	2. Pour mixture into pan lined with crust. Bake at 400° for 15 minutes. Reduce heat to 350° and bake an additional 30 minutes.
3 cups milk	
1 cup coconut	
Dash of salt	
2 teaspoons vanilla extract	
1 pie shell	

Cranberry Raisin Pie

From the Kitchen of Eunice Perry King
submitted by her son Reverend David King

This pie is a real favorite!

1 cup cranberries, cut in two
1 cup raisins
1 cup sugar
1 tablespoon flour
1 cup water
1 teaspoon vanilla extract
2 pie shells

1. Combine all ingredients.

2. Pour into a crust line pie pan. Cover with top crust. Bake, on bottom rack, at 400° for 10 minutes, then move to middle rack and reduce heat to 350° for 40 minutes or until done.

There were no cooking instructions with this recipe, however, these instructions were taken from The Boston Cooking School Cook Book by Fannie Merritt Farmer, dated 1836.

Ricotta Rice Pie

Angela M. Bailey

8 eggs
½ cup cooked rice, cooled
2 pounds ricotta cheese
2 cups sugar
  Juice of ½ lemon
¼ teaspoon cinnamon
¼ teaspoon vanilla
  Grated rind of 1 lemon (optional)
  Grated rind of 1 orange (optional)
1 (10 to 12-inch) unbaked pie shell (or 2 smaller ones)

1. Beat eggs until fluffy and set aside.

2. Combine remaining ingredients and add to egg mixture. Add grated rinds if desired.

3. Pour into unbaked pie shell. Bake at 350° for 1 hour.

Luscious Lemon Sponge Pie

From the Kitchen of Mary Kortekamp
submitted by her daughter Joy Reece

This is my sister Joan's favorite recipe. My mother was known for her baking. My sister Joan did not take after Mom and does not enjoy baking, however, this one she will attempt.

3 tablespoons butter

1½ cups sugar

⅛ teaspoon salt

⅓ cup lemon juice
Grated rind of 1 lemon (optional)

3 eggs, separated, reserve whites

3 tablespoons flour

1½ cups milk

1 (9-inch) unbaked pastry crust

1. In a large bowl, cream together butter, sugar and salt.

2. Add lemon juice, lemon rind and egg yolks. Beat until light and fluffy.

3. In a small bowl, mix flour with small amounts of milk and whisk until smooth.

4. Add remaining milk and combine with creamed mixture.

5. Fold in stiffly beaten egg whites.

6. Pour into unbaked pastry shell. Bake at 425° for 10 minutes. Reduce heat to 325° and bake an additional 45 minutes.

Dreamy High Pumpkin Pie

Nicole Crocker

I won first place at Keown's Orchard Pumpkin Pie Bake-Off.
This recipe was handed down from my husband Mark's aunt Louise Ewing,
who has passed away. It is a "Prize Winning" pie.

⅔ cup sugar
1 envelope unflavored gelatin
1 teaspoon cinnamon
½ teaspoon salt
¼ teaspoon nutmeg
3 egg yolks, separated, slightly beaten, reserve whites
¾ cup milk
1¼ cups canned pumpkin
3 egg whites, beaten stiff
⅓ cup sugar
1 (10-inch) pie crust
½ cup heavy cream, whipped
½ cup toasted coconut

1. In a large saucepan, combine sugar, gelatin, cinnamon, salt and nutmeg.

2. In a small bowl, combine egg yolks and milk and add to dry ingredients.

3. Cook, stirring constantly, until mixture thickens slightly.

4. Stir in pumpkin.

5. Chill until mixture mounds slightly when spooned, stirring often, about 30 minutes.

6. Beat egg whites, gradually add sugar, beat to stiff peaks.

7. Fold chilled pumpkin mixture into egg whites.

8. Pour into crust. Chill until firm. Top with whipped cream and coconut.

Fresh Strawberry Pie

Foppema's Farm, Northbridge, Massachusetts
submitted by Lisa Foppema

*This pie is always best when made with fresh picked strawberries
available only during a few short weeks between mid-June and early July.*

Crust

1½ cups flour
½ cup vegetable oil
2 tablespoons sugar
2 tablespoons milk
1 teaspoon salt

1. Combine all ingredients.

2. Press into a 10-inch pie plate and prick with fork. Bake at 450° for 8 to 10 minutes.

Filling

1 cup water
½ cup sugar
3 tablespoons cornstarch
2 tablespoons light corn syrup
5 tablespoons strawberry gelatin
1 quart strawberries, sliced

1. In a medium saucepan, combine water, sugar, cornstarch and corn syrup. Bring to a boil over medium heat until thickened.

2. Add gelatin and strawberries.

3. Pour into baked crust and refrigerate at least 3 hours before serving. Serve chilled.

Norwegian Crustless Apple Pie

Nancy Brigham

My friend Audrey gave me this recipe years ago and it is one of my favorites because it's so simple, quick to put together and delish!

¾ cup sugar
¾ cup brown sugar
1   cup flour
2   eggs
2   teaspoons baking powder
1   teaspoon vanilla extract
1   cup chopped nuts
2   cups cut-up apples, peeled

1. Mix all ingredients in order given.

2. Pour into two well-greased pie plates. Bake at 350° for 30 minutes.

Cool N' Easy Pie

From the Kitchen of Marie P. Chabot

This is a diabetic delight and treat. It will be appreciated by all. (Marie shared this recipe with us before her passing on August 1, 2003.)

⅔ cup boiling water
1   (3-ounce) package sugar-free gelatin, any flavor
½ cup cold water
    Ice cubes
1   (8-ounce) container light whipped topping, thawed
1   prepared 9-inch graham cracker crust

1. In a large bowl, combine boiling water and gelatin. Stir at least 2 minutes until dissolved.

2. Mix in cold water and ice to measure 1 cup; add to gelatin stirring until melted.

3. Whisk in whipped topping until smooth.

4. Refrigerate 15 to 20 minutes until mixture is thick. Spoon into crust. Refrigerate 4 hours or overnight.

Serves 8.

Key West Key Lime Pie

Cheryl Scott

It's best to use the juice of fresh fruit for this pie, but bottled Key lime juice can be substituted. The pie is also delicious frozen overnight and served semi-frozen.

1½ cups graham cracker crumbs (about 10 cracker sheets)

¾ cup sugar, divided

6 tablespoons butter, melted and cooled, plus more for pie plate

Pinch of salt

1 (14-ounce) can sweetened condensed milk

4 large eggs, separated

¾ cup fresh Key lime juice (about 20 Key limes)

¾ cup heavy cream

1. In a medium bowl, combine graham cracker crumbs, 3 tablespoons sugar, butter and salt.

2. Press into buttered pie plate. Bake at 375° about 12 minutes or until lightly browned. Cool completely on a wire rack.

3. In a bowl, combine condensed milk, yolks and lime juice.

4. Pour into crust. Bake at 325° for 15 to 17 minutes or until center is just set. Cool completely on a wire rack.

5. In a bowl of an electric mixer, whisk together remaining sugar and egg whites.

6. Place bowl over a pot of simmering water and stir until warm to the touch and sugar is dissolved.

7. Place bowl on mixer fitted with the whisk attachment and mix on medium-high speed until stiff peaks form and meringue is glossy, about 5 minutes.

8. Place cream in a chilled bowl and whisk until soft peaks form, being careful not to over-mix.

9. Gently whisk a third of the cream into meringue. Using a rubber spatula, fold in remaining cream.

10. Top pie with meringue mixture. Freeze just until topping is firm enough to slice.

Yields 1 (9-inch) pie.

Ice Cream Peanut Butter Pie with Peanut Butter Sauce

Sandy Paul

My mother's recipe served on special family occasions.

1   cup plus 1 tablespoon light or dark corn syrup
1   cup plus 6 tablespoons peanut butter
6   cups rice crispies
1   quart vanilla ice cream, softened (approximately)
1   cup sugar
½   teaspoon salt
¾   cup milk
¼   teaspoon vanilla extract

1. In a medium bowl, combine 1 cup corn syrup, 1 cup peanut butter and rice crispies.

2. Press ⅔ of mixture into a 9-inch pie plate.

3. Fill with ice cream and top with remaining mixture. Freeze.

4. In a medium saucepan, combine sugar, remaining corn syrup, salt and milk. Cook over low heat, stirring constantly, until thickened.

5. Add remaining peanut butter.

6. Remove from heat and add vanilla when cooled.

7. Slice pie and spoon sauce over individual slices.

Serves 8 to 10.

Pilgram Pumpkin Pie (Crustless)

Joan T. Johnson

*My father loved bread pudding and I loved making this recipe for him.
It gave him so much pleasure whenever I made this recipe. When baking this fond
memories spice the room along with the cinnamon, nutmeg and pumpkin. I serve
it with whipped cream, ice cream or sliced fresh fruit.*

1	(4 to 5-pound) short wide sugar pumpkin
2	tablespoons butter, melted
⅓	cup plus 2 tablespoons sugar, divided
2	cups milk
4	tablespoons butter
2	cups stale bread with crusts, cut into ½-inch cubes (about 3-4 slices)
3	eggs
⅔	cup raisins
¼	teaspoon salt
1	teaspoon cinnamon
½	teaspoon nutmeg

1. Clean out pumpkin and make a lid.

2. Brush the inside with melted butter and sprinkle with 2 tablespoons sugar. Put lid back on and place in baking pan; bake at 350° for 20 minutes.

3. Make the bread pudding by scalding the milk, add 4 tablespoons of butter and ⅓ cup sugar.

4. When the butter melts, pour the mixture over the bread cubes. Let stand for 5 minutes.

5. Beat eggs; mix in raisins, salt, cinnamon and nutmeg.

6. Combine with bread and fill the warm pumpkin.

7. Return to oven, uncovered. Bake for 1½ to 1¾ hours or until the custard is set. The custard will puff above the opening, but will sink down as it sets. Let stand for at least 10 minutes before serving. Slice into wedges to serve, much like a big wedge of pie.

Butter is mentioned twice in the ingredients. It is not a mistake.

Serves 8 to 10.

Raspberry Sour Cream Tart

Eileen Pastner

Crust

8 whole graham crackers, coarsely broken
¼ cup packed golden brown sugar
4 tablespoons unsalted butter, melted

1. Grind crackers and sugar in a processor until coarse crumbs form.

2. Add butter and process until crumbs are evenly moistened.

3. Press crumb mixture firmly onto bottom and up sides of a 9-inch in diameter tart pan with removable bottom.

4. Bake at 375° about 8 minutes or until crust is firm to touch. Cool on rack.

Filling and Topping

6 ounces cream cheese, room temperature
⅓ cup sugar
½ cup sour cream
2 teaspoons fresh lemon juice
½ teaspoon vanilla extract
2 (½-pint) baskets raspberries
¼ cup seedless raspberry jam

1. Using an electric mixer beat cream cheese and sugar in a medium bowl until smooth.

2. Beat in sour cream, lemon juice and vanilla extract.

3. Spread filling in cooled crust. Chill until firm, at least 4 hours. (Can be made 1 day ahead. Cover, keep chilled.)

4. Arrange berries over filling.

5. Whisk jam in a small bowl to a loose consistency. Drizzle over berries and serve immediately or chill up to 3 hours.

Serves 8.

Dutch Almond Tart

Rebecca Smith

Crust

1½ cups unbleached all-purpose flour
3 tablespoons sugar
⅛ teaspoon salt
7 tablespoons chilled solid vegetable shortening
5 tablespoons chilled unsalted butter, cut into pieces
6 tablespoons cold water (approximately)

1. Blend flour, sugar and salt in food processor.

2. Add shortening and butter and cut in using on/off turns until mixture resembles coarse meal.

3. Blend in enough water by tablespoons to bind dough; do not form ball.

4. Gather dough into ball and flatten into disk. Wrap in plastic and refrigerate for 1 hour. (Crust can be prepared 1 day in advance.)

5. Roll dough out on floured surface to a 13-inch round. Transfer dough to a 9-inch tart pan with removable bottom.

6. Press onto bottom and up sides of pan; trim edges.

7. Gather scraps and re-roll into 9 x 7-inch rectangle. Cut out ten 9-inch long, ½-inch wide strips.

8. Cover and refrigerate tart and strips while preparing filling.

Filling

6	tablespoons unsalted butter, room temperature
3	tablespoons solid vegetable shortening
½	cup plus 1 tablespoon almond paste
3	large eggs
6	tablespoons sugar
3½	tablespoons unbleached all-purpose flour
½	teaspoon grated lemon peel
½	cup apricot jam
1	tablespoon apricot jam, melted

1. Using an electric mixer, in a small bowl cream butter and shortening until light and fluffy.

2. In a medium bowl, beat almond paste until softened.

3. Gradually beat in eggs and then sugar. Continue beating until fluffy, about 5 minutes.

4. Beat in butter mixture.

5. Mix in flour and lemon peel.

6. Spread ½ cup jam over bottom of tart. Pour filling over.

7. Arrange 5 dough strips atop filling, spacing evenly. Repeat in opposite direction with remaining dough strips, creating lattice top.

8. Press dough strips at tart edges to seal.

9. Bake at 350° for 1 hour and 10 minutes or until golden brown. Transfer tart to rack. Brush lattice strips with melted jam. Cool completely.

Serves 8.

Cheesecake Fruit Tart

Susan Koopman

I found this recipe on the Internet. It had rave reviews.
It is truly a winner. It is very beautiful and delicious. I highly recommend it.

Crust

1½ cups flour
2   tablespoons sugar
⅛   teaspoon salt
10 tablespoons chilled unsalted
      butter, cut into ½ inch pieces
2   tablespoons ice water
      (approximately)
1   large egg yolk
¼   cup apple jelly

1. In a food processor, combine flour, sugar and salt.

2. Add butter and cut in, using on/off turns, until mixture resembles coarse meal.

3. Whisk 2 tablespoons ice water and egg yolk. Add to dry ingredients.

4. Blend until soft clumps form. Add more water if dough is dry by the teaspoon.

5. Gather dough into a ball and flatten into a disk. Wrap in plastic and refrigerate 1 hour.

6. Roll out dough on a lightly floured surface.

7. Transfer to tart pan with removable bottom. Press in overhang, turning double thick sides. Pierce crust all over with fork. Freeze for 30 minutes.

8. Remove from freezer and bake at 375° until golden brown. Spread jelly over bottom of crust and cool.

Filling

2 (8-ounce) packages cream cheese, room temperature
⅔ cup sugar
1 large egg
¼ teaspoon vanilla extract
½ cup sour cream

1. Using an electric mixer beat cream cheese until smooth.

2. Add sugar and beat until light and fluffy.

3. Beat in egg, then vanilla. Add sour cream and beat until blended.

4. Pour filling into tart crust. Bake at 350° for 35 minutes. The center should move slightly when pan is gently shaken. Cool and refrigerate at least 3 to 4 hours. (Can be prepared 1 day ahead. Cover and keep refrigerated.)

Topping

¼ cup apple jelly
1 pint strawberries
½ pint blackberries
2 kiwi
½ cup blueberries

1. Melt jelly in heavy saucepan over low heat. Brush over top of cheesecake.

2. Arrange the fruits decoratively around tart; brush with jelly if desired. Serve immediately or refrigerate up to 3 hours.

You can use whatever fruit you want. Mangos, peaches and raspberries are nice additions.

Serves 12.

Chocolate Turtle Tart

Ann Bouvier Achorn

A decatendly wicked, rich dessert for your favorite chocoholics.
For ease in portion control, I slice in half, then each half in half again
and then slice each quarter section into 3 slices.

Crust

1¾ cups pecans, toasted
⅓ cup sugar
4 tablespoons unsalted butter, melted and cooled

1. In a food processor, finely grind pecans with sugar.

2. Add butter and blend well.

3. Firmly press crumb mixture onto bottom and up sides of a 9-inch diameter (about 1¼-inch high) tart pan with removable bottom.

4. Bake at 350° for about 25 minutes or until golden brown. Cool.

If sides sink in, press back up with a fork.

Filling

1½ cups whipping cream
12 ounces bittersweet chocolate, chopped
½ cup finely chopped pecans (about 2 ounces)

1. In a heavy medium saucepan, bring cream to a simmer. Reduce heat to low.

2. Add chocolate and whisk until melted and smooth. Cool to lukewarm.

3. Pour filling into crust. Refrigerate 30 minutes.

4. Sprinkle pecans around the edge of filling, all the way around about 1-inch wide from sides. Refrigerate until firm, about 3 hours.

May be prepared 3 days ahead. Cover and keep refrigerated.

Sauce

1   stick unsalted butter
1   cup sugar
1   cup whipping cream
    Whipped cream for topping
       (optional)
    Johnny-jump-ups or pansies
       for garnish

1. In a medium saucepan, melt butter over medium low heat.

2. Add sugar and cook until deep golden brown, stirring occasionally, about 12 minutes.

3. Add cream and whisk vigorously until smooth; cool to lukewarm.

4. To serve, loosen tart pan sides and remove. Cut tart into small wedges and transfer to plates.

5. Spoon sauce over wedge, top with a dollop of whipped cream, if desired. Garnish with a Johnny-jump-ups or pansies.

Can be prepared 2 days ahead. Cover and refrigerate. Reheat before serving.

Serves 12.

Nana's Berry Tarts

Lisa Geraghty

This is a French-Canadian tradition. Tarts are only made and served at Christmas time. We still honor this tradition and look forward to them all year long.

2   boxes pie crust
1   (10-ounce) jar raspberry or strawberry seedless jam
2   cups confectioners' sugar
    Milk
¼   cup butter
¼   teaspoon vanilla extract

1. Make both boxes of pie crust according to package directions.

2. Divide in half and roll out into a thin rectangular shape to fit in a cookie sheet.

3. Spread a thin layer of jam.

4. Roll out remainder of dough in a rectangular shape. Place dough over jam; seal edges with a fork.

5. Poke many holes in the pastry with a fork. Bake at 425° for 10 minutes. Reduce heat to 350° and bake an additional 20 minutes.

6. After baking and while tarts are still warm, combine the remainder of ingredients and put in the warm oven until the butter melts. Stir until smooth.

7. Frost tarts.

You could make homemade pie crust like Nana did.

Yields 10 tarts.

Pecan Tartlets

From the Kitchen of Ruth Cotton Gurney
submitted by her daughter Pamela Gurney Farnum

1 (3-ounce) package cream cheese
1 stick butter
1 cup flour
1 egg, beaten
1 cup light brown sugar
¼ cup chopped pecans
1 teaspoon softened butter
1 teaspoon vanilla

1. In a large bowl, blend cream cheese and 1 stick of butter.

2. Add flour, mixing together with a fork or with your fingers.

3. Divide the dough into 24 parts; roll each into a small ball and press firmly into ungreased small muffin tins.

4. Beat together the egg, sugar, pecans, soft butter and vanilla.

5. Divide this mixture into the 24 shells. Bake at 350° for 25 minutes or until set.

6. Remove from oven and loosen edges with a sharp knife; let set five minutes before turning out of pan.

Yields 24 tartlets.

Waters Farm Apple Crisp

Taken from the Waters Farm Newsletter

Each year thousands of people turn out to West Sutton the first weekend in October for Waters Farm Days. This apple crisp is huge hit year after year. Volunteers are welcome to make a pan of Waters Farm Apple Crisp and deliver it to the farm for either Saturday or Sunday.

6	pounds apples, Gravenstein or Macoun
¾	cup granulated sugar
½	cup flour
1	teaspoon cinnamon
¼	teaspoon nutmeg

1. Peel and slice apples into a 13 x 9 x 2-inch aluminum foil pan (half steam-tray size pan).

2. In a small bowl, mix together well remaining ingredients.

3. Sprinkle over apples in pan. Mix in and pat down firmly, filling the corners.

Topping

1½	cups brown sugar
1	stick margarine
1	cup rolled oats
1	cup flour
½	teaspoon cinnamon
⅛	teaspoon nutmeg

1. Mix together topping ingredients with a pastry blender or hands to a crumbly consistency.

2. Cover apples with the mixture and pat down. Bake at 375° for 1 hour. Bake until light brown on top.

Baking time depends upon the firmness of the apples. You can test for doneness by inserting a sharp knife into apples, being careful not to puncture pan.

Yields 12 large servings.

Blueberry Crisp

Barbara MH Daigneault

Simple, simple, simple! I remember picking blueberries at
Hill Side Farm in West Sutton. It is so nice to have freshly picked blueberries
on hand all winter long to make this quick and easy dessert. Serve with a
smidgen of vanilla ice cream, low fat ice cream that is.

3	cups blueberries
2	tablespoons lemon juice
⅔	cup brown sugar
¾	teaspoon cinnamon
½	cup flour
½	cup oatmeal
⅓	cup softened butter
¼	teaspoon salt

1. Place blueberries in a greased 9 x 9-inch glass baking dish. Sprinkle with lemon juice.

2. In a small bowl, mix remaining ingredients forming a crumb-like mixture. Pour over blueberries.

3. Bake at 375° for 30 minutes.

Serves 8.

Rhubarb Crisp

Gladys L. Stewart

4	cups diced rhubarb
1	tablespoon flour
½	cup granulated sugar
1	tablespoon water
¾	cup sifted flour
⅔	cup firmly packed light brown sugar
½	cup sifted flour
¼	teaspoon cinnamon
¼	teaspoon salt
1	stick butter

1. Combine rhubarb with 1 tablespoon of flour, granulated sugar and water.

2. Place in a greased 10 x 6 x 2-inch baking dish.

3. Combine remaining ingredients, except butter. Mix well.

4. Cut in butter with a fork until mixture is crumbly. Sprinkle over rhubarb.

5. Bake at 350° for 45 to 50 minutes.

Serves 9.

Blueberry Crisp
with Oatmeal Almond Topping

Kim Hunkeler

3 cups fresh blueberries

2 tablespoons plus ¼ cup packed brown sugar

½ teaspoon cinnamon

½ cup quick oats

2 tablespoons flour

¼ teaspoon salt

2 tablespoons butter, chilled

¼ cup sliced almonds

Vanilla ice cream

1. Rinse blueberries in cold water. Drain allowing some water to remain on blueberries.

2. Place blueberries in a greased 9-inch pie plate. Sprinkle with 2 tablespoons of brown sugar and cinnamon. Stir until sugar coats blueberries.

3. Combine oats, flour, salt, remaining sugar and butter. Rub with fingers or mix with a fork until moist clumps form.

4. Stir in almonds. Sprinkle over blueberries evenly.

5. Bake at 350° for 35 minutes or until bubbly and golden brown. Serve warm with vanilla ice cream.

Almond Danish Puff

Nancy A. Johnson

*This is an old recipe of my mothers. She made it so well
and always served at gatherings or made it just for the family.*

Puff Pastry

2   cups flour, divided
2   sticks butter, divided
2   tablespoons plus 1 cup water
1   teaspoon almond extract
3   eggs

1. Cut ½ cup butter into 1 cup flour.

2. Sprinkle with 2 tablespoons of water. Mix with fork. Round into ball and divide in half.

3. On an ungreased baking sheet, pat halves into a 12 x 3-inch strip. Place 3 inches apart.

4. In a saucepan, heat ½ cup butter and 1 cup water into rolling boil.

5. Remove from heat. Quickly stir in almond extract and remaining 1 cup flour.

6. Stir vigorously over low heat until it forms into a ball, about 1 minute.

7. Remove from heat and beat in eggs all at once until smooth. Divide in half.

8. Spread halves evenly over strips, covering completely.

9. Bake at 350° for 60 minutes or until topping is crisp and brown. Cool and frost.

Frosting

1½ cups confectioners' sugar
2   tablespoons softened butter
1½ teaspoons almond extract
1-2 tablespoons warm water
    Slivered almonds

1. Beat all ingredients until smooth.

2. Frost pastry and top with slivered almonds.

Strawberry Rhubarb Puff

Evelyn L. Morris

3 cups sliced rhubarb
1 pint strawberries, sliced
1½-2 cups plus 2 tablespoons
    sugar
½ cup water
2 cups flour
3 teaspoon baking powder
1 teaspoon salt
⅓ cup oil
⅔ cup milk
2 tablespoons butter
    Cinnamon
    Whipped cream

1. Combine rhubarb, strawberries, 1½ to 2 cups sugar and water in a 9-inch square metal pan.

2. Cook on stove 5 minutes over medium-low heat.

3. Measure flour by dip-level-pour method. Mix flour, baking powder, salt and remaining 2 tablespoons of sugar.

4. Stir in oil and milk only until dry ingredients are moistened.

5. Drop onto hot fruit, making 9 biscuits. Make a hole in each biscuit and put a little butter and cinnamon in each.

6. Bake at 450° for 20 to 25 minutes. Serve with whipped cream.

Serves 6 to 8.

Grammie Edies' Shortcake Biscuits

Carol Botty

This recipe is at least 4 generations "passed down". My grandmother's mother had these in the house as a staple serving them at dinner. I use them as a special dessert for strawberry shortcake! Heaven with fresh whipped cream and just picked strawberries.

2	cups flour
4	teaspoons baking powder
1	teaspoon salt
1	teaspoon butter (not margarine)
1	teaspoon shortening
¾	cup whole milk

1. In a large bowl, combine dry ingredients and sift twice.

2. Work in butter and shortening with fingertips.

3. Gradually adding the milk, mixing to a soft dough consistency. Don't over mix or it will toughen up.

4. Toss dough on a lightly floured board and roll lightly to ½-inch thickness. Shape with biscuit cutter.

5. Place on greased cooked sheet. Bake at 350° for 12 to 15 minutes.

Butterscotch Thins

From the Kitchen of Ethel Hutchinson
submitted by her great niece Norma H. Baker

Here's another one of Aunt Ethel's favorite recipes. Whenever I went next door, she'd have a cookie tin filled with fresh cookies. All were good, but these were the best.

½	cup shortening
½	cup brown sugar
1	cup flour
⅓	cup sugar
1	egg
½	teaspoon baking powder
¼	teaspoon baking soda
¾	teaspoon vanilla extract

1. Combine all ingredients in a large bowl and mix well.

2. Shape into 1½-inch logs, chill thoroughly.

3. Slice thin and place on a greased cookie sheet. Bake at 350° for 10 minutes.

I prefer to slice the dough thicker for chewy cookies.

Almond Cookies

Joan Moroney

I received this recipe from my mother, who got it from her sister-in-law.
I am told the cookies are Italian cookies. I have no real proof.

2   eggs, divided
1   cup sugar
⅙   cup oil
1   cup whole almonds
1¼ cups flour
1   teaspoon baking powder
1   teaspoon cinnamon
1   teaspoon cloves

1. In a large bowl, combine 1 egg, sugar, oil and almonds.

2. Add flour, baking powder, cinnamon and cloves.

3. First sprinkle rolling surface and hands with flour. Roll into three strips.

3. Place on a cookie sheet.

4. Beat remaining egg with a few drops of water. Brush on top of roll.

5. Bake at 350° for 20 minutes. Slice at a slant as soon as possible.

A helpful hint: to keep cookies moist, place a piece of white bread on the bottom of the container.

Almond Crescents

From the Kitchen of Ethel Linder
submitted by her children Ken and Marie Linder

This recipe was handed down to Ethel from her mother Maria Anderson. This crescent cookie was prepared at Christmas time and always in the jar, ready to be enjoyed by the Linder family and friends.

1	cup sifted flour
½	cup sugar
⅛	teaspoon salt
⅔	cup ground blanched almonds
½	cup butter
1	egg yolk, slightly beaten, reserve white
¼	teaspoon almond extract
1	egg white, slightly beaten
½	cup very finely chopped almonds for coating

1. In a large bowl, combine flour, sugar, salt and nuts.

2. Cut in butter until mixture looks like cornmeal.

3. Add egg yolk and almond extract.

4. Place dough on wax paper and form into a ball. Roll out and cut into long strips, ½-inch wide by ½-inch thick. Then cut into 2-inch lengths.

5. Shape into crescents and dip in egg white and chopped almonds.

6. Bake on an ungreased baking sheet at 350° for 15 to 20 minutes.

Scandinavian Almond Bars

Sue Penterson

This has become a favorite Christmas cookie in our family.

Cookies

1¾ cups flour
2 teaspoon baking powder
¼ teaspoon salt
1 stick butter
1 cup sugar
1 egg
½ teaspoon almond extract
Milk
½ cup sliced almonds, coarsely chopped

1. Combine flour, baking powder and salt.

2. In a large mixer bowl, beat butter until softened.

3. Add sugar and beat until fluffy.

4. Add egg and almond extract and beat well.

5. Add flour mixture and beat until well mixed.

6. Divide dough into fourths. Form each into a 12-inch roll. Place two rolls 4 to 5 inches apart on an ungreased cookie sheet. Flatten until 3-inches wide. Repeat with remaining rolls.

7. Brush flattened rolls with milk and sprinkle with almonds.

8. Bake at 325° for 12 minutes or until edges are lightly browned.

9. While cookies are warm, cut them crosswise at a diagonal into 1-inch strips; cool.

10. Drizzle with Almond Icing.

Almond Icing

1 cup confectioners' sugar, sifted
¼ teaspoon almond extract
3-4 teaspoons milk

1. Stir together sugar, almond extract and enough milk to make icing of drizzling consistency.

Orange Almond Biscotti

J. Chicy-Natoli

1 cup sugar
1 stick butter (no substitutes)
½ cup toasted sliced almonds
1 tablespoon grated orange peel
2 eggs
3½ cups flour
1 teaspoon baking powder
½ teaspoon salt

1. In a large bowl, beat sugar and butter well.

2. Add remaining ingredients, beating well.

3. Divide dough in half. Shape into rectangle about 10 x 3 on an ungreased cooked sheet.

4. Bake at 350° for 20 minutes or until toothpick inserted in center comes out clean.

5. Cut into crosswise slices about ½-inch wide. Turn slices cut side down on cookie sheet. Cool on baking sheet 15 minutes.

6. Bake again for 15 minutes or until crisp and light brown. Remove from cookie sheet to wire rack. Cool. Store in an airtight container.

Cherry Nut Cookies

Dolores Rossetti

4 cups flour

6 teaspoons baking powder

1 cup sugar

¼ cup oil

2 large eggs

1 (8-ounce) package chopped walnuts

1 (10-ounce) jar maraschino cherries, chopped, reserve liquid

½ cup milk

1. In a large bowl, mix dry ingredients.

2. Add remaining ingredients, except ¼ cup chopped cherries and mix well.

3. Drop by the teaspoon onto a greased cookie sheet. Bake at 400° for 8 to 10 minutes. Cool on wire rack.

Frosting

1 (1-pound) box confectioners' sugar

¼ cup reserved cherry juice

¼ cup reserved chopped cherries
Milk

1. Combine confectioners' sugar, cherry juice and a few chopped cherries. Mix well.

You might need to add a few drops of milk to get the right consistency.

Crunchy Chocolate Chip Cookies

Sue Hebert

*Mouthwatering! These are not your basic
chocolate chip cookie, they are outstanding.*

3½ cups all-purpose flour
3   teaspoons baking soda
1   teaspoon salt
1   stick butter
1   stick margarine
1   cup firmly packed light brown
     sugar
1   cup granulated sugar
1   egg
1   tablespoon milk
2   teaspoons vanilla
½-1 cup vegetable oil
1   cup rice crispies
1   cup quick oats
1   (12-ounce) package
     semisweet chocolate chips

1. Sift together flour, baking soda and salt onto a sheet of wax paper. Set aside.

2. In a large bowl, beat butter, margarine, sugars, egg, milk and vanilla until blended.

3. Stir in the flour mixture alternating with oil until thoroughly mixed.

4. Stir in cereal, oats and chocolate chips.

5. Roll dough by teaspoonfuls into balls and place on an ungreased cookie sheet 2-inches apart.

6. Bake at 350° for 12 minutes or until golden brown. Cool on wire racks.

Yields 5 dozen.

Gram Grover's Soft Molasses Cookies

Jane Anderson

These cookies were a great favorite with all the Grover children, grandchildren and great grandchildren. Mrs. Grover was my grandmother, my mother's (Margaret Potter) mother.

5	cups sifted flour
¾	cup sugar
1	cup shortening
1	cup molasses
1	cup milk
1	tablespoon baking soda
2	teaspoons cinnamon
1	teaspoon ground ginger

1. In a large bowl, combine all ingredients and mix well.

2. Roll out thick and cut using a cookie cutter.

3. Bake on an ungreased cookie sheet at 325° for 15 minutes.

Batter must be refrigerated overnight.

Oatmeal Cranberry White Chocolate Chunk Cookies

Pam Adams

2	sticks butter or margarine, softened
1	cup brown sugar
2	eggs
2	cups oats
2	cups flour
½	teaspoon salt
1	teaspoon baking soda
1½	cups sweetened dried cranberries
1	cup white chocolate chips

1. Using an electric mixer beat butter or margarine and sugar together until light and fluffy.

2. Add eggs; mix well.

3. Combine oats, flour, salt and baking soda. Add to butter mixture in several additions. Mix well after each addition.

4. Stir in dried cranberries and chocolate chips.

5. Drop by rounded teaspoons onto ungreased cookie sheets. Bake at 375° for 10 to 12 minutes or until golden brown.

Yields 2½ dozen.

Antique Oatmeal Cookies

Helen Silun Ordung

This recipe was the first one on the Quaker Oats carton in 1938. I was just married and was asked to bake something for my husband's office girls for a food sale. I made these and none appeared on the bake sale table. Trying to find them, I was told the staff had eaten them. I made them for 30 years for the food sales. The recipe has changed many times over the years, but this one is the best.

2   sticks butter or margarine
2¼ cups sugar, divided
2   eggs
2   teaspoons vanilla
2   cups flour
¾   teaspoon salt
1½ teaspoons cinnamon, divided
1½ teaspoons baking powder
3   cups quick oats
1   cup chopped nut (optional)
1   cup raisins, halved (optional)

1. In a mixer, combine butter, 2 cups sugar, eggs and vanilla extract.

2. Add flour, salt, 1 teaspoon cinnamon and baking powder.

3. Add oatmeal and mix well. Allow to stand for 30 minutes.

4. Oil the palms of your hands and roll a round teaspoon of dough and place on a cookie sheet 2 inches apart.

5. In a shallow dish, combine remainder ¼ cup sugar and remainder ½ teaspoon of cinnamon.

6. Lightly moisten the bottom of a flat bottom glass to flatten the cookies. Dip the glass bottom in the sugar/cinnamon mixture and then flatten the cookie. Repeat this process until all the cookies are flattened.

7. Bake at 375° for 12 minutes or until lightly browned.

You may use 1 cup dark brown sugar and 1 cup granulated sugar in place of 2 cups granulated sugar.

Oreo Cookies (Whoopie Pies)

Carol Baker

2 boxes chocolate cake mix
  (no pudding added)
4 eggs
1½ cups solid shortening

1. Combine all ingredients.

2. Roll into 1-inch balls and place on a greased cookie sheet. Bake at 350° for 9 minutes. Cool on pan.

Filling
1 (8-ounce) package cream cheese
½ cup margarine
1 teaspoon vanilla extract
1 (1-pound) box confectioners' sugar

1. Combine cream cheese and margarine.

2. Add vanilla and confectioners' sugar; mix well.

3. Spoon onto cookie and cover with a cookie lid.

If you wrap these individually in plastic wrap, they will stay fresh much longer.

Yields approximately 4 dozen.

Easy Pecan Cookies

Jan Davagian

2 sticks butter, softened
½ cup confectioners' sugar
2 cups flour
¾ cup finely chopped pecans
  Confectioners' sugar for sprinkling

1. In a large bowl, combine all ingredients.

2. Roll out onto a lightly floured board to ¼-inch thick. Cut out (I use a floured glass) into small rounds.

3. Bake at 400° for 5 to 7 minutes.

4. Sprinkle with confectioners' sugar after baking. Remove to wire racks to cool.

Peanut Butter Kiss Cookies

Barbara MH Daigneault

This is your basic peanut butter kiss cookie and it is my favorite cookie. My Aunt Connie makes these for me every Christmas and I am literally very selective with whom I share these with.

1¾ cups flour
½ cup granulated sugar
½ cup brown sugar
½ cup butter
½ cup peanut butter
1 egg
2 tablespoons milk
1 teaspoon baking soda
½ teaspoon salt
1 teaspoon vanilla extract
48 chocolate kisses
¼ cup granulated sugar for coating

1. Combine all ingredients in a large bowl, except the kisses and sugar for coating.

2. Shape dough by teaspoonfuls into balls.

3. Roll balls in sugar and place on a greased cookie sheet. Bake at 375° for 10 to 12 minutes.

4. After baked, immediately top each cookie with a kiss. Press down firmly so cookies crack around the edges.

Yields 4 dozen.

Apricot Squares

Evelyn L. Morris

¾ cup butter
¾ cup sugar
2 cups plus 1 tablespoon flour
½ cup chopped nuts
⅓ cup coconut
1 egg
1 teaspoon vanilla extract
¼ teaspoon salt
1 (10-ounce) jar apricot preserves

1. In a large bowl, cream butter and sugar.

2. Add flour, nuts, coconut, egg, vanilla and salt.

3. Spread ½ ingredients in an ungreased 11 x 9-inch metal pan.

4. Spread preserves on top and then crumble remaining ingredients on top.

5. Bake at 350° for 35 to 45 minutes.

Thumb Cookies

Cynthia Jellesma

I have been eating these delicate cookies since I was a child and these are my favorite. They are so simple to make. This makes a small batch so I generally double this recipe.

½ cup cornstarch
½ cup confectioners' sugar
1 cup flour
¾ cup butter
½ cup raspberry jam

1. In a large bowl, sift together first 3 ingredients.

2. Cut in the butter with a pastry cutter.

3. Roll into balls by the teaspoonfuls and place on an ungreased cookie sheet. Flatten cookies gently with the palm of your hand.

4. Gently press a thumbprint in the center of the cookie and place a dollop of jam in the center.

5. Bake at 300° for 20 minutes or until the bottoms are golden brown.

Thimble Cookies

Liz Shannon-Charest

Baking cookies at Christmas time has become a fond tradition for my mother, sister and I. This recipe is from a Swedish cookbook of my mother's from Quinsigamond Village where she grew up. We've also been known for our friendly flour fights, bringing much laughter and a very messy floor. Despite my mothers warning, my sister and I can't resist eating the dough before it is baked, after all it's tradition.

2   sticks butter, softened
6   tablespoons heavy cream
2   cups flour
    Cinnamon and sugar

1. In a large bowl, combine butter, cream and flour. Mix to form dough.

2. Using a rolling pin, roll dough to ¼-inch thick. Cut circles out of dough with a shot glass. Cut another circle in the middle of each with a thimble (Cookies look like tiny, thin doughnuts.)

3. Bake at 350° for 10 minutes or until lightly brown.

4. Roll warm cookies in cinnamon and sugar. Place on wire rack to cool.

Gramma Grace's Graham Cracker Brownies

Nancy Brigham

*This is a 1940's war recipe from Grace Brigham's family.
It is long been a tradition at all our family gatherings.*

1   package graham crackers
    (22 2 x 2-inch crackers)
1   (6-ounce) package semisweet chocolate chips
1   cup raisins
1   (14-ounce) can sweetened condensed milk

1. Coarsely roll out graham crackers.

2. Add the remaining ingredients and mix well.

3. Pour into a greased 8 x 8-inch pan. Bake at 350° for 35 minutes.

Nuts and/or coconut can be added too!

Alaskan Logs

Ruth S. Putnam

¾ cup flour
1 cup sugar
1 teaspoon baking powder
¼ teaspoon salt
1 cup chopped pitted dates
1 cup chopped walnuts
3 eggs, well beaten
Granulated sugar for rolling

1. In a medium mixing bowl, sift dry ingredients.

2. Stir in remaining ingredients.

3. Pour into a greased 8 x 8-inch pan. Bake at 325° for 40 minutes. Cool on a wire rack for 5 to 10 minutes.

4. Cut into four equal squares and then quarter each square into 2-inch pieces by ½-inch equaling 52 pieces.

5. Form each piece into a log and press firmly, roll in granulated sugar.

These freeze well.

Magic Gooey Bars

From the Kitchen of Ruth Cotton Gurney
submitted by Barbara MH Daigneault

I can remember being in Bluebirds and Camp Fire Girls under the leadership of Mrs. Gurney. Some 40+ years later, I can still remember her making these delicious bars. I have this recipe in her handwriting and it makes it even more special to me.

1 stick margarine
1½ cups graham cracker crumbs
1 (14-ounce) can condensed milk
1 cup chocolate chips
1 cup coconut
1 cup chopped nuts

1. Melt margarine in a 13 x 9-inch pan. Sprinkle graham cracker crumbs over top.

2. Pour condensed milk over crumbs. Add remaining ingredients.

3. Bake at 350° for 20 to 25 minutes.

Grammy Irma's Apple Squares

From the Kitchen of Irma Whitney
submitted by her granddaughter Whitney (Melia) Margoupis

This is a recipe I inherited from my grandmother, someone known for her delicious jams, pies and squares. I always remember my gram being in the kitchen and we always were treated to something warm and delicious because of it.

1¾ cups sugar
3 eggs
2 cups flour
1 teaspoon cinnamon
1 teaspoon baking powder
½ teaspoon salt
1 teaspoon vanilla extract
1 cup vegetable oil
1 cup chopped nuts (optional)
2 cups diced apples

1. In a large bowl, beat sugar and eggs.

2. Add flour, cinnamon, baking powder and salt.

3. Add in oil and vanilla. Mix in walnuts and apples.

4. Spread into a greased 13 x 9-inch pan. Bake at 350° for 40 to 45 minutes.

Hermits

Georgia Perry

This is a family favorite.

¾ cup shortening
1½ cups sugar
2 tablespoons water
2 eggs, beaten
3 cups flour
½ teaspoon salt
¼ cup molasses
1 teaspoon baking soda
1 teaspoon cinnamon
1 teaspoon ground cloves
1 teaspoon ground ginger
1 cup raisins
½ cup chopped nuts

1. Cream together shortening and sugar.

2. Add molasses and water.

3. Add all but 1 tablespoon of egg. Add remaining ingredients; mix well.

4. Shape into 6 strips about the size of a frankfurter.

5. Place on two greased cookie sheets. Pat down with hand. Brush with remaining egg.

6. Bake at 350° for 20 minutes. Be sure not to overbake. Cut into six pieces each.

Yields 3 dozen.

Best Ever Brownies

Evelyn L. Morris

I am not sure where this recipe came from originally but it was passed on to me from my mother and I have passed it along to my girls and many more. These are excellent fudge brownies.

1 cup shortening
4 squares unsweetened chocolate
1½ cups flour
1 teaspoon salt
1 teaspoon baking powder
4 eggs
2 cups sugar
2 teaspoons vanilla extract
1 cup chopped nuts

1. Melt shortening and chocolate together; cool.

2. Sift dry ingredients together and set aside.

3. Beat eggs lightly, add sugar and vanilla.

4. Add shortening mixture, then dry ingredients.

5. Pour into a greased 11 x 9-inch metal pan. Bake at 350° for 30 minutes. Either mix nuts in or sprinkle on top.

Mom's Lemon Squares

Evelyn M. Reed

1 cup flour
1 stick butter
¼ cup confectioners' sugar
2 eggs
½ teaspoon baking powder
1 cup granulated sugar
2½ tablespoons lemon juice
Dash of salt
Confectioners' sugar for sprinkling

1. Sift together flour and sugar.

2. Blend in shortening.

3. Pat evenly into a greased 8 x 8-inch pan. Bake at 350° for 20 minutes.

4. Meanwhile, beat together remaining ingredients. Pour over the baked crust and return to the oven for an additional 20 to 25 minutes.

5. Cool on a wire rack. Cut into squares and sprinkle with confectioners' sugar.

Chocolate Vanilla Brownies

Ann Junilla

*My mother, Betty Sundquist, would make these
for every special event. They became known as Betty's Brownies.*

Brownies

1 cup shortening
2 cups sugar
4 eggs, beaten
2 cups flour
½ teaspoon salt
½ teaspoon vanilla extract
2 squares of unsweetened
   chocolate, melted

1. Cream together shortening and sugar.

2. Add eggs and mix.

3. Add flour, salt and vanilla. Divide the batter in half and set half aside.

4. Add melted chocolate to half of the batter and mix well.

5. Spread the chocolate batter on the bottom of a greased 11 x 9-inch metal pan.

6. Add vanilla batter over the chocolate batter.

7. Bake at 350° for 25 minutes.

Frosting

1 cup sugar
1 square semisweet chocolate
   Pinch of salt
¼ cup milk

1. In a medium saucepan, combine all ingredients and boil for 1 minute, then beat for 20 strokes and pour over hot brownies. Cool before cutting.

Chocolate Caramel Bars

Evelyn M. Reed

2¼ cups flour, divided
2 cups quick oats
1½ cups packed brown sugar
1 teaspoon baking soda
½ teaspoon salt
3 sticks cold butter or margarine
2 cups milk chocolate chips
1 cup chopped pecans
1 (12-ounce) jar caramel ice
    cream topping

1. In a bowl, combine 2 cups flour, oats, brown sugar, baking soda and salt. Cut in butter until crumbly; set half aside for topping.

2. Press the remaining half of crumb mixture into a greased 13 x 9-inch baking pan. Bake at 350° for 15 minutes.

3. After baking, sprinkle with chocolate chips and pecans.

4. Whisk caramel topping with remaining ¼ cup flour until smooth. Drizzle over chips and pecans.

5. Spread the remaining crumb mixture over the top and bake an additional 18 to 20 minutes or until golden brown. Cool for 2 hours before cutting.

Heathbar Crunch Bars

Donna L. Beckwith

*My closest friend brought this to our dinner party. We left this
dessert on the table, while drinking wine, picking away at it until there was
none left. During the entire time, we complained how full we all were.*

1 sleeve saltine crackers
2 sticks butter
1 cup brown sugar
1 (16-ounce) package semisweet
   chocolate chips
1 cup chopped walnuts

1. Line the edges of a cookie sheet
with foil. Line bottom of pan with
saltines until completely covered.

2. Melt butter and then add brown
sugar. Bring to a boil stirring
constantly until caramelized.

3. Pour over saltines. Bake at 400°
for 5 minutes.

4. Remove from oven; add
chocolate bits. Spread with
backside of a wooden spoon; add
nuts.

5. Refrigerate 2 hours. Break into
2-inch small pieces and serve.

Chinese Chews

Nancy Brigham

*I have no idea who named these squares, but they are
good and easy to make. Sometimes I add chocolate chips.*

1 cup sugar
1 stick butter or margarine
2 eggs
1 cup flour
1 cup chopped walnuts
⅔ cup chopped maraschino
   cherries

1. Combine all ingredients and
pour into a greased 8 x 8-inch pan.

2. Bake at 350° for 30 minutes.

Oatmeal Cheesecake Cranberry Bars

Cathy Brodeur

2 cups flour
1¼ cups quick oats
¾ cup packed brown sugar
2 sticks butter, softened
12 ounces cream cheese, softened
½ cup sugar
2 eggs
2 teaspoons lemon juice
1 teaspoon vanilla extract
1 (16-ounce) can whole berry
    cranberry sauce
2 teaspoons cornstarch

1. In a large mixing bowl, stir together flour, oatmeal and brown sugar.

2. Using a pastry blender cut in butter until mixture resembles coarse crumbs. Reserve 1½ cups of the crumbs.

3. Press remaining crumbs into a greased 13 x 9-inch pan. Bake at 350° for 15 minutes.

4. Meanwhile, beat cream cheese and sugar with mixer on medium speed until light and fluffy.

5. Beat in eggs, lemon juice and vanilla extract. Spread over baked crust.

6. Stir together cranberry sauce and cornstarch, spoon carefully over cream cheese layer. Sprinkle with reserved crumbs.

7. Bake an additional 40 minutes. Cool on a wire rack. Cover and chill at least 3 hours before cutting into bars.

Vanilla Cream Puffs

Cathleen Haddad

These puffs are a lovely presentation on a sterling silver tray and laced doily. Since first making theses 10 years ago, they have become a Thanksgiving and Christmas tradition. Many thanks to Katie for sharing this with me.

1   pint whipping cream
2   packages instant vanilla pudding
2   tablespoons of milk (if necessary)
1   package frozen phyllo pastry puff
1   cup confectioners' sugar for dusting

1. Using an electric mixer, whip the cream until almost thick.

2. Mix in the pudding by hand. If too thick add a couple of tablespoons of milk. Set aside.

3. Open phyllo pastry puff carefully and cut into bite-size pieces.

4. Place on a cookie sheet and bake at 350° for 15 minutes. Cool completely.

5. Cut phyllo puff in half and fill with creamed filling, using a spoon or a pastry bag.

6. Put tops back on. Dust with confectioners' sugar.

Walnut Strips

Carolyn Brigham

This recipe originated in the 1950's and was often served at afternoon coffee parties, so popular during this era.

Crust

1	stick butter
1	cup flour

1. Cream butter and flour.

2. Spread into a greased 8 x 8-inch pan. Bake at 350° for 10 minutes.

Filling

1	egg, beaten
¾	cup brown sugar
1	tablespoon sifted flour
⅛	teaspoon baking powder
¼	teaspoon salt
½	cup coconut
½	cup chopped walnuts
½	teaspoon vanilla extract

1. Combine all ingredients and put on top of the baked crust and bake an additional 15 to 20 minutes.

Frosting

1	tablespoon butter
¾	cup confectioners' sugar
1	tablespoon warm orange juice
½	teaspoon lemon juice
	Crushed walnuts for topping

1. Cream butter and add remaining ingredients.

2. Spread on top of cake and sprinkle with a few crushed walnuts.

Yields 12 to 16 squares.

Bread Pudding with Spiced Rum Sauce

Jane Palermo

This is a recipe I found that has brought all family members smiles. It is so good. It will be a keeper throughout our families to come. The spiced rum sauce is a sweetened version of the popular spirit flavor with such spices as vanilla, cinnamon and nutmeg. This sauce would also be sublime served over ice cream.

8   large eggs
3½ cups whole milk
2   cups sugar
1½ cups whipping cream
1   teaspoon vanilla extract
1   (1-pound) loaf cinnamon swirl
     bread, cut into 1-inch cubes
1   cup golden raisins

1. In a large bowl, whisk eggs.

2. Add the milk, sugar, cream and vanilla. Whisk until well blended.

3. Stir in the bread and raisins.

4. Pour mixture into a greased 13 x 9-inch baking dish. Cover and refrigerate 2 hours.

5. Bake, uncovered, at 350° for 1 hour 15 minutes until puffed and golden brown. Cool slightly.

6. Serve with Spiced Rum Sauce.

Spiced Rum Sauce

1   cup packed golden brown
     sugar
1   stick unsalted butter
½   cup whipping cream
2   tablespoons spiced or dark
     rum
¾   teaspoon cinnamon

1. In a medium saucepan, stir brown sugar and butter until melted and smooth, about 2 minutes.

2. Add cream, rum and cinnamon and bring to a simmer.

3. Simmer until the sauce thickens and is reduced to 1½ cups, about 5 minutes. Serve warm.

Sauce can be prepared 2 days in advance. Cover and refrigerate. Bring to a simmer before serving.

Serves 12.

Chocolate Pudding Dessert

Norma H. Baker

Everytime I bring this dessert somewhere, I get recipe requests.

1   stick butter, melted
1   cup flour
¾ cup chopped walnuts
1   (8-ounce) package cream
     cheese
2   (8-ounce) containers whipped
     topping, thawed, divided
1   cup confectioners' sugar
2   (3-ounce) boxes instant
     chocolate pudding
3   cups milk

1. Combine first 3 ingredients and spread into the bottom of a greased 13 x 9-inch pan.

2. Bake at 350° for 15 minutes. Cool.

3. Combine cream cheese, 1 container of whipped topping and confectioners' sugar. Mix well and spread very carefully over crust.

4. Combine pudding and milk and mix well with a whisk.

5. Spread over whipped topping mixture.

6. Top with remaining whipped topping. Refrigerate. Cut into squares.

Must be eaten the same day.

Pecan Bourbon Crème Brûlée

Ann Bouvier Achorn

9   large eggs
¾   cup sugar
3   tablespoons bourbon
1½ teaspoons vanilla
2½ cups whipping cream
6   tablespoons golden brown sugar
½   cup coarsely chopped pecans, toasted

1. Place six ¾-cup custard cups in a large roasting pan.

2. In a large bowl, whisk egg yolks, sugar, bourbon and vanilla to blend.

3. In a medium saucepan, bring whipping cream to a boil. Gradually whisk hot whipping cream into the egg yolk mixture.

4. Pour custard into custard dishes, dividing equally.

5. Pour enough hot water into roasting pan to come halfway up the sides of the cups.

6. Bake at 350° about 30 minutes or until just set in the center.

7. Remove from water and cool completely. Cover and refrigerate at least 6 hours. (Can be prepared 2 days ahead. Keep covered and refrigerated.)

8. To serve, preheat broiler and arrange custard cups on a baking sheet. Sprinkle with 1 tablespoon brown sugar evenly over each.

9. Broil until sugar melts and turns dark brown, rotating baking sheet for even browning, watching very closely, about 2 to 3 minutes.

10. Sprinkle each with toasted pecans. Serve.

Caramelize the sugar no more that 2 hours before serving, otherwise it starts breaking down soon after that. Do not double this recipe.

Serves 6.

White Chocolate Crème Brûlée

Audrey Mingolla

5 large egg yolks
½ cup plus 2 tablespoons sugar, divided
2 cups whipping cream
3 ounces imported white chocolate, finely chopped
¼ teaspoon vanilla

1. In a medium bowl, whisk egg yolks and ¼ cup sugar; set aside.

2. Bring cream and remaining ¼ cup sugar to a simmer in a heavy saucepan.

3. Reduce heat to low, gradually add the chocolate and whisk until smooth.

4. Gradually add to the yolk mixture. Add vanilla.

5. Ladle into four 10-ounce custard cups. Place in a water bath half way up the sides. Bake at 300° for about 1 hour. Add 5 to 10 minutes longer if doubled.

6. Remove, cool and refrigerate overnight.

7. Sprinkle ½ tablespoon of sugar over each; place under broiler until sugar caramelizes, about 2 minutes.

Serves 4.

Indian Meal Pudding

Deb Hebert

This recipe is one of the oldest New England dishes and it dates back to the Pilgrim days, when cornmeal, the principle ingredient, was known as "Indian meal" in reference to America's native peoples, who taught the settlers how to grow corn. It tastes somewhat like pumpkin pie, without the pastry. This is a favorite Thanksgiving tradition in our family.

2	cups milk
3	tablespoons yellow cornmeal
2	tablespoons butter
3	tablespoons molasses
¼	teaspoon ground ginger
¼	teaspoon ground nutmeg
¼	teaspoon cinnamon
½	teaspoon salt
¼	cup sugar
2	eggs, beaten
	Vanilla ice cream

1. In a medium saucepan, heat milk.

2. Add cornmeal and cook while stirring for 15 minutes.

3. Add remaining ingredients and stir until well mixed.

4. Pour into a greased baking casserole. Bake at 400° for 30 minutes.

5. Serve warm with vanilla ice cream.

Whipped cream may be substituted for vanilla ice cream.

Grapenut Custard Pudding

From the Kitchen of Ruth Cotton Gurney
submitted by her daughter Pamela Gurney Farnum

4   cups milk
4   eggs
¼   teaspoon nutmeg
½   teaspoon cinnamon
1   teaspoon vanilla extract
¾   cup sugar
    Dash of salt
¾   cup grapenuts

1. Scald milk; at the same time boil a pan of water for a water bath.

2. Lightly beat eggs with a whisk.

3. Add nutmeg, cinnamon, vanilla, sugar and salt.

4. Beat eggs and add scalded milk, stirring to mix.

5. Place grapenuts in the bottom of a greased 1½-quart casserole. Add 6 cups of custard.

6. Place casserole dish into a water bath. Bake at 350° for 45 minutes to 1 hour. To test for doneness, insert a knife into the center and if it comes out clean, it's done.

You may use lemon or orange extract and a sprinkle of grated rind in place of vanilla extract. Bread cubes or coconut for may be used in place of grapenuts. If you make a double batch, cook at least 1 hour.

Serves 8.

Grandma's Sweet and Creamy Rice Pudding

Leeni Gravlin-Dunn

This recipe came from a community cookbook in Ohio, where my sister lived at the time. No one seems to know whose Grandma created the recipe, but it wasn't ours. This recipe has become a holiday tradition for Thanksgiving, Christmas and Easter. This dessert tastes even better the second day, if there's any left.

1   cup dry white rice
½   cup raisins (optional)
2½ cups cold water
½   teaspoon salt
1   pint half & half
¾   cup sugar
14   large marshmallows

1. In a large saucepan, combine rice, raisins, water and salt. Cover and cook over high heat until it starts to boil. Turn heat down to low and simmer for 15 to 20 minutes or until water is gone.

2. Stir in half & half, sugar and marshmallows. Continue to cook, stirring occasionally, until cream bubbles and all marshmallows are melted.

3. Remove from heat and let stand for 30 minutes. Stir and serve.

Layererd Jello Squares

Norma H. Baker

I tend to make this for family events when I know they'll be lots of children, but truth be told, I think the adults eat as many as the younger ones.

1   (6-ounce) package cherry or
    raspberry jello
5   cups boiling water, divided
2   envelopes of unflavored gelatin
½   pint heavy cream
1   cup sugar
1   teaspoon vanilla extract
½   pint sour cream
1   (6-ounce) package orange jello

1. Dissolve cherry jello in 2 cups of boiling water. Pour into an 11 x 9-inch glass baking pan. Chill until firm.

2. Dissolve unflavored gelatin in 1 cup of boiling water and set aside.

3. Heat cream until bubbles form around the inside of the pan. Remove from heat and add sugar, vanilla and unflavored gelatin mix; mix well.

4. Add sour cream and stir until well blended. Pour over chilled and firm cherry layer. Let chill until very firm.

5. Lastly, dissolve orange jello in 2 cups of boiling water and pour over layers.

6. Chill completely. Cut into squares to serve.

Any flavored jello can be used to create a colorful theme.

Banana Split Dessert

From the Kitchen of Marie P. Chabot

A great summer dessert and a sure success!
(Marie shared this recipe with us before her passing on August 1, 2003.)

2   cups graham cracker crumbs
1   stick butter, melted
½   cup chocolate syrup
2   cups confectioners' sugar
1   stick butter, softened
2   eggs
3   bananas, sliced
1   (8-ounce) can crushed
    pineapple, drained
1   (8-ounce) container whipped
    topping, thawed
½   cup chopped nuts
1   cup chopped cherries

1. In a small bowl, combine cracker crumbs and melted butter.

2. Press into a greased 13 x 9-inch pan. Bake at 350° for 5 to 7 minutes. Cool completely.

3. Drizzle with chocolate syrup.

4. In another small bowl, combine sugar and softened butter; beat until light.

5. Add eggs and beat until fluffy. Spread evenly over chocolate syrup.

6. Add sliced bananas over filling and spread pineapple over bananas.

7. Cover entire pan with whipped topping. Sprinkle with nuts and garnish with cherries.

8. Refrigerate until ready to serve.

Serves 12.

Lemon Chocolate Dessert

Janet A. Whittier

It's easy on calories and carry only in cold weather.

1   (14½-ounce) can evaporated
    milk
1   (3-ounce) package lemon
    gelatin
¾   cup sugar
1½ cups boiling water
3   tablespoons lemon juice
25 chocolate wafers, crushed fine
1   tablespoon grated lemon rind
4   tablespoons butter, melted

1. Chill evaporated milk in refrigerator overnight.

2. Dissolve gelatin and sugar in boiling water. Chill until almost completely set.

3. Stir in lemon juice and rind.

4. In a large bowl, whip milk until it resembles soft whipped cream.

5. Add gelatin mixture and continue whipping for about 2 minutes.

6. Place wafer crumbs in the bottom of a 13 x 9-inch pan, reserving about 1 tablespoon crumbs.

7. Add melted butter, mix and press firmly into bottom of pan.

8. Pour in whipped lemon mixture and sprinkle with remaining crumbs. Refrigerate until ready to serve.

Use chocolate wafers that are thin icebox size, 2⅜-inch in diameter.

Serves 15 to 18.

Raspberry Dessert

From the Kitchen of Lillian Mann Jernberg
submitted by her family

Lillian Mann was "the bakers' daughter". Her family started Helen's Bakery in Quinsigamond Village. She was always happiest when making some sweet Swedish delight for her family. Forget the veggies, dessert was the mainstay. Often her recipes lacked detail because "she just knew". When Lillian made this dessert we all would "straighten up the edges" as we took turns having just a little more.

1   (12-ounce) box vanilla wafers, crushed very fine, divided

1   stick butter, softened

2   eggs

2   cups confectioners' sugar

1   teaspoon vanilla

4   boxes sweetened frozen raspberries, thawed and drained

8   ounces whipping cream

2   tablespoons granulated sugar (approximately)

½   cup chopped walnuts (optional)

1. Pat two-thirds of the wafer crumbs into the bottom of a 13 x 9-inch glass baking dish.

2. Cream butter, eggs and confectioners' sugar. Add vanilla.

3. Spread mixture over wafers with a wet spoon or knife.

4. Layer berries over mixture.

5. Beat the whipping cream and sweeten with granulated sugar to your liking.

6. Spread over berries.

7. Mix remaining wafer crumbs with nuts and sprinkle on top. Refrigerate.

You may use a combination of raspberries and strawberries.

Serves 12.

Cherry Strawberry Dessert

Evelyn L. Morris

*This recipe is worth the prep time. Each step is
quick you just need to plan the oven and refrigerator time.*

Meringue Crust

6	eggs whites
½	teaspoon cream of tartar
¼	teaspoon salt
¼-½ cup sugar	

1. Beat egg whites, cream of tartar and salt until frothy.

2. Gradually add sugar, beating until stiff, about 10 to 15 minutes.

3. Spread in a greased 13 x 9-inch pan. Bake at 275° for 60 minutes.

4. Turn oven off and leave in pan in oven for 12 hours.

Filling

1	(6-ounce) package cream cheese
½	cup sugar
1	teaspoon vanilla extract
2	cups whipped cream
2	cups miniature marshmallows

1. Mix cream cheese, sugar and vanilla extract.

2. Fold in whipped cream and marshmallows.

3. Spread over meringue crust and refrigerate for 12 hours or overnight.

Topping

1	(21-ounce) can cherry pie filling
2	cups sliced fresh strawberries
1	teaspoon lemon juice

1. Mix cherry pie mix, strawberries and lemon juice.

2. Spread on top of second layer and serve.

You may substitute one 16-ounce package of frozen strawberries for fresh. This recipe also freezes well.

Serves 12 to 15.

Basic Custard Ice Cream

Ethel M. O'Day

This is my aunt's recipe from Maine. We always had her homemade ice cream for the 4th of July picnic. The kids and men always took turns turning the crank. I also made this at the Sutton Historical Society picnic held at the Eight Lots School about 9 years ago. This was a huge success and everyone said it brought back childhood memories.

1½ cups milk
3 eggs
¾ cup sugar
½ teaspoon salt
1 tablespoon vanilla
3 cups light cream
Crushed ice
Rock salt

1. Scald milk and set aside.

2. Beat eggs, add sugar and salt. Gradually add milk to egg mixture.

3. Cook over hot water stirring constantly until mixture thickens and coats a spoon; cool.

4. Add vanilla and cream.

5. Using a hand crank ice cream freezer; place dasher in freezer can.

6. Add custard mixture. Cover.

7. Adjust the crank. Using 8 parts crushed ice to 1 part rock salt. Pack around freezer can. Turn the crank rapidly. Freeze until mush.

8. Drain off any liquid, repack 4 parts ice to 1 part salt and pack firmly around freezer can. Cover freezer with burlap or newspaper and let stand 3 to 4 hours.

Strawberry or Peach Ice Cream - follow recipe above adding 2 cups mashed sweetened strawberries or peaches before pouring into freezer can. Chocolate Ice Cream - follow recipe above adding 2 squares of melted unsweetened chocolate to hot custard mixture. Coffee Ice Cream - follow recipe above substituting 1 cup strong coffee brew for 1 cup milk.

Poire d' Helene

Barbara MH Daigneault

When you read through the ingredients, you might think
canned pears, oh my. Let me tell you, the blend of this combination is "to die for".
This is an elegant ending to a formal dinner party or Christmas dinner.
Serve in crystal dessert dishes or balloon glasses.

2 (15-ounce) cans of pears, in
   natural pear juice, drained
8 tablespoons Grand Marnier,
   divided
1 quart vanilla ice cream
8 tablespoons milk chocolate
   sauce
   Vanilla Ice cream

1. Divide pears evenly among
4 dessert dishes.

2. Drizzle with 2 tablespoons of
Grand Marnier. Cover and allow to
marinate in refrigerator for at least
6 hours.

3. When ready to serve, place 1
scoop of ice cream on top of the
pears and drizzle with warmed milk
chocolate sauce.

Use a good quality chocolate sauce.

Serves 4.

Delicious Date Nut Balls

Cheryl Bedard

I got this recipe years ago in Home Economics, a
class taught at Sutton High School by Mrs. Agnes Davagian.

1 stick butter
1 cup sugar
1 cup chopped dates
1 cup chopped walnuts
1 egg
1 teaspoon vanilla extract
2 cups rice crispies
½ cup shredded coconut

1. In a 2-quart saucepan, combine
first 5 ingredients. Cook for 8
minutes, stirring constantly.

2. Cool 1 minute and add vanilla
extract and rice crispies.

3. When cool enough to handle,
roll into 1-inch balls and roll in
coconut.

Grandma's Rum Balls

Chris Rice

My father's mother made these at Christmas. As a child,
I wasn't crazy about the flavor, but as an adult they taste pretty good.

1   (6-ounce) package semisweet
    chocolate chips
½   cup sour cream
    Pinch of salt
4   tablespoons butter
2   cups crushed vanilla wafers
1   cup confectioners' sugar
¼   cup cocoa
¼   cup rum

1. In a double boiler, melt the chocolate chips.

2. Add sour cream, salt and butter; mix well.

3. Add wafers, sugar, cocoa and rum. Mix well.

4. Remove from heat. Roll into balls when cooled enough to handle.

5. Store in refrigerator.

Microwave Peanut Brittle

Debbi Abbott Holmgren

This is an easy recipe that makes a great gift - yummy!

1   cup sugar
½   cup white corn syrup
1   cup raw Spanish peanuts
¼   teaspoon salt
3   tablespoons butter or
    margarine
½   teaspoon vanilla
1   teaspoon baking soda

1. In a large glass bowl, combine the first 4 ingredients and mix well.

2. Microwave on high for 5 minutes. Remove from microwave; stir. Microwave on high for 5 more minutes.

3. Take out and add the butter and vanilla. Mix well, return to the microwave and cook on high for 2 more minutes.

4. Immediately add the baking soda. Stir well and quickly spread on a greased cookie sheet.

5. Cool completely before breaking into pieces.

You can purchase these peanuts at a health food store.

Trade Fudge

Helen Silun Ordung

I received this recipe from David Hale Fanning Girls Trade School in Worcester, Massachusetts in 1932, where I graduated at the age of 13. The teacher would tell us not to make this too often or we would get fat. This is a favorite I make for First Congregational Church of Sutton's choir.

1½ cups sugar
2½ tablespoons cocoa
½ cup milk
1 tablespoon light corn syrup
1 teaspoon vanilla
1 tablespoon butter

1. In a saucepan, combine sugar, cocoa, milk and corn syrup. Stir on stove until mixture begins to boil. Cook without stirring to 238 degrees until a firm ball forms in cold water.

2. Set in pan of cold water, add vanilla and butter and do not stir.

3. When thoroughly cooled to 110 degrees, beat briskly until creamy.

4. The instant it appears dull, put in a buttered pan or on buttered wax paper. Cut in squares immediately.

At the same time you add the vanilla and butter, you may add any of the following: ½ cup chopped nuts, ½ cup raisins, ½ cup cut up marshmallows or ½ cup candied fruit. As much as a cup can be used.

Caramel Corn

Debbi Abbott Holmgren

1 cup popcorn kernels
1 cup brown sugar
1 stick margarine
¼ cup light corn syrup
½ teaspoon salt
¼ teaspoon baking soda

1. Pop the kernels in an air popper and place in a large paper bag.

2. In a saucepan, combine the brown sugar, margarine, corn syrup and salt. Bring to a boil and cook for 1 minute. Remove from heat and add baking soda. Stir well.

3. Pour caramel mixture over the cooked popcorn. Mix well.

4. Fold over the bag and cook in the microwave on high for 3 minutes, stirring well after each minute.

5. Empty onto a cookie sheet and allow to cool.

Cow Chips

Melissa Nydam

This is so simple to make and anyone who loves sweets can't resist these.

1 (16-ounce) bag chocolate chips
1 (16-ounce) bag peanut butter chips
1 (16-ounce) bag butterscotch chips
3 cups honey roasted peanuts

1. In a large saucepan, melt all chips together over low heat and add nuts.

2. Drop by the spoonful on a wax paper-lined cookie sheet.

3. Set until firm.

Best to store in refrigerator.

Peppermint Kisses

Cathy Eaton

This is a delicious candy for Christmas! I make these every year.

2 egg whites
⅛ teaspoon salt
⅛ teaspoon cream of tartar
½ cup sugar, divided
2 candy canes, crushed

1. In a large bowl, beat egg whites until foamy. Add salt and cream of tartar. Beat until soft peaks form.

2. Beat in sugar, 1 tablespoon at a time, until stiff, glossy and meringue texture.

3. Spoon into a food storage bag and cut a 1-inch hole in the corner. Squeeze ½-inch kisses of meringue onto ungreased, foil-lined baking sheet. Sprinkle with crushed candy cane.

4. Bake at 225° for 1½ hour to 2 hours or until dry but not brown.

Store in airtight container.

Yields 3 dozen.

U. S. Measurement Equivalents

Pinch/dash	1⁄16 teaspoon
½ teaspoon	30 drops
1 teaspoon	⅓ tablespoon
3 teaspoons	1 tablespoon
½ tablespoon	1½ teaspoons
1 tablespoon	3 teaspoons; ½ fluid ounce
2 tablespoons	⅛ cup; 1 fluid ounce
3 tablespoons	1½ fluid ounces; 1 jigger
jigger	1½ fluid ounces; 3 tablespoons
4 tablespoons	¼ cup; 2 fluid ounces
5⅓ tablespoons	⅓ cup; 5 tablespoons plus 1 teaspoon
8 tablespoons	½ cup; 4 fluid ounces
10⅔ tablespoons	⅔ cup; 10 tablespoons plus 2 teaspoons
12 tablespoons	¾ cup; 6 fluid ounces
16 tablespoons	1 cup; 8 fluid ounces; ½ pint
⅛ cup	2 tablespoons; 1 fluid ounce
¼ cup	4 tablespoons; 2 fluid ounces
⅓ cup	5 tablespoons plus 1 teaspoon
⅜ cup	¼ cup plus 2 tablespoons
½ cup	8 tablespoons; 4 fluid ounces
⅔ cup	10 tablespoons plus 2 teaspoons
⅝ cup	½ cup plus 2 tablespoons
¾ cup	12 tablespoons; 6 fluid ounces
⅞ cup	¼ cup plus 2 tablespoons
1 cup	16 tablespoons; ½ pint; 8 fluid ounces
2 cups	1 pint; 16 fluid ounces
3 cups	1½ pints; 24 fluid ounces
4 cups	1 quart; 32 fluid ounces
8 cups	2 quarts; 64 fluid ounces
1 pint	2 cups; 16 fluid ounces
2 pints	1 quart; 32 fluid ounces
1 quart	2 pints; 4 cups; 32 fluid ounces
4 quarts	1 gallon; 8 pints
1 gallon	4 quarts; 8 pints; 16 cups; 128 fluid ounces
8 quarts	1 peck
4 pecks	1 bushel

Mother's Apron

Do you remember Mother's Aprons? Always big, they were, and their uses myriad. Besides, the foremost purpose, the protection of the dress beneath, it was a holder for removing pots and pans from the oven, it was wonderful for drying children's tears and, yes, even for wiping small noses and shooing flies.

From the hen house it carried eggs, fuzzy chicks, ducklings or goslings, — sometimes half hatched eggs to be finished in the warming oven. It's folds provided an ideal hiding place for shy children and when guests lingered on chilly days, the apron was wrapped around mother's arms.

Innumerable times it wiped a perspiring brow bent over a hot, wood burning stove. Chips and kindling came to the kitchen stove in the ample garment, as did fresh peas and string beans from the garden — often they were podded and stemmed in the lap the apron covered. Windfall apples, kindling chips and corn cobs were gathered in it, and wild flowers.

Chairs were hastily dusted with its corner when unexpected company was sighted. Waving it aloft was as good as a dinner bell to call the men from the fields. Big, they were. Yes, and useful. Now, I'm wondering — will any modern, frilled apron provoke such nostalgic memories?

Taken from *Stories and Recipes of the Great Depression of the 1930's* written by Rita Van Amber.

Index

C

𝒬

𝑅

S

T

Seasons of Thyme

P.O. Box 463
Sutton, Massachusetts 01590
www.seasonsofthyme.net

Please send _____ copy (ies)   @ $24.95 each _____

                 Shipping and handling   @ $ 4.00 each _____

Massachusetts residents add 5% sales tax   @ $ 1.25 each _____

                                          TOTAL _____

Name _____

Address _____

City _____ State _____ Zip _____

Tele _____

Please make check payable to *Seasons of Thyme*.
For additional ordering options, please visit our website.

- -

Seasons of Thyme

P.O. Box 463
Sutton, Massachusetts 01590
www.seasonsofthyme.net

Please send _____ copy (ies)   @ $24.95 each _____

                 Shipping and handling   @ $ 4.00 each _____

Massachusetts residents add 5% sales tax   @ $ 1.25 each _____

                                          TOTAL _____

Name _____

Address _____

City _____ State _____ Zip _____

Tele _____

Please make check payable to *Seasons of Thyme*.
For additional ordering options, please visit our website.